BEST
by
NUMBER

Who wore what ... with distinction

SportingNews
BOOKS

CREDITS

Ron Smith, the primary author for *Best by Number*, is a Senior Editor for Sporting News.

Editor: Joe Hoppel.
Book design: Chad Painter.
Cover design: Michael Behrens.
Photo editors: Albert Dickson, Michael McNamara, Sean Gallagher.
Contributing writers: Dale Bye, Shawn Reid.
Copy editors: Corrie Anderson, Erin Farrell, Ryan Fagan, Tom Dienhart, Bob Hille, Dan Graf, Dave Bukovich, Matt Crossman, Jessica Daues, Zach Bodendieck, Katie Koss.
Page design and layout: Chad Painter, Bob Parajon, David Niehaus.
Photo research: Jim Meier.
Prepress specialists: Steve Romer, Vern Kasal, Cindy Jones, Russ Carr.

PHOTO CREDITS

Albert Dickson/TSN: 10T, 31BL, 40, 44, 57BR, 60B, 62B, 64B, 72B, 76B, 78B, 79 (2), 92-93, 105B, 106T, 107L, 114R, 121M, 142B, 147L, 155TL, 157L, 181TR, 193BR, 201BL, 204T, 212, 213T, 221R

Jay Drowns/TSN: 51R, 71ML, 123L, 126BR, 145T, 155R, 163B, 218B

Bob Leverone/TSN: 6-7, 27, 28L, 28T, 34-35, 42B, 49M, 51L, 71BL, 95R, 101R, 115M, 127BR, 129T, 152T, 163T, 165R, 169T, 171T, 175R, 189TL, 198, 199 (2), 200B, 201BR, 205BL, 215R, 222-223

Robert Seale/TSN: back cover, 6TR, 19T, 35M, 39B, 56R, 57TR, 60TR, 60M, 65TR, 70-71, 74-75, 80-81, 82L, 83BM, 84-85, 87B, 101L, 105T, 117M, 117TR, 140TL, 141R, 149BR, 150, 157TR, 174B, 181L, 197BR

Michael McNamara/TSN: 33R, 140-141, 155BL, 198B

Doug DeVoe/TSN Archives: 139M

Sean Gallagher/TSN Archives: 136BR

Craig Hacker/TSN Archives: 66B

Elsa Hasch/TSN Archives: 175M

Ed Nessen/TSN Archives: 39L, 45BR, 159B

Rich Pilling/TSN Archives: 8B, 23 (3), 28B, 35R, 37R, 49B, 56L, 66T, 67L, 73B, 86 (2), 89R, 90L, 95L, 99R, 103BL, 103TL, 115R, 133B, 135R, 142-143, 172L, 196-197, 201T, 203BL, 205T, 218T, 222B

Dilip Vishwanat/TSN Archives: 15 (2), 52B, 98, 117B, 119R, 144B, 158B, 159T, 181BR, 186B, 190B, 205R, 217R, 223BR

John Cordes for TSN: 125R, 178B, 180B

Jay Crihfield for TSN: 171B

John Dunn for TSN: 29R, 123R, 157BR, 197T, 213B

Cliff Grassmick for TSN: 177B, 211R

Craig Hacker for TSN: 173

Tom Hauck for TSN: 197BL

Harold Hinson for TSN: 45T, 69T, 136TL, 146-147

M. David Leeds for TSN: 61T

John Locker for TSN: 182B

Alan Marler for TSN: 77M

Craig Melvin for TSN: 191BR

James Nielsen for TSN: 22T, 65L

Erik Perel for TSN: 91L

Scott Rovak for TSN: 152B

Bill Wippert for TSN: 162B

Malcolm Emmons: 6TM, 12, 16-17, 29T, 36-37, 41R, 50B, 54-55, 57L, 58-59, 64-65, 72-73, 77BL, 78T, 88-89, 108-109, 125BL, 126T, 128T, 134-135, 144T, 149M, 151, 161, 162, 172R, 176L, 177M, 183 (2), 185, 186T, 191T, 195R, 207, 209

AP/Wide World Photos: 21, 53B, 73L, 81R, 87L, 110L, 131M, 132-133, 211L

Duane Burleson/AP/Wide World Photos: 17

Kevork Djansezian/AP/Wide World Photos: 184B

Mark Duncan/AP/Wide World Photos: 18T

Chris Gardner/AP/Wide World Photos: 189R

Julian Gonzalez/Detroit Free Press/AP/Wide World Photos: 165BL

Marc Matheny/AP/Wide World Photos: 61BR

Lennox McClendon/AP/Wide World Photos: 131TR

Amy Sancetta/AP/Wide World Photos: 83L

Reed Saxon/AP/Wide World Photos: 131BL

Lynne Sladky/AP/Wide World Photos: 100R

Robert Sorbo/AP/Wide World Photos: 127T

Peter Southwick/AP/Wide World Photos: 115L

Pat Sullivan/AP/Wide World Photos: 43R

Suzanne Vlamis/AP/Wide World Photos: 120

Dusan Vranic/AP/Wide World Photos: 49TL

Allsport UK/Getty Images: 50T

Bruce Bennett Studios/Getty Images: 31BR, 102

Bruce Bennett/Getty Images: 220-221

Andrew D. Bernstein/NBAE via Getty Images: 35BL

Jonathan Daniel/Getty Images: 216

Melchior DiGiacomo/Getty Images: 46L

Don Emmert/AFP/Getty Images: 42L

Focus On Sport/Getty Images: 13, 51T, 68T, 96B

John Giamundo/Getty Images: 45BL

Otto Greule/Getty Images: 61BL

Jim Gund/Getty Images: 113R

Walter Iooss Jr./NBAE via Getty Images: 42TR, 71R, 110-111

Jed Jacobsohn/Getty Images: 73TR

Kidwiler Collection/Diamond Images/Getty Images: 168B

Fernando Medina/NBAE via Getty Images: 55R

Doug Pensinger/Getty Images: 187BM

Rich Pilling/MLB Photos via Getty Images: 103M, 154

Rich Pilling/NBAE via Getty Images: 112-113

Mike Powell/Getty Images: 6TL, 107R

David Stluka/Getty Images: 204B

Michael Zagaris/Getty Images: 18L

PhotoFile: 194

US Presswire: 52T

Malcolm Emmons/US Presswire: 104, 174-175

Tony Tomsic/US Presswire: 62T, 83R, 93L, 110B, 184T, 210

Bettmann/Corbis: 24-25

Gregg Newton/Corbis: 14

Anthony Baker: 25

Vernon J. Biever: 170

Frank Bryan: 43TL

Louis DeLuca: 215L

Gary G. Dineen/Winning Image: 24

Jeff Fishbein: 133TR

George Gojkovich: 53T

Ed Mailliard: 54B

Al Messerschmidt: 116, 158

Robert L. Miller: 22

Ronald L. Mrowiec: 76TL, 94-95, 180

Niagra University: 177M

Kevin W. Reece: 38R

Charlie Ryan: 46T

Bud Skinner: 69B

Medford Taylor: 10-11

Tony Tomsic: 192T

Peter Travers: 18B

Don Wingfield: 22L

TSN Archives: back flap, 6BL, 8T, 9, 19B, 20-21, 26-27, 29BL, 30, 31T, 32-33 34T, 34B, 38L, 39TR, 41L, 43BR, 45M, 46BR, 47R, 48, 53R, 59R, 63 (2), 65M, 67R, 68B, 75R, 77BR, 82R, 85R, 87TR, 90R, 91T, 92B, 93R, 96, 97 (2), 100L, 104B, 106B, 109R, 111BL, 111BR, 114L, 118 (2), 119L, 121R, 122, 124, 125T, 128B, 129BL, 130, 137 (3), 138-139, 140BL, 141BL, 143M, 143BR, 145BR, 147R, 148-149, 149BL, 153, 156, 159R, 160, 164 (2), 166, 167, 168, 169BL, 169BR, 171R, 176R, 178-179, 179 (2), 182T, 187TL, 187R, 188, 189BL, 190T, 192B, 193TL, 195BL, 195M, 200T, 202, 203T, 203BR, 206, 208, 214, 217L, 219T, 222L, 224

Copyright ©2006 by Sporting News, a division of Vulcan Sports Media, Inc., 10176 Corporate Square Drive, Suite 200, St. Louis, MO 63132. All rights reserved. Printed in Italy.

Sporting News is a registered trademark of Vulcan Sports Media, Inc.

ISBN: 0-89204-848-4

10 9 8 7 6 5 4 3

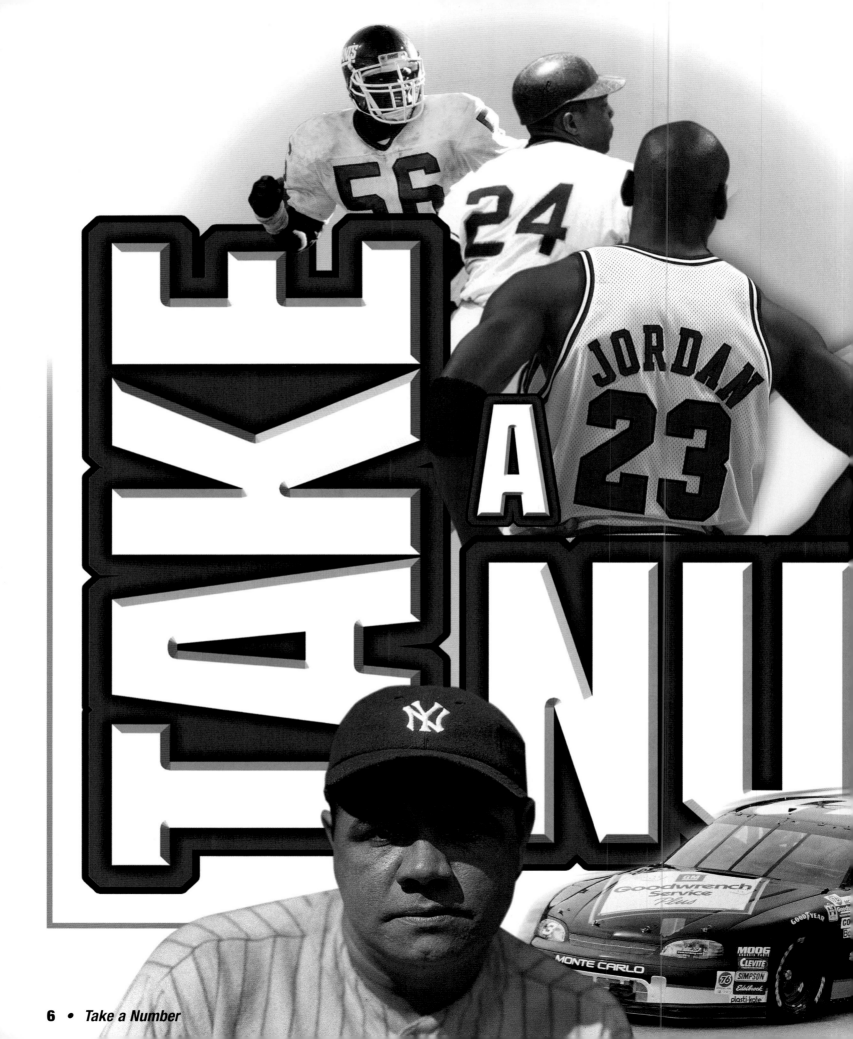

HOW WE DID WHAT WE DID

Pick a number, any number. We did, and that's why everything you ever needed to know about digital digression in sports can be found in this book.

We operate by the "best athlete available" philosophy, which means regional allegiances, short-term popularity and reputation have been ignored in our selection of numerical No. 1s for every digit, 0 through 99, across all sports. Go ahead and disagree, we don't mind. But be prepared to argue the justifications we offer for each of our choices.

We also offer best-of-the-rest selections for each of the numbers presented under the heading *Elite*. The elite listings, which appear alphabetically and unranked, are not all-inclusive and do not always include star-caliber athletes who are mentioned elsewhere on the pages.

There also are short stories about numbers and athletes associated with them, as well as "Fast Facts" that provide trivial details and unusual informational tidbits. Streamers across the bottom of pages flash the names of other *Notables* who had long or prominent associations with the numerals of choice.

WHAT'S ON THE BACK OF A UNIFORM OFTEN HAS EMOTIONAL—AND EVEN ECONOMIC—MEANING

Oklahoma fans remember him as Boz, the cool, hip and charismatic No. 44 who mesmerized college football with his intimidating linebacker play and outrageous personality. Seattle fans remember him as Brian Bosworth, the smaller, slower and more confused 55 who was outrageously disappointing during a three-year NFL career with the Seattle Seahawks. Blame it on 11 unwanted digits.

"No. 44 made me feel better. It made me run faster. I felt more confident out there," said Bosworth, who insists his professional downfall was accelerated by the NFL's restrictive numbering system. "People might not think it's a big deal, but to me it's a very big deal."

Welcome to the sports fast lane, where numbers

HE GETS ONLY A FRACTION OF NUMERICAL RESPECT

Uniform number fascination is not confined to the stars. Any self-respecting baseball fan probably can recall the number worn by *Eddie Gaedel*, whose major league experience was limited to one game, one plate appearance—more than a half century ago.

The greatest promotional stunt in baseball history started off innocently enough between games of an August 19, 1951, doubleheader at St. Louis' Sportsman's Park. Browns owner Bill Veeck, who had promised an extravaganza to celebrate the American League's 50th anniversary, staged a circus-themed show that ended with a 3-foot-7 midget, dressed in a Browns uniform, popping out of a papier-mache birthday cake and scurrying to the St. Louis dugout.

But it wasn't until the bottom of the first inning of the nightcap, after Detroit had gone quietly in the top half, that 18,369 fans caught the full impact of Veeck's "show." Suddenly the announcer's voice echoed through the park: "Batting for Frank Saucier, number one-eighth, Eddie Gaedel." And sure enough, the 65-pound cake-popping midget approached the plate swinging three toy bats.

After umpire Ed Hurley questioned St. Louis manager Zack Taylor, who produced an official A.L. contract, the game continued with Tigers lefthander Bob Cain battling his composure and the almost nonexistent strike zone. Gaedel walked on four pitches.

Jim Delsing was announced as a pinch runner for Gaedel, who was released the next day when A.L. president Will Harridge ruled that the contract was not in the best interest of baseball.

provide the standards by which athletes are judged as well as the badge by which many are identified. They often get personal.

"Numbers go all the way back to the beginning of civilization," said sports psychologist Dr. Richard Lustberg. "There's a proclivity to get attached to numbers, just like colors, clothes and things like that. Numbers have a sentimental value and, of course, a superstitious value. Players' identities become merged with their uniform numbers,

Bosworth

along with the idea that those numbers make them play and look better."

Emotional links to numbers are not uncommon. Washington running back Clinton Portis paid $38,000 to keep his No. 26 after being traded to the Redskins by the Denver Broncos, and other exorbitant sums have changed hands after sometimes-intense negotiations. Uniform numbers have been traded for vacations, fishing trips, home-improvement projects, suits, dinners, cases of beer and enough Rolex watches to subsidize a Yankee Stadium giveaway. Atlanta coach Fredi Gonzalez graciously gave up his 33 to new Braves outfielder Brian Jordan, only to be surprised by a thank-you gift—a $40,000 motorcycle.

All of which demonstrates how mentally ingrained numbers have become with the American psyche. Not only do fans identify sports heroes with their numbers, the digits become a fashion statement, marketing tool and alter-ego for the athlete. Red Grange was, still is and always will be No. 77. No. 23 is interchangeable with Michael Jordan, as is 5 with Joe DiMaggio, 24 with Willie Mays, 43 with Richard Petty and 56 with Lawrence Taylor. And who among us would fail to

5 JOE DiMAGGIO 5

identify the pinstriped No. 3 of the Yankees' Bambino?

"A lot of kids get attached to a number because it was the first one they were given in sports," Lustberg says. "Others like it because it was their father's number. Maybe it represents their birthday or an association with an athlete. I liked Willie Mays because my father was a big Giants fan. It's all about a comfort level and some athletes have paid a lot of money for that comfort."

Some athletes become one with their numbers by design, others through long-term association. Check out your autograph collection and see how many signatures are accompanied by numbers. Check out the jewelry, the license plates, the business cards and, yes, even the tattoos of the modern athletes. "They walk around with necklaces with a big old 45 on their neck," said former Dallas quarterback Troy Aikman, "and they have vanity plates on their trucks and whatever with their numbers."

For Aikman, the number association has become automatic—and borderline annoying.

"I have companies that at times will send me a golf bag, for instance," he said. "And they always want to put 8 on it. They put the name and then they put 8. Or when you ask the phone company for a number or you're getting a mobile number, they always want to put 8s in it. They just do it. And they think that 8 is how you're identified. I get turned off by it.

"Whenever I've done logos for my (automobile) dealership, they've tried to work in an 8. I said, 'I don't want an 8. My name's Troy. I don't need an 8 on every single thing I own. I wore the number 8 and that's fine. But I'm not identified by the number 8.'"

Blame it on the Galloping Ghost. It was Grange who showed us more than 80 years ago how a number can become intrinsically tied to an athlete. After his otherworldly performance for Illinois in a 1924 game against Michigan, No. 77 enhanced his national stature when he endorsed a myriad of products ranging from toys and clothes to drinks and candy. While Grange was raking in the dough from his side ventures, he found time to give the

"Numbers go all the way back to the beginning of civilization."
—Dr. Richard Lustberg, a sports psychologist

fledgling NFL credibility as its first legitimate superstar.

That was before major league baseball even stitched on its first permanent number, more than two decades before the National Basketball Association played its first game. Grange ran wild against the Wolverines the same year the National Hockey League made its United States debut in Boston, 13 years after the first Indy 500 and many miles before NASCAR's first good ol' boys revved their engines.

While college football had been tinkering with uniform

? MAX PATKIN ?
Longtime baseball showman Max Patkin, who had all the answers when it came to entertaining fans, proved that everyone in uniform didn't need to wear a number. Patkin displayed his many antics in countless major league and minor league ballparks.

6 **JULIUS ERVING** 6

numbers since the early 1900s, baseball limped slowly into the "scorecard era." In 1916, the Cleveland Indians experimented with numbers on their left uniform sleeves; apparently displeased with fan response, they tried the right sleeves in 1917. The St. Louis Cardinals also numbered their sleeves in 1924, but permanent digits did not appear on baseball uniforms until 1929, when the Yankees of Babe Ruth and Lou Gehrig assigned numbers according to the players' spots in the batting order.

No. 1 Earle Combs, No. 2 Mark Koenig, No. 3 Ruth, No. 4 Gehrig, No. 5 Bob Meusel, No. 6 Tony Lazzeri, No. 7 Leo Durocher and No. 8 Johnny Grabowski. Yes, that Leo Durocher, who would go on to later fame as a cranky, high-maintenance No. 2.

By 1932, all of baseball was digitalized, five years before numbers became mandatory in college football. By 1946, when the NBA played its first season as the Basketball Association of America, Gehrig's No. 4 had already been retired by the Yankees, Ruth's 3 had already reached icon status and the numerical values of such greats as Bronko Nagurski (3), George Mikan (99) and Howie Morenz (7) already were locked into the sports consciousness.

The NFL, in an attempt to make order out of numerical chaos, instituted a system in 1952 that provided number ranges for each position, giving "nationally known players" an exemption. In 1973, *all* players were required to wear numbers in the following ranges: quarterbacks and kickers, 1-19; running backs and defensive backs, 20-49; centers and linebackers, 50-59; defensive linemen and interior offensive linemen, excluding centers, 60-79; wide receivers and tight ends, 80-89. The system has been amended slightly over the years, but not enough to ease Bosworth's pain in 1987.

Other sports have stayed away from such restrictive systems, though the NCAA in 1957-58 legislated against any basketball digit above 5—a concession to the number of fingers on a referee's hand. In auto racing, numbers are owned by NASCAR and issued to car owners, who in turn choose

Mantle wasn't wearing No. 6 by choice; it was assigned to him as the natural followup to New York's numerical icon sequence of 3, 4, 5, ___ .

their drivers, thus ensuring that few will carry the same number throughout their careers.

Check those old hockey programs and you'll find that goalies traditionally wore No. 1. Not anymore. Any two-digit number is fair game now, with only the NFL maintaining a semblance of order. And many of today's numbers are chosen with an eye toward marketing opportunities. Prominent college football and basketball draft picks actively lobby (and sometimes pay big money) to keep their numbers, often because of endorsement deals already in place. Coming baseball attractions maneuver to improve their digital status. And other future stars, such as Gretzky/Lemieux clone Sidney Crosby, create their own little numerical niche (does anybody else wear 87?).

Call it the Michael Jordan syndrome. His Airness carved a business empire out of his high-wire basketball act, and now another 23, LeBron James, is "being just like Mike." And while athletes dabble in acting, music and broadcasting, they can only watch and marvel over the replica jersey craze that has swept through the hip-hop world and Generations X and Y while tapping into the pockets of virtually every sports fan in the universe.

There's gold in them thar shirts.

Gold wasn't on the mind of Cliff Mapes, who is best remembered in baseball circles for his uniform number meandering in the late 1940s and early '50s. Mapes, a light-hitting rookie outfielder for the Yankees in 1948, watched in amazement on June 13 as the number he had worn for the last 2½ months—3—was retired for Ruth during ceremonies in honor of Yankee Stadium's 25th anniversary.

Mapes obligingly switched to 13 for the remainder of 1948, then to 7 at the start of 1949. He still was wearing that number in 1951 when a rookie outfielder wearing No. 6 made his Yankees debut. Mickey Mantle's path to immortality was cleared late in '51 when Mapes was traded to the St. Louis Browns, a brief sojourn before his career-ending 1952 season in Detroit—where he wore the No. 5 that had not yet

DREAM TEAM NUMBERS A NIGHTMARE FOR MOST

Only one member of basketball's original Dream Team, which swept through the 1992 Olympic Games like a runaway train, was able to play at Barcelona while wearing his trademark uniform number. Utah's John Stockton wore his familiar No. 12 while the other 11 players sported digits that ranged from 4 through 15, as governed by international rules.

At least three players would have been shut out of their NBA numbers, anyway. Magic Johnson and Karl Malone both wore 32 in the NBA, while Larry Bird, Patrick Ewing and Scottie Pippen all were 33s.

Christian Laettner, the former Duke star who was between his final college season and first in the NBA, also wore 32 for the Blue Devils.

NBA No.	Olympic No.	Player
34	14	Charles Barkley
33	7	Larry Bird
22	10	Clyde Drexler
33	6	Patrick Ewing
32	15	Magic Johnson
23	*9*	*Michael Jordan*
	4	Christian Laettner
32	11	Karl Malone
17	13	Chris Mullin
33	8	Scottie Pippen
50	5	David Robinson
12	12	John Stockton

been retired for Hank Greenberg.

Which only illustrates how fickle this numbers business can be. Mantle wasn't wearing No. 6 by choice; it was assigned to him as the natural followup to New York's numerical icon sequence of 3, 4, 5, __. Already faced with the psychological burden of following DiMaggio in center field, the Mick opted to break the sequence with his switch to 7.

Ernie Accorsi, general manager of the NFL's New York Giants and a self-admitted uniform numbers guru, said Hank Aaron once told him his switch from No. 5 (as a rookie in 1954) to 44 (in '55) also was because of DiMaggio, who apparently cast a 900-mile-long shadow from the Bronx to Milwaukee.

Mantle and Aaron were anticipated superstars who were fortunate enough to have a say in their uniform number destiny. But most Baby Boomer big leaguers were handed their first uniforms by grizzled equipment men who gave them the option of earning a "better number" later or lifting the assigned digit to elite status.

Tom Seaver literally found his uniform No. 41 hanging in an assigned locker in his first Mets spring training at St. Petersburg, Fla. Phil Niekro recalls being handed No. 35, no discussion, when he was called up by the Braves in 1964. Bob Gibson didn't have a say about his 45, or Jackie Robinson his 42. The system really has not changed much over the years.

"If it's a minor league kid, we don't worry a great deal about what number they are," said Buddy Bates, former equipment manager of the St. Louis Cardinals. "We just try to put them in a number that's open. I would keep jerseys with just numbers on them in case we made a trade in the middle of the night. Then I'd just slap a name on it the next day.

"The only time that a number is a little bit of a headache is when you acquire a veteran guy and you have to juggle numbers. That can get a little sticky sometimes."

Bates recalled a situation late in the 2000 season when the Cardinals acquired veteran Will Clark, whose familiar No. 22 was being worn by veteran catcher Mike Matheny.

"I'll tell you what a big leaguer Mike Matheny is," Bates said. "He came to me when he heard we had acquired Will, and I was sitting there agonizing over how to handle this because I knew Will had seniority on him. And he said, 'Look Buddy, I heard about Will Clark, and I want him to have 22. What do you have? And I was like, 'Whew! I dodged a bullet there.' And I had right there in front of me a list of numbers and Mike said, 'Aw, 44 is fine.' "

Sometimes, however, players are not so gracious. At which point the experienced equipment man resorts to a tried-and-true formula. "Your lead-pipe, drop-dead absolute no-argument way of handling number issues is seniority," Bates said. "And if all else fails, sometimes you just have to say, 'Mike Matheny, this is Will Clark. Come back in 15 minutes and tell me what you're doing.' "

Baseball might be a little more traditional in number distribution than other sports, which often bend over backward to fulfill requests for the now-generation athlete.

Many players simply want the same number they had in college; others want a number that shows their affinity for a favorite childhood star, or a current athlete who shares a common heritage or position. And then there are the off-the-wall requests, which range from the bizarre to the obvious.

Birthdates, anniversaries and draft years are popular number sources, as are superstitions. Confirmed three-aholic Larry Walker, the former outfielder who appreciates the power of a lucky number, wore 33 throughout his career with the Expos, Rockies and Cardinals. "I'd wear 333 if they'd let me," Walker once said. Colorful closer Turk Wendell once showed his affinity for 99 by signing a three-year New York Mets contract with a potential value of $9,999,999.99. Former Chicago White Sox outfielder Carlos May wore No. 17 so the back of his uniform would read, "May 17"—his birthday—and several Czech and Russian hockey defectors wear uniform numbers reflecting the year they gained their freedom. If you're a hockey player named Jordin Tootoo, what number are you going to ask for?

Sometimes numbers happen by accident.

"I was 10 growing up," Aikman said. "When I went to the University of Oklahoma, there was an upperclassman who had 10, so I couldn't get it. I wore 18. It was just given to me, there was no rhyme or reason. And then when I transferred to UCLA, I wanted 10 and couldn't get it there, either. So I said, 'All right, I'll be 13.' Dan Marino was my favorite quarterback. And 13 was retired there (for Kenny Washington) and I couldn't have that number.

"I just said, 'What's available?' I picked 8. It wasn't because of anybody. I didn't know many people wearing 8. I liked the single digit and thought it was kind of cool. So I went with 8 and that's that."

For New England quarterback Tom Brady, 12 seemed to be a preordained right of passage.

"I think I showed up my first day and I had a 12 in my locker," he told a writer for the *Providence Journal-Bulletin*. "I just said, 'Wow … 12.' I really didn't pick 12. But my mom said there's been a lot of great 12s. So

I stuck with 12. It's just a standard quarterback number."

Whereas Baby Boomer generation stars often stayed with one team for their entire careers, today's athletes are very mobile—thanks to the empowering free-agent market—and their paychecks very thick. That often leads to big-money negotiations when a player moves from one team to another and finds his number already in use. His only other option is to get creative, which some do by turning numbers upside down, reversing them (yeah, 81 really does look like 18 in the mirror) and even staying "connected" by way of illogical mathematical formulas.

When the perfect connection between player and number occurs, the reward is great. Ask any former superstar the highlight of his career short of Hall of Fame induction and he'll probably point toward the rafters. There's no greater rush for an athlete than to step onto the ice … or the court … or the field years later and listen to fans reaffirm their affection.

No team knows more about retired numbers than the Boston Celtics, who have taken 21 out of circulation while honoring 20 players, a coach and an owner. The Yankees lead baseball with 15 retired numbers, the Chicago Bears are tops in the NFL with 13 and the Boston Bruins and Montreal Canadiens lead the NHL with 10 apiece.

All of which begs the argument advanced with passion by actor Patrick McGoohan's frustrated character, known only to viewers as Number 6, in the 1968 television series *The Prisoner*. "I am not a number. I am a person," he pleaded.

McGoohan's Number 6 probably wouldn't have appreciated his spiritual connection to such accomplished former 6s as Bill Russell, Stan Musial, Dr. J and Al Kaline. And it's doubtful he would have understood the value of digital decor.

But for most athletes, something special occurs when their numbers align, like the planets, and signal that all's well in the sports universe.

Confirmed three-aholic Larry Walker, the former outfielder who appreciates the power of a lucky number, wore 33 throughout his career with the Expos, Rockies and Cardinals.

Wendell

Os

JIM OTTO

Otto was a 255-pound palindrome—and proud of it. He also could spell his name with the double zeroes (0tt0) he promoted proudly as his Oakland Raiders uniform number for 14 years (he wore 50 in his 1960 debut season). Besides being the most fashionably chic center in football history,

Otto was a Hall of Fame performer—the constant in an offense that helped the Raiders win the 1967 AFL championship and post a 115-42-11 regular-season record from 1963 through his retirement in 1974. Ol' Double Zero was tough as an old boot, a bulldog who fought through 10 broken noses and numerous knee operations to start all 210 of his team's regular-season games, all 13 postseason contests and 12 all-star games/Pro Bowls over 15 seasons. With all due respect to NBA great Robert Parish, 00 belongs to Otto. He's the one, after all, who made something out of nothing.

PLIMPTON WAS 'ZEROED IN' AS PAPER LION

The 40th anniversary reunion was held on the weekend of September 20-21, 2003. About 40 former Detroit players gathered in Dearborn, Mich., with author *George Plimpton*, who in 1963 had participated as a backup quarterback in the Lions' training camp while gathering material for a book he would title *Paper Lion*.

Giving the festivities a special touch was an unexpected discovery. Only a week earlier, the long-missing blue-and-silver No. 0 shirt Plimpton had worn in 1963 was found in the bottom of a beat-up, multi-layered equipment trunk in a storage room at the Lions' Allen Park complex. The trunk was marked, "Tiger Stadium."

At the Saturday night reunion celebration attended by such former stars as Alex Karras, Joe Schmidt, John Gordy and Roger Brown, team president Matt Millen and coach Steve Mariucci presented the jersey to Plimpton, who reminisced about his training camp experiences. Players recalled that Plimpton worked out with the quarterbacks and took frequent timeouts to jot down ideas in his ever-present notebook.

The next day, Plimpton and Karras served as honorary co-captains for the Lions' game against Minnesota. Karras, a former star defensive tackle, had a big role in the 1968 movie version of *Paper Lion*, which helped launch his acting career.

Four days later, Lions players and officials were shocked to learn that Plimpton, a bona fide member of their exclusive football fraternity, had died in his Manhattan apartment. He was 76.

NOTABLE 0s JACK CLARK 0s ERIC MONTROSS 0s JOHNNY MOORE 0s GILBERT ARENAS 0s

EliteOs

Parish

Burrough

(00) KEN BURROUGH: This career double zero still ranks third on the Oilers/Titans career receiving yardage list. His 1,063 yards in 1975 led the NFL.

(00) KEVIN DUCKWORTH: This 7-foot 00 was a Trail Blazer, but not in the world of uniform numbers.

(00) JEFF LEONARD: "Je-e-ef-rey, Je-e-ef-rey" didn't discover 00 until 1987, the season he warmed the hearts of Giants fans with his ever-present scowl and Cardinals fans with his defiant "one-flap-down" home run trot in the NLCS. Leonard was 00 through his four career-ending seasons—with the Giants, Brewers and Mariners.

(00) GREG OSTERTAG: The big, lumbering backup center doubled up on the "O" connection with his name and played some serious Jazz for more than a decade.

(00) ROBERT PARISH: From Golden State to Boston to Charlotte to Chicago, Parish was remarkably consistent in a 00-worthy career covering an NBA-record 21 seasons and 1,611 games. The Chief played for four championship teams—three with the Celtics and one with the Bulls.

(0) ODDIBE McDOWELL: The number-name connection made him

FAST FACTS

Moore

F The zero fad started early in New York, where nine Giants players wore the non-number—from halfback *Phil White* in 1925 to tackle *Lou Eaton* in 1945. No Giant has worn 0 since.

F The two-zeroes-are-better-than-one notion got its NFL start when Washington halfback *Steve Bagarus* first sported 00 on his jersey in 1945. Pittsburgh back *Johnny Clement* followed Bagarus' lead a year later.

F Dramatizing his "I'm starting all over" declaration in 1978 after he was traded from the Pirates to the Rangers, sweet-swinging *Al Oliver* started a revolution of sorts when he switched from his longtime No. 16 to 0. A.O. stayed true to his 0 tolerance for the final eight seasons of his 18-year career.

F *Jim Otto* had his trademark double zero and running back *Johnny Olszewski* and outfielder

JERRY HAIRSTON 0s OSCAR GAMBLE 0s PAUL DADE 0s TONY DELK 0s

Ostertag

BOBO SHOWS ZERO TOLERANCE IS ACCEPTABLE

His real name was *Louis Norman Newsom*, but friends knew him simply as Bobo. That's because the former righthander called everyone else "Bobo"—perhaps a result of never staying in one place long enough to memorize names. He was a baseball nomad who brought personality and fun to the game in the 1930s, '40s and '50s.

"Nomad" is an understatement. In 20 major league seasons, the 6-2, 230-pound workhorse pitched for nine teams, changed uniforms 16 times and wore 11 numbers. Newsom made five stops in Washington, prompting his boast that he had more terms in the nation's capital than Franklin D. Roosevelt. He also pitched for the St. Louis Browns three times and the Philadelphia Athletics and Brooklyn Dodgers twice. It was during his third Washington stop that he made history of a different kind.

In 1943, Newsom became the first baseball player—maybe the first team athlete ever—to wear 00. Senators owner Clark Griffith, always looking for ideas to promote his often-doormat team, gave his blessing to the idea and Bobo reprised the number when he returned to Washington in 1946 and '47. Newsom, nearing the end of his career, didn't have much success with the double zeroes.

That wasn't the case with the No. 12 he wore in 1940, when he posted a 21-5 record for Detroit and won two games in a seven-game World Series loss to Cincinnati. Newsom also wore Nos. 8, 15, 16, 20, 21, 29, 33, 34 and 48 in a career that produced a 211-222 record.

visible in Texas from 1985-88, but he was a journeyman No. 20 with Cleveland and No. 1 with Atlanta before falling off the big-league charts.

(0) JOHNNY OLSZEWSKI: Johnny O. was a boring No. 36 for the Chicago Cardinals from 1953-57, a more recognizable 0 for the remainder of his career with Washington, Detroit and Denver. His rushing performance was steady, no matter what number he was wearing.

(0) ORLANDO WOOLRIDGE: The high-skying forward bounced around the NBA for 13 years, but always remained loyal to his zero roots.

Al Oliver also sported name-inspired 0s over the final years of their NFL and MLB careers. But the NBA's Big O, *Oscar Robertson*, resisted the temptation and remained true to his career Nos. 14 and 1.

F The 00s worn by Boston center *Robert Parish* and San Antonio guard *Johnny Moore* are the only "zero jerseys" retired by teams in the four major professional sports. Parish and football's *Jim Otto* are the only "zero athletes" in pro halls of fame.

FRANKLIN STUBBS 0s CLIFF JOHNSON

Newsom

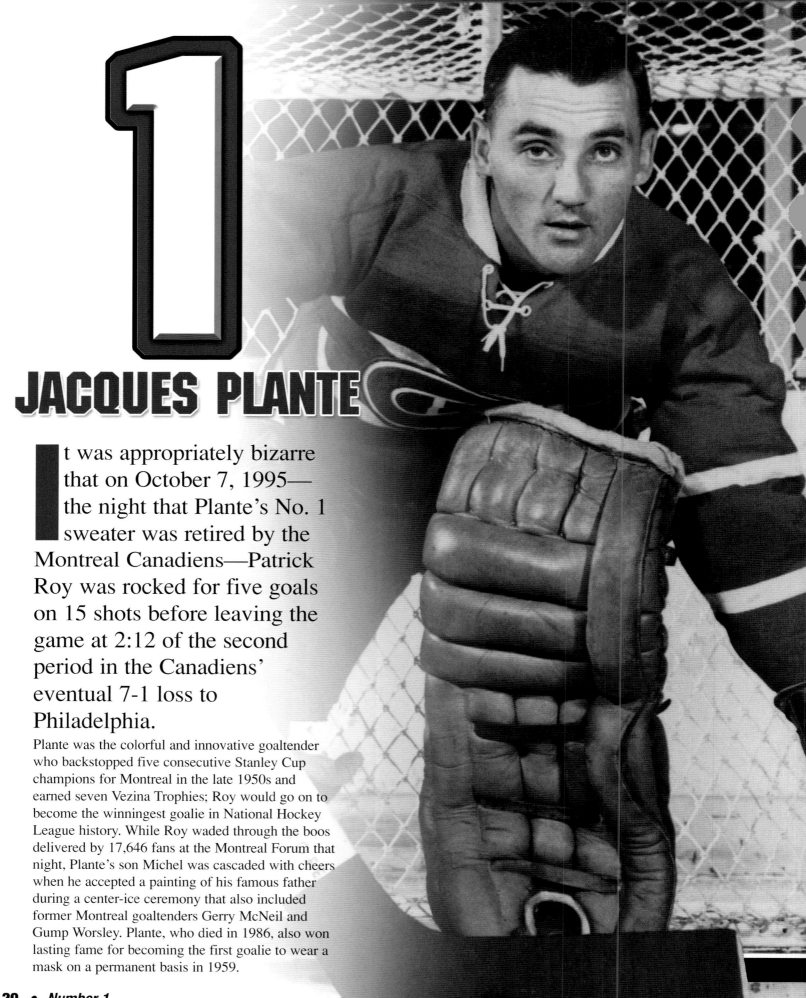

1

JACQUES PLANTE

It was appropriately bizarre that on October 7, 1995—the night that Plante's No. 1 sweater was retired by the Montreal Canadiens—Patrick Roy was rocked for five goals on 15 shots before leaving the game at 2:12 of the second period in the Canadiens' eventual 7-1 loss to Philadelphia.

Plante was the colorful and innovative goaltender who backstopped five consecutive Stanley Cup champions for Montreal in the late 1950s and earned seven Vezina Trophies; Roy would go on to become the winningest goalie in National Hockey League history. While Roy waded through the boos delivered by 17,646 fans at the Montreal Forum that night, Plante's son Michel was cascaded with cheers when he accepted a painting of his famous father during a center-ice ceremony that also included former Montreal goaltenders Gerry McNeil and Gump Worsley. Plante, who died in 1986, also won lasting fame for becoming the first goalie to wear a mask on a permanent basis in 1959.

1A IN YOUR DERBY PROGRAM ... NO. 1 AT THE FINISH LINE

This was no gimmick. When jockey Ron Turcotte guided *Secretariat* into the 10 gate for the start of the 1973 Kentucky Derby at Louisville's Churchill Downs, Big Red was wearing saddle cloth 1A. Go ahead, check that old program. Secretariat, one of horse racing's most revered thoroughbreds, 1A. The explanation centers on the rules of the time.

Secretariat was a Kentucky Derby "entry" with Angle Light, meaning that because both horses were trained by Lucien Laurin, they were coupled on tickets with bettors getting a 2-for-1 deal. Shecky Greene and My Gallant also were a Derby "entry" because of a common trainer.

When post positions were drawn before the Derby, Angle Light received 2, Secretariat 10, Shecky Greene 11 and My Gallant 12. Post positions typically corresponded to numbers in the betting program, except when "entries" were involved. The entry with the lowest post draw (Angle Light) was given the authentic 1 in the program; the horse it was coupled with (Secretariat) received 1A. Shecky Greene thus was the authentic 2 and My Gallant 2C.

The rest of the field was numbered according to post position: 1 post Restless Jet getting 3 in the program; 3 post Warbucks getting 4 in the program, and so on. What looks odd in retrospect might not have raised eyebrows on the day of the race. Angle Light had stunned Secretariat followers two weeks earlier in the Wood Memorial, and Sham had won the Santa Anita Derby.

Secretariat won the Derby by 2½ lengths over Sham, becoming the first horse to finish the 1¼-mile race in under 2 minutes. The Triple Crown quest was on.

Elite 1s

RICHIE ASHBURN: Even after Philly's Whiz Kids fizzled, center fielder Ashburn sizzled.

BOBBY DOERR: This Hall of Fame second baseman was a key contributor (six 100-RBI seasons) to an outstanding Red Sox offense from 1937-51, and he played nifty defense, too.

EDDIE GIACOMIN: The former Rangers goalie was so popular he had to cover his ears when New York fans chanted his name at his number-retirement ceremony in 1989.

GLENN HALL: He invented butterfly goaltending, which turned this moth into one of hockey's brightest stars.

BILLY MARTIN: The only manager cocky enough to deal with George Steinbrenner five times and crazy enough to say, "One's a born liar, the other is convicted" in reference to his star player (Reggie Jackson) and his boss (Steinbrenner). Martin, the feisty Yankees second baseman, won four World Series titles; Martin, the cocky Yankees manager, won another.

TRACY McGRADY: All it took for T-Mac to strut his NBA stuff was getting out of cousin Vinny's shadow in Toronto.

BERNIE PARENT: He was a Broad Street Bully, but only when guarding the nets from pucks and intruders.

McGrady

Martin

FAST FACTS

Anfernee Hardaway, who had worn uniform No. 25 in two seasons at Memphis State, asked for No. 1 in 1993 when he was traded to Orlando after being picked third overall by Golden State in the NBA draft. Call it a marketing plan. Hardaway wanted to play off his nickname, Penny.

Oscar Robertson, No. 14 during his 10 seasons with the Cincinnati Royals, switched to 1 in 1970 when traded to the Milwaukee Bucks

Robertson

because guard Jon McGlocklin already had 14. Robertson, who helped the Bucks to the 1971 NBA championship, is one of only two NBA players (Julius Erving is the other) to have different uniform numbers retired by two teams.

The first major leaguer to wear No. 1 on a permanent basis was center fielder **Earle Combs**, the New York Yankees' leadoff man in 1929. Those Yankees were the first team to wear

JOHNNY BOWER | **LISA LESLIE** | **LOU WHITAKER** | **BOBBY AVILA** | **GARRY TEMPLETON** | **BUMP WILLS** | **CHAUNCEY**

PEE WEE REESE: The heart and soul of the 1940-58 Dodgers was the first to see what everyone else would soon enough: Jackie belonged.

TERRY SAWCHUK: Pre-Patrick Roy, his 447 victories were an NHL record. His 103 career shutouts still are.

OZZIE SMITH: St. Louis' Wizard redefined a position while making a valid claim as the greatest defensive shortstop ever.

GUMP WORSLEY: It helps to be crazy if you want to be a goaltender in the NHL, according to Worsley in his autobiography. That might explain the 250 or so stitches he needed in his face and the stubborn determination to play without a mask until the final season of his 21-year career.

GARO YEPREMIAN: In contrast to most of the 1972 Dolphins, the colorful kicker is best remembered for being imperfect. He helped the Redskins score their only touchdown of Super Bowl 7.

Smith

'ONE DOG' SHOWS DIPLOMATIC SIDE

To Chicago White Sox fans, speedy center fielder *Lance Johnson* is remembered as "One Dog," a tribute to the No. 1 he wore on his uniform and a comment made by Sox broadcaster Ken Harrelson that compared his running style to a greyhound he had seen at a dog track. To New York fans, Johnson is remembered for a gesture he made in 1996 when a former Mets No. 1, longtime outfielder Mookie Wilson, was inducted into the team's Hall of Fame.

Johnson, playing his first season with the Mets after eight with the White Sox, voluntarily switched to No. 51 for an August 31 game against San Francisco so that Wilson would be the only No. 1 on the field during his induction ceremonies. Johnson chose 51 as a tribute to St. Louis Cardinals center fielder Willie McGee.

Wilson, who called Johnson's gesture "a nice thing to do," had watched One Dog wipe out his team single-season record for triples earlier in the season en route to a major league-leading 21. Johnson also finished the season with a National League-best 227 hits, thus becoming the first player to lead both the A.L. (186 in 1995) and N.L. in that category.

Johnson

Moon

permanent uniform numbers, which were issued according to the player's spot in the batting order.

Ⓕ Highly desired uniform No. 1 has never been worn by a Boston Celtics player. The number was set aside to honor original team owner *Walter Brown*.

Ⓕ The most prominent No. 1 in NFL history? Try *Warren Moon*, who passed for 49,325 yards—fourth best all-time—and 291 touchdowns over a 17-year Hall of Fame career with Houston, Minnesota, Seattle and Kansas City.

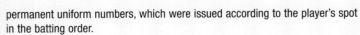

BILLUPS | **DEL CRANDALL** | **GARY ANDERSON** | **JERRY ROYSTER** | **JIM LANDIS** | **DICK GREEN**

2
SECRETARIAT

Perhaps you were expecting Derek Jeter or Moses Malone? Granted, Secretariat's saddle cloth numbers varied from race to race during his Triple Crown run in 1973, but never has a No. 2 provided a more mesmerizing performance than the day Big Red rampaged to a 31-length victory in the Belmont Stakes. We're talking chills-up-and-down-the-spine mesmerizing. No athlete of any shape, color or form ever dominated as thoroughly as the chestnut colt with the star on his forehead. "He's moving like a tremendous machine," announcer Chic Anderson said with almost breathless anticipation near the end of Big Red's history-making jaunt. And nobody who watched that race will ever forget. How utterly sensational was Secretariat during his romp to the first Triple Crown in a quarter century? More than three decades later, he still holds the record for the current distances run in the Kentucky Derby and Belmont. We're talking absolute domination—by the greatest horse in racing history.

FAST FACTS

F **Danny Ainge** is best remembered for his No. 44 days as a member of the Boston Celtics. But there's a No. 2 uniform packed away neatly in his closet. That's the digit he wore in his three seasons (1979-81) as a light-hitting infielder/outfielder for the Toronto Blue Jays.

F No. 2 has never been worn by a Boston Celtics player. It is retired in honor of longtime coach, president and general manager **Red Auerbach**.

Payton

NOTABLE 2s JERRY REMY 2 JUNIOR BRIDGEMAN 2 FRANK CROSETTI 2 FREDDIE PATEK 2

Elite 2s

LEO DUROCHER: This Lip was rarely zipped during a 41-year major league playing and managing career.

ALEX ENGLISH: Know which NBA player scored the most points (19,682) in the 1980s? Here are a couple of hints: He played for the Denver Nuggets, and his initials are "A.E."

NELLIE FOX: Baseball's ultimate little guy (5-9, 150 pounds) earned his keep by rarely striking out, advancing runners and playing great defense. In 1959, the second baseman was the A.L. MVP and catalyst for the first White Sox team to reach the World Series since 1919.

CHARLEY GEHRINGER: If Hall of Fame second basemen were produced on assembly lines, chances are they would look like Detroit's "Mechanical Man."

DOUG HARVEY: A defenseman with an attitude and seven Norris Trophies to prove it. Hall of Famer Harvey was the big No. 2 for six Montreal Stanley Cup champions.

BILLY HERMAN: It was brains over brawn for this Hall of Fame second baseman, who "quarterbacked" Chicago Cubs teams that won three N.L. pennants in the 1930s.

DEREK JETER: This heady shortstop is wearing one of the two single-digit numbers not retired by the Yankees. Soon No. 6 will be the only holdout.

TOMMY LASORDA: After testing 11, 23, 27, 29 and 52 as a player and coach, Lasorda spent his Dodgers managerial career wearing No. 2 as a tribute to Durocher.

BRIAN LEETCH: The longtime Rangers defenseman became the first American-born player to win the Conn Smythe Trophy in 1994.

AL MacINNIS: When the king of the 100-mph slap shot let fly, NHL opponents sang the Blues. And MacInnis stood out at Calgary, too.

RED SCHOENDIENST: A ham sandwich and glass of milk—that's all it took to lure this Hall of Fame second baseman to the Cardinals organization.

EDDIE SHORE: This 1930s Boston defenseman, a four-time Hart Trophy (MVP) winner who intimidated with defense and offense, was scarier than a cemetery on Halloween.

RUSTY WALLACE: Famous for his intense rivalry with Dale Earnhardt, Wallace never backed down from the Intimidator and finished in the top 20 in Winston/Nextel Cup points in each of his final 22 seasons.

AL UNSER: Patience and super-quick pit stops were the formula that led to four Indy 500 wins, two (1970, 1978) while driving No. 2 cars.

F Former guard *Gary Payton*, No. 20 through most of his college career at Oregon State and professional career, actually wore No. 2 as a 1990-91 NBA rookie with Seattle. With veteran Quintin Dailey wearing 20, Payton chose to celebrate his status as the No. 2 overall pick in the draft.

F Kicker *Teddy Garcia* became the first Minnesota Viking to wear No. 2 in 1989, 28 years after the team played its first NFL game.

NO FO, FO, FO

When *Moses Malone* was traded by Houston to Philadelphia before the 1982-83 season, 76ers forward Bobby Jones was wearing No. 24, Moses' number with the Rockets. So the rugged 6-10 center switched to 2. Then he went out and showed that determination, skill and raw power play well with any number.

In his first regular season with the 76ers, Malone averaged 24.5 points and 15.3 rebounds while helping his team post an NBA-best 65-17 record. He was rewarded with his third MVP award. And he made history of a different sort when 76ers coach Billy Cunningham asked him what he expected in the 1983 playoffs.

Malone, a man of few words, looked at his coach and said, "Fo, fo, fo." Cunningham smiled, Philadelphia fans rejoiced and the 76ers adopted it as their anthem. Then Malone and forward Julius Erving led the way as the team steamrolled its way to a championship. The Sixers drew a first-round bye, swept New York, beat Milwaukee in five games and swept the defending champion Los Angeles Lakers in the Finals. Not quite "fo, fo, fo," but close.

How quickly things change! The joy of that victory was tempered three years later when Malone was traded to Washington. At a news conference, he was handed a Bullets jersey with the No. 2. "I had this number in Philly; it's a 76ers number. I think I'll change it to No. 4," said Malone, who did just that.

MITCH RICHMOND 2 ZOILO VERSALLES 2 MALIK SEALY 2 STEVE CHRISTIE 2 STACEY AUGMON 2 RED ROLFE 2 RICK LEY

3
BABE RUTH

The New York Yankees clearly waited too long to retire Ruth's number. What were they thinking?

Bud Metheny with the Babe's number? Roy Weatherly? Cliff Mapes? These guys were benchwarmers, not fit to sharpen the Bambino's spikes. George Selkirk, the first player to wear No. 3 after Ruth, at least was a starter and contributor to five World Series championships. But Selkirk was known as Twinkletoes, a nice nickname for someone not wearing the Sultan of Swat's number. The Yankees finally came to their senses in 1948 when they retired No. 3 at Yankee Stadium on a festive day celebrating the ballpark's 25th anniversary. The Yankees simply acknowledged the obvious: Other athletes—for other teams or in other sports—might wear the number, but there is no doubt who the all-time No. 3 really is.

NOTABLE 3s J.C.

NO. 2 CHEVY SET A FAST PACE FOR EARNHARDT'S LEGACY

Racing fans will forever associate *Dale Earnhardt* with the black No. 3 Goodwrench Chevrolet that he drove to four Winston Cup points championships and his only Daytona 500 title in 1998. But Earnhardt's first NASCAR success was achieved in a blue-and-yellow No. 2 Chevy that he drove to a surprising points title in 1980 for owner Rod Osturlund.

Ironically, more than a quarter century later, that remains the only No. 2 car to win a Winston Cup or Nextel Cup championship.

Earnhardt was a second-year phenom when he won for Osturlund, the year after he was named NASCAR's top rookie driver. The '80 Winston Cup triumph was a startling feat for the inexperienced Earnhardt, who defied predictions of a late collapse and held off three-time champion Cale Yarborough by 19 points. That would be his last championship association with No. 2.

Earnhardt didn't start driving Richard Childress' No. 3 Chevrolet until 1984 and went black in 1988 when Goodwrench became the primary sponsor—a relationship that lasted until his 2001 death in a crash during the Daytona 500.

TREMBLAY 3 FRANK FRISCH 3 JOSE VIDRO 3 PETE GOGOLAK 3 ALAN TRAMMELL 3 DWYANE WADE 3 DICK McAULIFFE

Elite3s

Iverson

EARL AVERILL: Indians outfielder Averill, the strong, silent type, let his bat do the talking in a Hall of Fame career in the 1930s and '40s.

TONY CANADEO: The Gray Ghost of Gonzaga did it all for the Packers in the 1940s and '50s—he ran, passed, punted, defended passes and returned kicks, perhaps explaining his prematurely gray hair. There was no gray area in his 1974 election to the Pro Football Hall of Fame.

WILLIE DAVIS: This smooth and speedy center fielder made life easier for the Koufax-Drysdale Dodgers of the 1960s.

JIMMIE FOXX: They called him "The Beast," and Yankees pitcher Lefty Gomez claimed Foxx once broke an outfield bleacher seat with a batted ball.

BUD HARRELSON: The light-hitting New York shortstop who fought Pete Rose in the 1973 NLCS was symbolic of the uphill battle the Mets fought against the future Big Red Machine.

ALLEN IVERSON: NBA scoring titles,

Marbury

FAST FACTS

F *Dennis Johnson*, whose No. 3 is retired by the Boston Celtics, said he chose the number when he reached Boston in 1983 because there were three people in his family and he was beginning play for his third team.

F Hall of Fame broadcaster *Curt Gowdy* wore No. 3 when he was a starter for the University of Wyoming basketball team from 1940-42.

Baines

F *Harold Baines* wore No. 3 longer than any other player in the four major team sports. Baines wore it in all or parts of 22 seasons with the White Sox, Rangers, A's, Orioles and Indians.

F *Bronko Nagurski* was the first prominent No. 3 in Chicago Bears history—he wore it from 1930-37 and in 1943—but not the first. Nagurski was preceded by two backs, *Robert Koehler* (1920-21) and *Ed Sternaman* (1922-27).

EDGAR RENTERIA 3 *MARK MOSELEY*

3 *BUD HARRELSON* 3 *DRAZEN PETROVIC*

cool and attitude—this 76ers lightweight (6-0, 165) has got game.

DARYLE LAMONICA: More than three decades after Lamonica's retirement, Raiders owner Al Davis still is looking for another "Mad Bomber."

STEPHON MARBURY: Don't tell "Starbury" there's a better point guard in the NBA—you'll have an argument on your hands.

DALE MURPHY: A five-tool center fielder who won MVP awards for the Braves in 1982 and '83.

JAN STENERUD: A ski-jumping scholarship at Montana State evolved into a Hall of Fame kicking career for this Chiefs great. One of the pioneers of soccer-style kicking, Stenerud took 3 because that's how many points field goals are worth and how many times he tapped his feet before each kick.

BILL TERRY: This John McGraw protege and antagonist had championship tools: He could hit, field and lead, as he demonstrated as a manager during his Hall of Fame career.

Lamonica

Killebrew

BOOMER DOES BABE

David Wells professed strong feeling for Babe Ruth and his No. 3, even though he had never worn it. Edgar Renteria was emotionally attached to the digit, which he had worn for eight of his nine major league seasons. Unfortunately for Renteria, he signed his free-agent contract with Boston on December 17, 2004, three days after Wells had signed his.

Boomer swept into Boston and asked for No. 3, which had been denied to him by the New York Yankees—for obvious reasons. He was granted his wish, becoming the first Red Sox pitcher to wear a single-digit number since 1932 and only the second ever. Renteria settled for 16, the number he had worn for Florida as a rookie in 1996.

The power of 3 was not apparent for Wells, a portly lefthander and free spirit who could not otherwise match Ruth's pitching prowess for the Red Sox (1914-19) over the first two months of the 2005 season. The power of 16 also eluded Renteria, a shortstop who had thrived wearing 3 over the previous six seasons with St. Louis. A slumping Renteria heard Wells might be willing to give up his number and negotiations opened.

When Wells took the mound for his May 29 start at Yankee Stadium, he was wearing 16, Renteria 3. Wells worked 8⅓ innings in a 7-2 win—his first since April 20—and Renteria went 4-for-5 and hit a home run.

Rumor had it that the desire to switch numbers was not entirely mutual. Renteria, insiders said, had to sweeten the deal with money—reportedly in the five-figure range.

F **Harmon Killebrew** is the only player to wear No. 3 for the Minnesota Twins. In the franchise's history, though, the digit was modeled pre-Killebrew by two other Hall of Famers. Heinie Manush wore it for four seasons (1931 and 1933-35) and Al Simmons for one (1937) when the team was located in Washington.

4
LOU GEHRIG

What's not to like about this choice? More than six decades after his untimely death, Gehrig remains one of the most romanticized figures in sports history, not to mention one of baseball's greatest stars. His legacy is as durable as the ironman records he posted in the 1920s and '30s for the New York Yankees. Gehrig also was the game's original No. 4 and the first player ever to have a uniform number retired. He practically invented the concept of the cleanup hitter, batting fourth (thus No. 4) behind Babe Ruth—a 3-4 combination unmatched before or since. There's no denying Bobby Orr's impact on hockey, or the incredible ironman exploits of a modern-day No. 4, Green Bay quarterback Brett Favre. But the pinstripe magic and his heart-wrenching demise swing this battle of titans to Gehrig—"the luckiest man on the face of the Earth."

FAST FACTS

F *Jim Harbaugh*, who played quarterback for five teams during his 15-year NFL career, wore No. 4 because he was a huge fan of former hockey great Bobby Orr.

F When *Paul Molitor* was inducted into the baseball Hall of Fame in 2004, he became the 22nd member of that elite club to have worn No. 4 for at least one season. Molitor wore it for 18 of his 21 big-league years.

F *Billy Williams* lifted No. 26 to prominence in his 16 seasons with the Chicago Cubs, but the Hall of Fame outfielder played 18 games in his 1959 big-league debut wearing uniform No. 4.

F Uniform No. 4 has been retired by eight major league teams—more than any other number.

NOTABLE 4s JOE DUMARS 4 HAROLD REYNOLDS 4 MARTY MARION 4 SCOTT STEVENS 4 CARNEY LANSFORD 4 ROB BLAKE

LUKE APPLING: The more "Old Aches and Pains" complained, the better he played shortstop in his Hall of Fame career with the White Sox.

JEAN BELIVEAU: Montreal's stylish center won two regular-season MVPs and led the Canadiens to 10 Stanley Cups in the 1950s and '60s. Few can match his Hall of Fame accomplishments.

JOE CRONIN: He began his baseball career in 1926 as a shortstop and ended it almost half a century later as president of the A.L. In between, Cronin compiled a .301 average for the Pirates, Senators and Red Sox, topped 100 RBIs eight times, became a player/manager (Washington, 1933) at the tender age of 26 and earned Hall of Fame election.

RALPH KINER: The slugging Pittsburgh outfielder won or shared home run titles in his first seven major league seasons, a feat no player has matched.

MARTY MARION: The best defensive shortstop of the 1940s won an MVP award (in 1944, despite hitting just .267) and three World Series rings with the Cardinals.

SIDNEY MONCRIEF: The heart and soul of Milwaukee Bucks teams that won seven division titles in the 1980s. His outstanding defense was a mirror image of his offense.

MEL OTT: John McGraw groomed him as the backbone of the Giants' offense, a role he filled from

Favre

1926-47. Mr. Consistent was the N.L's first 500-homer man.

REGGIE ROBY: Linebacker-sized punters who can boom the ball are prized commodities. Nobody was better than Roby for the first two-thirds of his career with the Dolphins.

DOLPH SCHAYES: Basketball's first ironman also was the NBA's first true power forward and its career scoring leader before Bob Pettit passed him in 1963.

JERRY SLOAN: Utah's bulldog coach got his start as a tenacious guard for the Bulls.

DUKE SNIDER: In New York in the '50s, he was the center field equal of Willie Mays and Mickey Mantle. That's pretty lofty status for an artful Dodger.

EARL WEAVER: Weaver's tantrums and umpire baiting are legendary, but they didn't prevent him from guiding the Orioles to four A.L. pennants and one World Series title.

Snider

🄵 Green Bay quarterback *Brett Favre*, unable to get his high school No. 10 at the University of Southern Mississippi, took the only number left—4. "You take what you can get," he explained.

A FINAL TRIBUTE FOR BOSTON'S NO. 4

It was a classic *Bobby Orr* memory, right up there with his suspended-in-air Stanley Cup-deciding goal in 1970, the eight Norris Trophies he earned as the NHL's top defenseman and the three Hart Trophies he won as the league's MVP. This one came at the advanced age of 47 when the Boston icon gathered with former Bruins teammates and 14,448 fans on September 26, 1995, to pay final respects to 67-year-old Boston Garden.

When Orr's No. 4 banner was lowered from the rafters as the climactic end to an emotional night of tributes, the reality hit everyone like a 100-mph slap shot to the gut. In a matter of minutes, the venerable Garden would close its doors for a final time. Ray Bourque, a later-era defenseman, skated out to retrieve the banner and in turn presented it to Orr, who skated one final lap around the ice. The crowd erupted, a roar that rose to a building-shaking crescendo.

The night, billed as the Garden's "Last Hurrah," started with an exhibition game that featured former Boston stars wearing their familiar jerseys and uniform numbers. But center stage belonged to Orr, the pioneering defenseman who revolutionized his sport. Orr greeted fans at the door in his No. 4 jersey, spent considerable time in front of cameras and interviewers and departed—in classic Orr style—to the emotional chants of "Bob-by, Bob-by, Bob-by."

Orr

🄴 **ADAM VINATIERI** 🄴 **RUDY YORK** 🄴 **CHARLIE MAXWELL** 🄴 **JACKIE JENSEN** 🄴 **BOBBY GRICH** 🄴 **CHRIS WEBBER** 🄴 **DALE BERRA**

Best by Number • **31**

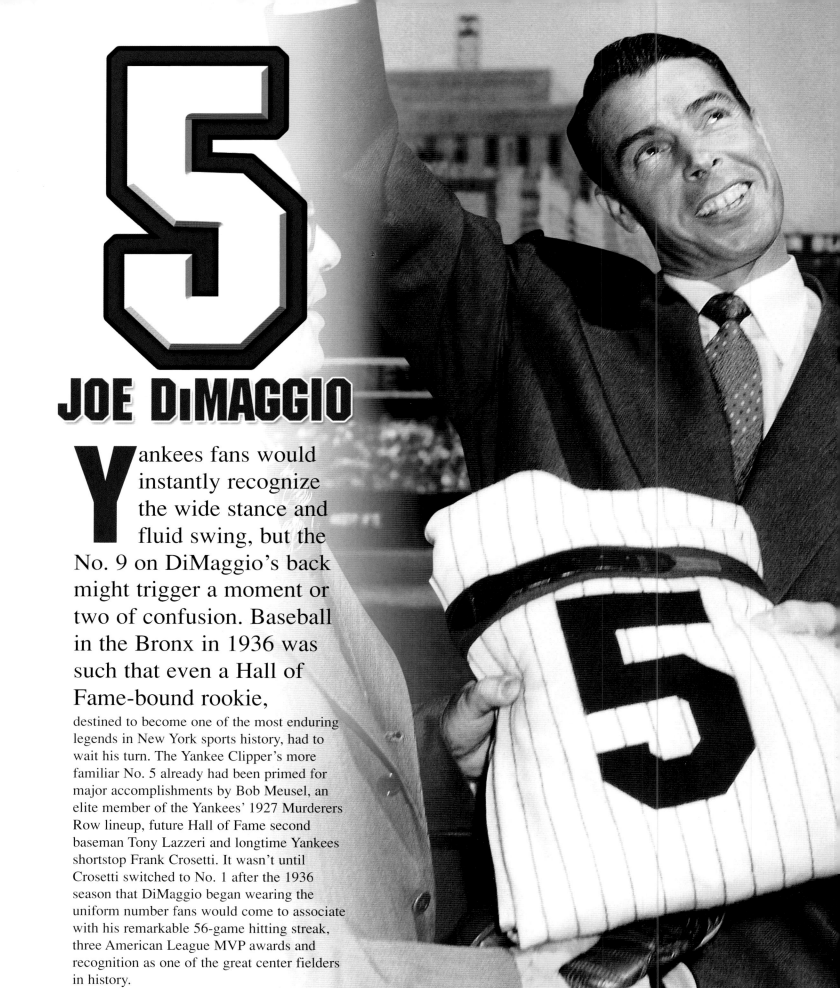

5

JOE DiMAGGIO

Yankees fans would instantly recognize the wide stance and fluid swing, but the No. 9 on DiMaggio's back might trigger a moment or two of confusion. Baseball in the Bronx in 1936 was such that even a Hall of Fame-bound rookie,

destined to become one of the most enduring legends in New York sports history, had to wait his turn. The Yankee Clipper's more familiar No. 5 already had been primed for major accomplishments by Bob Meusel, an elite member of the Yankees' 1927 Murderers Row lineup, future Hall of Fame second baseman Tony Lazzeri and longtime Yankees shortstop Frank Crosetti. It wasn't until Crosetti switched to No. 1 after the 1936 season that DiMaggio began wearing the uniform number fans would come to associate with his remarkable 56-game hitting streak, three American League MVP awards and recognition as one of the great center fielders in history.

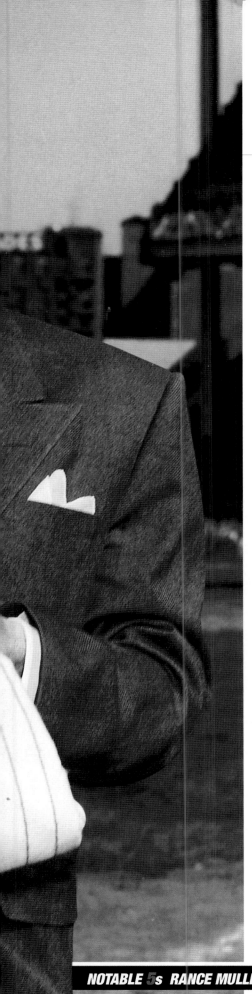

'NO. 5' PUJOLS JUSTIFIES NUMERICAL PROMOTION

He could have been a 32, an elite society in the long history of sports numbers. But St. Louis general manager Walt Jocketty had a different vision for **Albert Pujols**. The Cardinals' young slugger was far from a sure-bet superstar in the spring of 2001 when Jocketty spotted his Hall of Fame potential.

Pujols came to camp as a long-shot 68 and ended it by making the Cardinals' opening day roster, prompting then equipment manager Buddy Bates to switch his number to 32. Pujols had been outstanding throughout the spring, more than justifying the numerical promotion. But an excited Jocketty had even lower aspirations.

"Walt had never in the time we worked together told me what to do," Bates recalled, "and he asked me the day before we were breaking camp, 'What number did you put Pujols in?' I told him I had him in 32 and Walt kind of winced. And I said, 'What's the matter?'

And he said, 'You don't have anything better?' So I asked him what he was going to do with (outfielder Quinton) McCracken. He said, 'Well, we're going to let him go.' I told him that would open up No. 5 and he said, 'That's perfect.'

"And that's how he got 5. I would like to take credit for that, but I can't. Walt was behind that."

Through the 2005 season, Jocketty's lofty expectations for his young star had been far exceeded, with Pujols matching the early career statistics of such superstars as Joe DiMaggio and Ted Williams.

Elite 5s

JEFF BAGWELL: The biggest buzz among Houston's "Killer B's" comes from this hard-hitting first baseman, who has anchored the Astros' offense for a decade and a half.

LOU BOUDREAU: Cleveland's most recent World Series championship was orchestrated in 1948 by this Hall of Fame shortstop, the last player/manager to win a title.

DIT CLAPPER: A member of Boston's first championship team in 1928-29, the durable Hall of Famer played 21 grueling seasons for the Bruins.

HANK GREENBERG: Injuries and war service limited the big Tigers first baseman to 331 career home runs but didn't keep him from reaching the Hall of Fame.

PAUL HORNUNG: Football's "Golden Boy" never had a problem scoring—by running, kicking, passing or getting a young lady's phone number.

TERRY LABONTE: Terry and Bobby are the only brothers to capture Winston Cup titles. Terry drove his No. 5 car to victory in 1996.

GUY LAPOINTE: An important defensive cog in the Canadiens' championship machine of the 1970s.

GEORGE McAFEE: A now-you-see-

Dick and Tom Van Arsdale

him-now-you-don't runner who helped the World War II-era Bears win three championships.

DONOVAN McNABB: The Eagle has landed near the top of NFL quarterback charts.

DENIS POTVIN: Bobby Orr might have been the first defenseman to dominate games offensively, but Islanders great Potvin was the first to score 1,000 points.

BROOKS ROBINSON: His 16 straight Gold Gloves suggest he's the best fielding third baseman of all time. Need a refresher

McNabb

FAST FACTS

When the Cincinnati Reds retired the No. 5 jersey of catcher *Johnny Bench* in 1984, he became the first player to be so honored in the 115-year history of the franchise.

Quarterback *Heath Shuler* wore No. 5 throughout his five NFL seasons with Washington and New Orleans. The number preference, which dated back to the seventh grade, was a tribute to baseball star George Brett.

Bench

When *Bill Walton* was traded by San Diego to Boston in 1985, he wanted the No. 32 he had worn at UCLA and with the Portland Trail Blazers and Clippers. But 32 belonged to Celtics power forward Kevin McHale. So Walton got creative. He added 3 plus 2 and came up with 5.

Jason Kidd's 5 is one of three University of California basketball numbers to be retired—even though he left Cal after two years.

PAT LEAHY 5 JEFF GARCIA 5 GEORGE

SCOTT 5 ROD LANGWAY 5 ROY SMALLEY 5

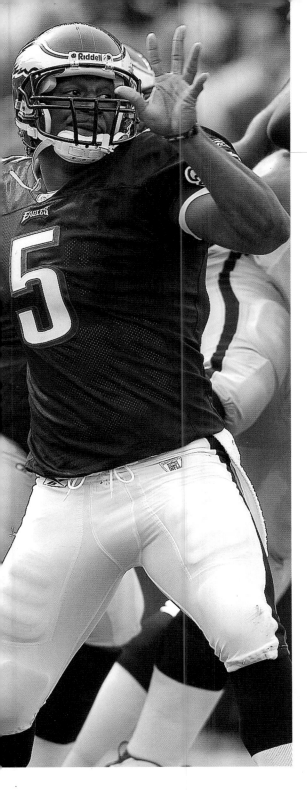

course? Check out his performance in the 1970 World Series.

MENDY RUDOLPH: Before NBA refs became emotionless robots, this old-school official ruled his games with an iron fist and—gasp!—personality.

DICK AND TOM VAN ARSDALE: Separated at NBA birth (Dick played his first season with the Knicks, Tom with the Pistons), the identical twins remained connected through their No. 5 uniforms for 11 seasons. In 1976-77—the 12th and final season for both—they played together at Phoenix with Dick, a longtime member of the Suns, keeping his 5 and Tom switching to 4.

Bagwell

Walton

(F) Canadiens great **Bernie "Boom Boom" Geoffrion** died on March 11, 2006—the day he was scheduled to have his No. 5 sweater retired at Montreal's Bell Centre. At Geoffrion's request, the ceremony went on, with members of his family receiving a long, emotional ovation.

BRETT WAITS HIS TURN, MAKES 5 A ROYAL PAIN

When *George Brett* was recalled from the minor leagues for good early in the 1974 season, he simply wanted to be like Brooks—from the magic glove Brooks Robinson flashed as the star third baseman for the Baltimore Orioles to the No. 5 he wore on his uniform jersey. Good things, he discovered, come to those who wait.

Brett's third base defense needed a lot of work to measure up to Robinson's, and No. 5 already was being worn by Kansas City journeyman outfielder Richie Scheinblum. So Brett wore No. 25 and began flashing the intensity, determination and bat speed that eventually would give him Hall of Fame status alongside the man he admired.

Midway through the 1974 season, Scheinblum left Kansas City and Royals equipment manager Al Zych asked Brett if he wanted to switch numbers. Brett began wearing No. 5 the next spring, an association that would last 19 years. Now the most celebrated number in Kansas City history has been retired by the Royals and occupies a place of honor below the Kauffman Stadium scoreboard.

And how does Brett think he measures up on the long list of outstanding baseball No. 5s?

"A couple of years ago, we played a game at Dyersville, Iowa, at the Field of Dreams," Brett told *Kansas City Star* writer Pete Grathoff in 1999. "I was No. 5 and Brooks was No. 15."

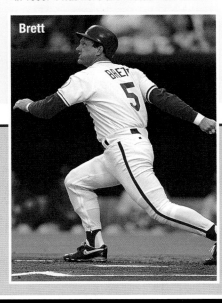

Brett

6

BILL RUSSELL

The number hangs from the Garden rafters, alongside the 11 championship banners Bill Russell helped the Boston Celtics secure from 1956-69, both as a player and the first black coach in NBA history. Befitting the complex, introspective and sometimes-aloof manner of the greatest defensive center in NBA history, the number was retired in two installments. The first ceremony was March 12, 1972, in an empty Boston Garden, the way Russell wanted because of bitterness over perceived racial prejudice during his career. Only a few players and friends participated. The second was a rededication on May 26, 1999—a *show* emceed by actor Bill Cosby and witnessed by thousands of fans and basketball luminaries such as John Havlicek, Oscar Robertson, Kareem Abdul-Jabbar, Larry Bird, Julius Erving and Bob Cousy.

GARVEY GETS DIGITAL CLOSURE FROM PADRES

Steve Garvey always had a flair for marketing. So it wasn't surprising in 1983 when Garvey, who had just signed a free-agent contract with San Diego, sought out Padres infielder Tim Flannery and asked if he would give up his uniform No. 6, the digit that had become synonymous with Garvey during his 14-year run as the Los Angeles Dodgers' All-Star first baseman. Flannery needed incentive. So Garvey bought him a three-piece suit. The deal consummated, Garvey wore No. 6 for five more seasons, during which he extended his National League-record playing streak to 1,207 consecutive games and delivered a Game 4-winning home run in the 1984 NLCS.

After his retirement in 1987, Garvey was told by team president Chub Feeney that his No. 6 uniform would be retired—well, kind of. Keith Moreland was wearing the number and Feeney asked Garvey if he had any problem with the outfielder keeping it through the remainder of the season. Garvey suggested that was not a good idea. So Feeney had another brainstorm. He suggested Moreland could remove his jersey during a home-plate ceremony and present it to Garvey, who responded that he really didn't want a uniform with Moreland's name across the back.

In the end, Moreland switched from 6 to 7 in an April 16, 1988, pregame ceremony on Steve Garvey Night at Jack Murphy Stadium. Feeney presented Garvey a framed picture of jersey No. 6 and showered him with gifts, including a 1988 Mercedes-Benz.

Ironically, the first number retired by the Padres has never been retired by the Dodgers.

NOTABLE *6s JOHNNY CALLISON* 6 *ROLF BENIRSCHKE* 6 *ANDY CAREY* 6

Elite 6s

Musial

SAL BANDO: The clutch-hitting third baseman should have won a Nobel Peace Prize after surviving Charlie Finley and all those clubhouse characters in Oakland.

CLETE BOYER: New York fans loved watching Mantle and Maris hit the ball out of the park. Yankees pitchers loved watching Boyer play sparkling defense at third base.

WALTER DAVIS: The sweet-shooting swingman averaged 18.9 points and was a quiet, steady leader over 15 seasons with the Suns, Nuggets and Trail Blazers.

CARL FURILLO: The Dodgers were so impressed with the rifle-armed right fielder, they bought an entire minor league team to get him. Furillo became a cornerstone for the great Brooklyn teams of the 1940s and '50s.

JOE GORDON: The 1942 A.L. MVP, a great-fielding second baseman with power, was a key member of powerhouse Yankees teams.

Erving

FAST FACTS

F In 2001, **Rob Bell** and **Wayne Gomes**, midseason acquisitions by Texas and San Francisco, shared an unusual distinction as pitchers wearing single-digit numbers—Bell 6 and Gomes 2. After the season, they shared another distinction—ERAs higher than their uniform numbers. Bell's was 7.18 in 18 games for the Rangers; Gomes' was 8.40 in 13 games for the Giants.

F **Julius Erving** is one of two players who have had different numbers retired by two NBA teams. Dr. J was No. 6 for the Philadelphia 76ers, 32 in his ABA days with the New York/New Jersey Nets franchise. Oscar Robertson was honored by the Cincinnati Royals (now Sacramento Kings) as 14, the Milwaukee Bucks as 1.

PHIL HOUSLEY 6 **RON FAIRLY** 6 **WILLIE WILSON** 6 **BRANDI CHASTAIN** 6 **RENNIE STENNETT** 6 **ANDREW BOGUT** 6 **ROY WHITE**

QUEST FOR 6 HAS A LUCKY ENDING

Catcher *John Flaherty* always had an affinity for 6. So, naturally, he requested the number when he was called up by the Boston Red Sox in 1992. No dice. Former Red Sox shortstop Johnny Pesky worked as a roving instructor for the organization and still was wearing the number. So Flaherty opted for 15.

Flaherty was traded to Detroit in 1994, but again his 6 yearning went unfulfilled. The Tigers had retired the number for Al Kaline. In San Diego two years later, Flaherty again was denied because the number had been retired for Steve Garvey. When at last Flaherty got the opportunity to switch to 6 after a 1997 trade to Tampa Bay, he did a sudden about-face.

In the true spirit of superstitious baseball players, he chose to go with 23—because he had compiled a 27-game hitting streak while wearing that number for the Padres.

Kaline

AL KALINE: Without him in the 1950s and '60s, all those years of Yankees domination would have been tougher to swallow for Detroit fans.

TONY LAZZERI: Though his big-league home run totals never matched his prolific minor league numbers, "Poosh 'Em Up" Tony was a big run producer for the Murderers Row Yankees.

STAN MUSIAL: When your nickname is "The Man," that says it all.

TONY OLIVA: The Twins outfielder was one of the best all-around players in the 1960s until his knees started giving out. After that, he merely was one of the game's best hitters.

RICO PETROCELLI: This Red Sox favorite, one of the few shortstops with offensive pop in the 1960s, knew how to feed the Green Monster.

F Two NBA teams, the Orlando Magic and Sacramento Kings, have retired No. 6 as a tribute to their fans (the "sixth man").

F New York Yankees great *Mickey Mantle* wore No. 6 in his 1951 rookie season before switching to 7.

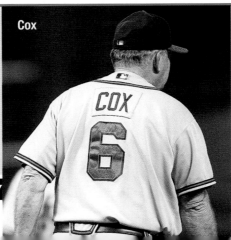

Cox

F The two major league managers whose teams have posted the most victories over the last decade (1996 through 2005) wear No. 6—Atlanta's *Bobby Cox* (977) and New York's Joe Torre (982).

F Washington All-American quarterback *Sonny Sixkiller* was so popular in 1971 that a song written by a local disc jockey—"The Ballad of Sonny Sixkiller"—remained on the charts for weeks in Seattle. Sixkiller, of course, wore No. 6.

6 PAUL BLAIR 6 KEVIN BUTLER 6 JOHNNY PESKY   6 KENYON MARTIN 6 BOB RODGERS

7

JOHN ELWAY

Elway. Elway. Elway. Whisper the word three times, open your eyes and watch looming defeat transform into heart-pounding victory.

Mickey Mantle? His romantic, pinstripe aura captivated boomers, but Super John gets a now-generation edge in this numerical battle of titans. We're talking legends here, and the mystique of Mantle has yielded center stage to the savvy, cool-under-pressure magic of Elway. Mantle was brilliant, but the New York Yankees' great teams of the 1950s and '60s featured many gifted players; Elway, the ultimate field general, did the heavy lifting for Denver teams that reached three Super Bowls in the 1980s and won two in the '90s. Choose your poison. But Elway's physical tools, comeback heroics, immunity to pressure, improvisational skills and leadership abilities are hard to top. Denver's No. 7 performed Mile High magic for 16 years—with that cocky smile and a twitch or two of his powerful right arm.

Mantle

SPURRIER'S DIGITAL FAUX PAS TICKS OFF WASHINGTON FANS

When Steve Spurrier coached at the University of Florida, he said he didn't believe uniform numbers should be retired and demonstrated his conviction by "unretiring" his own No. 11. But that numerological indifference did not play well in the spring of 2002 when Spurrier was the new coach of the NFL's Washington Redskins.

Fans were shocked during a minicamp when new quarterback Danny Wuerffel, Florida's 1996 Heisman Trophy winner, took the field wearing No. 7—his old college number and the digit he wore with the New Orleans Saints and Green Bay Packers. In Washington, 7 is synonymous with *Joe Theismann*, and nobody had worn it since Theismann's retirement after the 1985 season.

The public reaction was loud and clear. Only Sammy Baugh's 33 had been retired by the Redskins, but other numbers—including 7—had been kept out of circulation as an unofficial tribute to esteemed players. When it was later revealed that a new signee, quarterback Shane Matthews, was planning to wear Sonny Jurgensen's revered No. 9, fans decided enough was enough—and Spurrier did an about-face.

He declared famous Redskins numbers off-limits, and Wuerffel switched to 17 and Matthews to 6. But something got lost in translation. Tight end Leonard Stephens played the 2002 season wearing 49, the number that had been mothballed since 1968 in honor of Hall of Famer Bobby Mitchell. When a "deeply hurt" Mitchell "retired" as Redskins assistant general manager in February 2003, Spurrier apologized for the mistake.

Theismann

NOTABLE **7**s   DOM DiMAGGIO **7** PAUL COFFEY **7** BOB WATERFIELD **7** DON MONEY **7** STEVE YEAGER **7** RON JAWORSKI

Elite 7s

MORTEN ANDERSEN: The Great Dane is the second leading scorer in NFL history and No. 1 all-time in career games, to boot.

NATE ARCHIBALD: His skills didn't match his nickname. "Tiny," the only player ever to lead the NBA in assists and points in the same season, helped the Celtics capture a championship in 1981.

BILL BARBER: This do-it-all Broad Street Bully left wing credited his strength to shoveling his homemade rink as a kid.

DAVID BECKHAM: Almost famous? He's married to a pop star, he's a fashion trendsetter, he's the captain of the English national soccer team and he plays for Real Madrid, the most prominent soccer team in the world.

CRAIG BIGGIO: A gamer, a catalyst, an instigator and the ultimate Astro—not to mention he's one of those Killer B's.

DUTCH CLARK: This triple-threat quarterback led the Lions to the 1935 NFL championship.

PHIL ESPOSITO: Moving this high-scoring Bruin from in front of the net required a forklift, or at least a Zamboni.

ROD GILBERT: Gilbert is remembered as part of the Rangers' GAG (goal-a-game) Line in the 1960s and '70s.

MEL HEIN: The "Lou Gehrig of the NFL" played every minute of every Giants game at center and linebacker from

Archibald

Beckham

FAST FACTS

Redman

F Florida State coach **Bobby Bowden** was a versatile No. 7 when he earned Little All-American honors while playing quarterback for Birmingham-based Howard College (now Samford University) in the late 1940s and early '50s.

F Actor **Mark Harmon**, son of former Heisman Trophy winner Tom Harmon, wore No. 7 when he played quarterback for UCLA in 1972 and '73.

F When quarterback **Chris Redman** was drafted by the Baltimore Ravens in 2000, he chose uniform No. 7 because of his birthdate—7-7-77.

F Any list of memorable hockey No. 7s would have to include **Reggie Dunlop**, the aging and crusty player/coach of the Charlestown Chiefs in the 1977 movie *Slap Shot*.

MARK BELANGER 7 **NEAL BROTEN** 7 **DICK STUART** 7 **AL ROSEN** 7 **BERT JONES** 7 **KEITH TKACHUK** 7 **ED KRANEPOOL** 7

Esposito

basketball fans at New York's Madison Square Garden in 1936.

MICKEY MANTLE: The Mick was a legendary centerpiece for seven Yankee championships.

HOWIE MORENZ: The Canadiens' first superstar and one of the NHL's first real gate attractions. The high-scoring center was recovering from a broken leg in 1937 when he suffered a fatal heart attack.

JOE MEDWICK: Everything was Ducky for this Gas House Gang enforcer in 1937, when he won the National League's last Triple Crown.

JERMAINE O'NEAL: How did he spend so much time on the Portland bench and still develop into an NBA star?

IVAN RODRIGUEZ: Pudge is to Gold Gloves what Roger Clemens is to Cy Youngs. Baseball's ultimate defensive catcher of the 1990s also is a career .300 hitter.

BEN ROETHLISBERGER: Big Ben is a true man of steel. Just ask Bill Cowher and all those Pittsburgh fans who watched him deliver a victory in Super Bowl 40.

CHANGING OF GUARD GIVES O'BRIEN JET LAG

For Ken O'Brien, March 18, 1993, might fall under the classification of "bad day." There he was, relaxing at his home in Sacramento, unaware that 3,000 miles away *Boomer Esiason* was being introduced to New York fans as the new Jets quarterback. Not only was he being introduced, Esiason was posing for pictures wearing a jersey with O'Brien's No. 7.

Losing a job is one thing; getting embarrassed is quite another. Even Esiason, who had worn No. 7 for nine years with the Cincinnati Bengals, was embarrassed—"I'm assuming his number and I'll wear it proudly," he said awkwardly—and he was on the good side of this boot. O'Brien had worn 7 since 1984, the year after the Jets picked him in the first round of the draft, and he ranked second on the team's all-time passing charts.

Jets coach Bruce Coslet, who had maintained a frosty relationship with O'Brien since taking control of the team in 1990, said the veteran quarterback had been told his days were numbered. But several Jets players were unhappy about the "tacky" uniform exchange while the popular O'Brien still was on the roster.

O'Brien was traded two weeks later to Green Bay for a fifth-round draft pick.

1931-45 and introduced blocking techniques that are still in use today.

TED LINDSAY: Detroit's Terrible Ted, all 5-8 and 160 pounds of him, could trade goals—and punches—with any NHL player in the 1940s and '50s.

HANK LUISETTI: A game that's now played above the rim should pay tribute to Stanford's No. 7, who introduced his revolutionary running one-handed shots to

Halas

One of the first No. 7s in NFL history was none other than *George Halas*, whose Hall of Fame resume lists league founder, player, coach and longtime owner of the Chicago Bears. Papa Bear wore 7 as a Bears end from 1920-28.

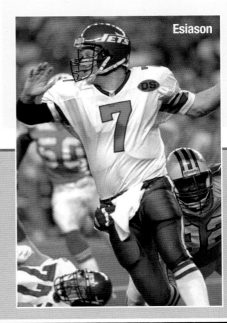

Esiason

KEVIN JOHNSON 7 DAN PASTORINI 7 MICHAEL VICK 7 DAMASO GARCIA 7 BOBBY WINE 7 BINGO SMITH 7 RICK MARTIN

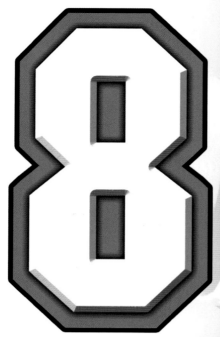

8

CAL RIPKEN

Turn that No. 8 on its side and you have the symbol for infinity, which pretty much goes to the heart of this former Baltimore shortstop and third baseman.

Ripken was like the Energizer Bunny—he kept playing … and playing … and playing in a major league-record 2,632 consecutive games. One of the most popular players in Orioles history—Baltimore-area Little Leaguers were known to burst into tears every year when their uniforms were issued without a No. 8—Ripken gets the nod over such baseball heavyweights as Carl Yastrzemski, Yogi Berra and Joe Morgan even though he wasn't a real number cruncher. He wore 16, 7 and 12 in his first three minor league stops and No. 5 at Rochester before his 1981 big-league debut. Since 5 was retired for Brooks Robinson, Ripken simply accepted the number he was handed and lifted it to ironman distinction.

FAST FACTS

F After a 1-for-4 debut wearing No. 8 for the Chicago Cubs in 2004, infielder **Nomar Garciaparra** negotiated a uniform switch with catcher Michael Barrett. In their next game, Barrett wore 8 and Garciaparra sported the No. 5 he had worn for nine seasons in Boston.

F No. 8 is the only single-digit number that has not been retired by an NBA team.

F In 1983, **Carl Yastrzemski**'s final major league season, his road uniform No. 8 was stolen four times from visiting clubhouses. The last theft occurred at Yankee Stadium.

F The leading scorer in Kansas City Chiefs history with 1,466 points is No. 8—14-year kicker **Nick Lowery**.

NOTABLE 8s BARCLAY PLAGER 8 ANDY ETCHEBARREN 8 BOOTS DAY 8 DOUG RISEBROUGH 8 JOHN ROSEBORO 8

Elite 8s

Earnhardt Jr.

BOSS HELPS NEELY FIND NUMERICAL HAPPINESS

Uniform No. 8 worked out well for former Boston right winger *Cam Neely*. But when he was traded to the Bruins in 1986, Neely had much higher expectations. Neely, whose jersey number was retired by the Bruins in January 2004, had grown up in British Columbia admiring Vancouver forward Stan Smyl, who wore No. 12. But 12 wasn't available when Neely played juniors, so he flipped it and went with 21. That's the number he stayed with in 1983 when he began playing for the Canucks.

The Boston trade forced a numerological dilemma: Defenseman Frank Simonetti had 21 and Neely was assigned No. 8. But when Simonetti was sent to the minors, Neely saw his opening and asked if he could switch to 21. The trainer told him he would get back to him in a couple of days.

He did—with a news flash. Boston general manager Harry Sinden had decided he "liked" Neely in No. 8 and wanted him to continue wearing it.

"OK, cool," Neely responded and spent the next 10 years creating memories as the only No. 8 most Boston hockey fans will remember.

Neely

Only two players wore No. 8 at Montreal before catcher *Gary Carter*—1969 infielder Kevin Collins and the always memorable Boots Day, an outfielder from 1971-74.

TROY AIKMAN: Calm, cool and efficient—no wonder this Cowboys quarterback won three Super Bowls and election to the Hall of Fame.

WALT BELLAMY: He played his career in the shadow of Chamberlain and Russell, but Bellamy was a Hall of Famer, too.

Berra

YOGI BERRA: Count 'em: 10 championship rings. Now go ahead and laugh at this lovable former Yankees catcher all you want.

BOB BOONE: Mr. Steady behind the plate for 19 big-league seasons.

MARK BRUNELL: He looks and plays like Steve Young, but the talent around him never has resembled the 49ers of the 1980s and early '90s.

KOBE BRYANT: The best high school-to-NBA player ever—just ask Shaq.

BILL DICKEY: Everybody remembers Yogi, but his Yankees mentor was a Hall of Famer, too.

DALE EARNHARDT JR.: Junior has it all—youth, good looks, luck, success, pedigree. The idea of living up to the Earnhardt racing legend is intimidating, but he has time on his side.

RAY GUY: When they put your name on the collegiate player-of-the-year award for your position, that's a pretty good indication of respect. Guy, the Raiders' punter for 14 years, had plenty of that.

ARCHIE MANNING: His quarterback sons might end up with better passing numbers, but Archie can say one thing they can't: He was a Saint.

JOE MORGAN: The little second baseman greased the wheels of Cincinnati's Big Red Machine with his power, speed and baseball savvy.

WILLIE STARGELL: Pittsburgh's Pops made everybody feel at home—everyone except opposing pitchers.

LARRY WILSON: This 1960s St. Louis Cardinal was a cleverly disguised wrecking machine and pioneer of the safety blitz.

STEVE YOUNG: The San Francisco quarterback replaced a legend and thrived. The mobile lefty was simply Super in 1994.

Young

DAVEY O'BRIEN 8 *RON LeFLORE* 8 *TONY TAYLOR* 8 *MARC TARDIF* 8 *GARY CARTER* 8 *RAY FOSSE* 8 *BILL GOLDSWORTHY*

HOCKEY TRINITY
GORDIE HOWE · BOBBY HULL · ROCKET RICHARD

Sorry, Boston. Your No. 9, as special as Ted Williams was to generations of baseball fans, is no match for the Hockey Trinity— Richard, Howe and Hull. No number has dominated the psyche of a sport like 9, hockey's symbol of excellence in the 1940s, '50s and '60s. It was a cultural phenomenon. The best player on every team in every league wore No. 9. It was a right of passage, the dream digit of every kid who wanted to match the passion of Richard, skate like Howe or shoot like the Golden Jet. So powerful was the number that it spawned a whole new generation of superstar 9s—and even a 99. No player in Quebec can wear the number in national competitions in honor of Richard, a member of eight Montreal Stanley Cup champions, and two NHL franchises—Chicago and Phoenix— have retired Hull's 9. Howe? Well, the former Detroit great is known universally as Mr. Hockey.

WILLIAMS INSPIRED HOBBS CHARACTER

Actor Robert Redford has always had an affinity for *Ted Williams*. So it wasn't a big surprise when his movie *The Natural* hit the big screen in 1984 with Redford's character, Roy Hobbs, wearing uniform No. 9 and pounding home runs from a modified Williams batting stance.

"As a kid growing up in California from a poor background and a Mexican neighborhood, sports was always my way out," Redford told *Denver Post* writer Stephen Singular in 1986. "I loved Ted Williams, and what I loved most was that he was good and had that arrogance because he knew he was good."

Redford was so enamored with Williams that he wrote a foreword for the 2002 book, Ted Williams: The Pursuit of Perfection, and included sprinklings of the Splendid Splinter throughout *The Natural*. In one scene in the movie, as an injured Hobbs recuperates in the hospital, he says all he wants is to walk down the street and hear people say, "There goes Roy Hobbs, the best hitter there ever was in this game."

That's a line straight from the mouth of Williams, who came ever so close to succeeding in that quest. In his book foreword, Redford writes, "... when I made *The Natural*, I dedicated my number to (Williams). It was the least I could do."

NOTABLE 9s **CHARLIE KELLER** 9 **DAN MAJERLE** 9 **HANK BLALOCK** 9 **MINNIE MINOSO** 9 **CLARK GILLIES**

Elite 9s

JOHN BUCYK: He hasn't played since 1978, but Bucyk still is the Bruins' all-time leading goal scorer.

BILL ELLIOTT: They love him; they really love him. How else can you explain Elliott being voted NASCAR's "Most Popular Driver" 16 times? He has backed it up with 44 career wins.

MIA HAMM: It takes a lot to make American girls think something is cool. Mia, like, so totally did that for soccer.

REGGIE JACKSON: While knocking heads with owner Charlie Finley during his pre-44 days in Oakland, young Mr. October began his ascent toward the upper echelon of baseball's home run charts.

SONNY JURGENSEN: Three decades after throwing his final spiral, the former Eagles and Redskins star still is regarded as one of the greatest pure passers to play in the NFL.

PAUL KARIYA: He's hockey's ultimate proof that speed and skill make up for size.

BILL MAZEROSKI: In 1960, the smooth-fielding Pirates second baseman fulfilled the universal baseball dream: He beat the Yankees with a World Series-winning home run.

LANNY McDONALD: Going out as a member of Calgary's Stanley Cup champion had to be sweet after spending an entire career coming *thisclose* to claiming the crown.

JIM McMAHON: The offbeat, rebellious and unpredictable McMahon in 1985 accomplished what no other Bears

FAST FACTS

F When Ted Williams took over the managerial reins of the Washington Senators in 1969, 6-7, 250-pound slugger *Frank Howard* gave him the number off his back. Howard traded the 9 he had worn for four seasons for 33.

F A premonition? While playing for the Kansas City Athletics in 1959, a year before he was traded to the New York Yankees and two years before he broke Babe Ruth's single-season

Maris

JOE ADCOCK 9 WALLY MOON 9 MATT BAHR 9 VON HAYES 9 TERRY PENDLETON 9 BILL WADE 9 GRAIG NETTLES

Hamm

Smoker

In professional sports, where uniform number switches typically are governed by whims, superstitions and fortuitous personnel changes, *Jeff Smoker* offers this unusual reason for going from 9 to 15: He was forced to change.

Smoker, St. Louis' sixth-round draft choice out of Michigan State in 2004, had worn No. 9 in college and kept it during his rookie season with the Rams. Coach Mike Martz had encouraged him to change numbers, but the third-string quarterback never detected any urgency. Then, before the first practice of a June minicamp in 2005, Smoker got a different kind of message.

"I kind of just kept putting it off," he said, "and I kind of showed up and that number was in my locker. So, I guess I'll be 15."

Martz, it seemed, had issues with 9. That was the number worn by former Rams quarterback Joe Germaine, who was slated to be Kurt Warner's backup in 2001. But Martz lost patience with Germaine, yanked him out of a nationally televised exhibition game against Kansas City, chewed him out on the sideline and soon traded him to the Chiefs.

After Smoker's uniform change, Martz said his feelings went beyond Germaine. He said he also remembered several college quarterbacks who had failed while wearing 9. Smoker, perhaps miscast as 15, was cut, re-signed and cut again by the Rams before and during the 2005 season.

quarterback has ever done—win a Super Bowl.

STEVE McNAIR: Knock him down and he'll get right back up—and complete more passes for the Tennessee Titans.

MINNIE MINOSO: He played in the majors in five decades, but Minoso's .298 career average shows he was more than a novelty act.

MIKE MODANO: Star or North Star, the veteran center still has plenty of wattage.

BOB PETTIT: The skinny go-to forward/center for the St. Louis Hawks was the first NBA player to score 20,000 points.

ENOS SLAUGHTER: Everyone knows about his 1946 mad dash, but he posted a lifetime .300 average and could have approached 3,000 hits if not for the three seasons he lost to World War II.

home run record as No. 9, *Roger Maris* wore No. 3.

F St. Louis Rams wide receiver *Torry Holt* wore 9 in high school after watching Michael Jordan wear it for the U.S. team in the 1984 Olympic Games. Unable to get 9 at North Carolina State, Holt squared it and took uniform No. 81.

Santiago

F New York Jets quarterback *Jay Fiedler* wears 9 because that was Roy Hobbs' number in *The Natural*, one of his favorite movies.

F In 1991 and '92, his final two seasons with San Diego, and 1993 and '94, his two seasons with the Florida Marlins, catcher *Benito Santiago* wore No. 09—because, he reasoned, his single-digit 9 was always obscured by the backstrap of his chest protector.

10

PELE

To family and friends, he's Edson Arantes do Nascimento. To the international sports community, he's Pele, No. 10, the greatest soccer player who ever lived and the man who, amazingly, made Americans care about the sport.

Care, of course, is relative. Americans love their heroes, and Pele, by all accounts, was that and much more. So when the former Brazilian World Cup hero and club star came out of retirement in 1975 to perform his goal-scoring magic for the New York Cosmos, Giants Stadium filled to the brim every time he played and the North American Soccer League got a national TV contract. The professional soccer craze Pele inspired during his two seasons in the U.S. lost its momentum, but his influence remains strongly rooted at the amateur level. Youth soccer still is the rage throughout the country with kids clamoring for jersey No. 10, which is sure to magically transform them into their team's ultimate playmaker.

FAST FACTS

F **King Hill**, a 12-year NFL quarterback who spent eight games with Minnesota in 1968, is the only Vikings player other than **Fran Tarkenton** to wear No. 10. Tarkenton was playing quarterback for the New York Giants that season.

F Montreal great **Jean Beliveau**, after playing his final NHL season in 1970-71, offered his No. 4 jersey to hot prospect Guy Lafleur, who had worn 4 in the Quebec Junior League. Lafleur

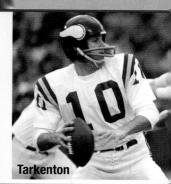

Tarkenton

NOTABLE 10s   RON CEY 10 BOB LOVE 10 TOMMY BRIDGES 10 NORM NIXON 10 SHERM LOLLAR 10 BRAD VAN PELT

Elite 10s

LUCKY JEFF FEAGLES

Clearly, New York Giants punter *Jeff Feagles* is a lucky-number magnet—an adept negotiator who knows how to pin his adversary against the goal line.

It all started with Feagles' affection for 10, a number he was unable to get in his first six NFL seasons with New England and Philadelphia. Feagles finally became a 10 in 1994 with Arizona and wore it for four seasons with the Cardinals, five with Seattle and in 2003 with the Giants.

Before the 2004 draft, however, Feagles was approached by Giants officials and asked if he would give his number to quarterback Eli Manning, the soon-to-be top overall pick who had worn it at Mississippi. Sure, Feagles would be happy to work out a deal. Future icons with lots of money make for good financial dealings.

Feagles negotiated for a family trip to Florida—six airline tickets, a house for the week, car rental, food—all expenses paid, probably worth around $12,000.

So Feagles switched to 17 for the 2004 season—because that would mark his 17th year in the NFL. End of story? Hardly. In 2005, the Giants signed former Pittsburgh wide receiver Plaxico Burress, who wanted No. 17 to commemorate the date of the deal. So Feagles called Burress' agent, Drew Rosenhaus, and told him he wanted to build an outdoor kitchen for his new house. How about trading No. 17 for a kitchen? Rosenhaus agreed.

Again Feagles switched numbers, to 18 in 2005 to commemorate his 18th NFL season. Future bids will be welcome.

Feagles

SPARKY ANDERSON: He wore No. 10 for only nine of his 28 big-league seasons, but during that span he drove Cincinnati's Big Red Machine.

ROBERTO BAGGIO: Italy's soccer great couldn't bring home a World Cup title.

ALEX DELVECCHIO: His reward for 23 seasons as a center for the Red Wings: the glory of the 1950s as well as the disappointment of the 1970s.

WALT FRAZIER: Imagine: an NBA star who would rather play defense and hit the open man than make highlight reels. Clyde quarterbacked two Knicks championship teams in the 1970s.

LEFTY GROVE: What was scarier, his temper or his fastball?

CHIPPER JONES: Quiet, consistent, excellent—the epitome of everything the Braves have been since 1991.

TONY LA RUSSA: He's not the most popular manager in Cardinals history, but he is No. 2 on the team's win list and No. 3 in all-time victories behind Connie Mack and John McGraw..

RONALDO: Should he feel bad that he's the second-best striker in his country's history—considering No. 1 is Pele?

RON SANTO: If Ernie is Mr. Cub, Santo is Mr. Cub Jr.—five Gold Gloves, 337 home runs for the North Siders and, of course, no World Series appearances.

Frazier

MIGUEL TEJADA: While Jeter, A-Rod and Nomar were getting the attention, Tejada began posting numbers that matched up with any of them. And no one can top his enthusiasm.

LLOYD WANER: He had less power than New York during its 1977 blackout, but he still posted a career average of .316. When it comes to hits, he and older brother Paul are the most prolific siblings of all-time.

JOJO WHITE: JoJo made the Celtics go-go in the 1970s with his discipline and playmaking ability.

VINCE YOUNG: His tour de force in the January 4, 2006, Rose Bowl was—what else?—Texas-sized domination.

ZINEDINE ZIDANE: Sports hero scenarios don't get any better: Superstar Zidane scored two goals in the 1998 World Cup championship game for France, the host country.

Jones

declined Beliveau's generosity and went on to create a special niche for No. 10 in Canadiens' lore.

F If you want to spot the top playmakers at a soccer game, look for the center forwards wearing No. 10. A numbering system based on position and long-standing tradition dictates that the Pele and *Diego Maradona* types will typically flash that "most perfect" double digit.

F When Minnesota acquired closer *Jeff Reardon* in 1987, he asked for 41—the number worn by Twins manager *Tom Kelly*. Kelly switched to 10, claiming Reardon wasn't the real reason: "All the women will say, 'There goes Tom Kelly. He's a 10.'"

F The Yankees retired 10 for former shortstop *Phil Rizzuto*, but it was worn first by another Hall of Famer. Catcher Bill Dickey was 10 in 1929, the first year the Yankees wore permanent numbers.

10 MAURICE CHEEKS **10** JIM SUNDBERG **10** STEVE BARTKOWSKI **10** ANDRE DAWSON **10** JIM ZORN **10** RUSTY STAUB

11

ISIAH THOMAS

He wore it in high school, wore it while leading the Indiana Hoosiers to the 1981 NCAA championship and wore it throughout a stellar 13-year career with the Detroit Pistons that netted two National Basketball Association titles.

If that's not enough to win your vote for this Bad Boy over such worthy contenders as Elvin Hayes, Carl Hubbell, Luis Aparicio and Norm Van Brocklin, consider this: Thomas is the Pistons' franchise leader in points, assists and steals and one of the NBA-honored 50 Greatest Players in history. Thomas' fondness for 11 traces back to Sam Puckett, a smooth-shooting high school guard young Isiah admired while growing up on Chicago's tough West Side. His passion for the number intensified greatly in 1984 when No. 11 became the league's richest point guard by signing an 11-year contract for an estimated $1.1 million per year.

FAST FACTS

F **Barry Larkin,** whose association with 11 began in Little League and ran all the way through his 19 seasons with Cincinnati, was called "Snake Eyes" by Reds teammates.

F When **Jim Leyland** became manager of the Florida Marlins in 1997, he took uniform No. 11 because outfield star Gary Sheffield was wearing his more familiar No. 10. When Sheffield was traded by Los Angeles to Atlanta in 2002, he,

Larkin

NOTABLE *11s* **LUIS APARICIO** *11* **BRIAN SUTTER** *11* **HECTOR LOPEZ** *11* **EDGAR MARTINEZ** *11* **DANNY WHITE** *11* **TOBY HARRAH**

Elite 11s

LUIS APARICIO:
For years, he was the prototype for shortstops—a pesky leadoff hitter who could run opponents to death on the basepaths and break their heart on defense.

PAUL ARIZIN:
The early NBA star with the "Renoir jump shot" was a two-time scoring champion and 10-time All-Star.

DREW BLEDSOE:
A quarterback with staying power. Bledsoe, seldom mentioned among the game's elite, has thrown for more than 40,000 yards.

DAUNTE CULPEPPER:
This quarterback might offer the best combination of size, speed, toughness and arm strength in the modern era.

LEFTY GOMEZ:
The skinny lefthander with the quick tongue and blazing fastball was a Yankees workhorse in the 1930s.

ELVIN HAYES:
The Big E mastered the turnaround J and scored 27,313 points in the NBA.

CARL HUBBELL:
In 1930s New York, King Carl's screwball ruled the National League.

MARK MESSIER:
Once he and Wayne Gretzky left Edmonton, Messier did something The Great One never could—win

Hayes

another Stanley Cup.

YAO MING:
Yes, Houston, we have liftoff. It's always easier to fight the NBA wars with a 7-5, 296-pound Rocket.

HAL McRAE:
It's difficult to say who was more afraid of the Royals' rugged outfielder/DH—pitchers or second basemen trying to turn a double play.

GILBERT PERREAULT:
The "Original Sabre" as Buffalo's first draft pick in 1970, Perreault still is the best non-goalie in team history.

PHIL SIMMS:
Unable to get his college No. 12, Simms simply lifted 11 to prominence as a Super Bowl-winning quarterback for the Giants.

STEVE SPURRIER:
Spurrier the coach had nothing on Spurrier the quarterback, who won a Heisman Trophy while guiding Florida in 1966.

NORM VAN BROCKLIN:
The Dutchman's career ended in 1960, but the former Rams and Eagles quarterback still holds the NFL's single-game record for passing yards (554 in 1951).

PAUL WANER:
How good of a hitter was this Pirates outfielder? Even Ted Williams went to Big Poison for advice.

WISTERTS HAD BIG TEN TEAMS SEEING TRIPLE

Oh brother! That's the reaction college football fans must have had in the 1930s and '40s when those dratted *Wistert brothers* kept popping up on Michigan rosters, all wearing No. 11 and delivering serious punishment from their hand-me-down tackle positions.

This deja vu-all-over-again story begins in 1933, when a 6-2, 210-pound senior named *Francis "Whitey" Wistert* earned consensus All-American honors for the Wolverines. Michigan finished 7-0-1 that year, a perfect season marred only by a scoreless tie against Minnesota.

Big Ten coaches probably did a double take in 1942 when *Albert Wistert*, Whitey's 6-2, 212-pound youngest brother, became a consensus All-American for a Michigan team that went 7-3. Six years later, 6-3, 223-pound *Alvin Wistert* showed up at Michigan and earned consecutive consensus All-American citations—as a junior tackle for Michigan's 9-0 national championship team of 1948 and as a senior captain for the 6-2-1 team of 1949.

Strangely, Alvin—also known as Moose—was the middle brother. Family obligations and six years in the Marine Corps during World War II dictated a late start in his education and he finished his college career at age 33.

Only one of the Wisterts went on to the NFL—Albert, who excelled from 1943-51 as the primary blocker for Philadelphia Eagles Hall of Fame running back Steve Van Buren.

The Wisterts' 11 is one of five numbers to be retired by the University of Michigan.

Radio broadcasts enabled Josephine Wistert to follow her sons' football exploits at Michigan.

too, switched to 11 because Chipper Jones was wearing 10.

In his two seasons with the Boston Celtics (1946-47 and 1947-48), future actor *Chuck Connors* wore No. 11. Ironically, in each week's opening segment of his later hit television series *The Rifleman*, 11 shots were fired by his rapid-fire rifle.

No. 11 cars have won more Winston Cup/NEXTEL Cup championships than any other number. *Ned Jarrett* drove his 11 car to victory in 1961 and '65; *Cale Yarborough* won a record three straight titles from 1976-78, and *Darrell Waltrip's* 11 won in 1981, '82 and '85.

Yarborough

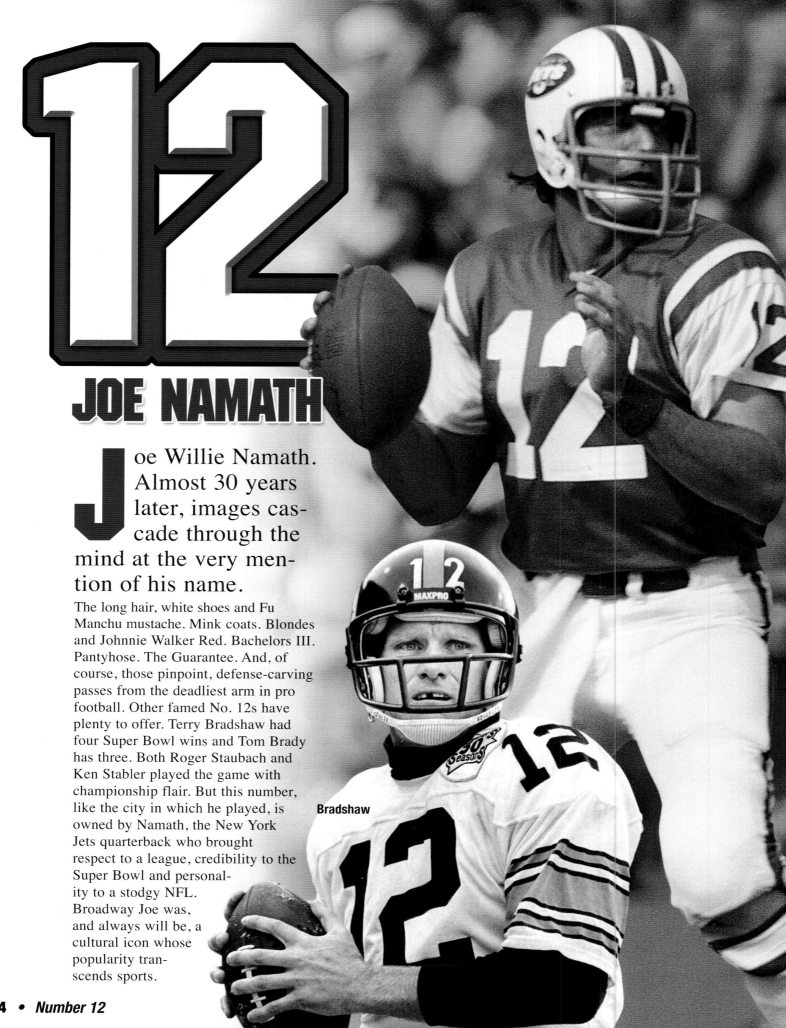

12

JOE NAMATH

Joe Willie Namath. Almost 30 years later, images cascade through the mind at the very mention of his name.

The long hair, white shoes and Fu Manchu mustache. Mink coats. Blondes and Johnnie Walker Red. Bachelors III. Pantyhose. The Guarantee. And, of course, those pinpoint, defense-carving passes from the deadliest arm in pro football. Other famed No. 12s have plenty to offer. Terry Bradshaw had four Super Bowl wins and Tom Brady has three. Both Roger Staubach and Ken Stabler played the game with championship flair. But this number, like the city in which he played, is owned by Namath, the New York Jets quarterback who brought respect to a league, credibility to the Super Bowl and personality to a stodgy NFL. Broadway Joe was, and always will be, a cultural icon whose popularity transcends sports.

Bradshaw

SUPERMAN STILL SOARS WITHOUT HIS 'S'

Anybody who questions whether Superman was still "Super" without his "S" need only check out what happened on Valentine's Day in 1990 at Orlando Arena. That was the night Chicago superman *Michael Jordan* took the floor for a game against the Magic wearing uniform No. 12—11 excrutiating digits removed from his customary 23—and scored 49 points in a 135-129 overtime loss.

Jordan was forced to switch numbers when a thief picked off his game jersey, which had been laid out by a locker room attendant about two hours before game time. A desperate Jordan spotted a youngster in the crowd wearing a 23 replica jersey and borrowed it, but the shirt was too small. So for the first time in his professional career, he took the floor wearing a number other than 23.

"That has never happened to me before," he said. "It's pretty irritating because you're accustomed to certain things and you don't like to have things misplaced."

Wearing the Bulls' reserve jersey, Jordan hit 21 of 43 shots and topped his NBA-leading average by 16.2 points. The 49 points were a team record for players wearing that number.

NOTABLE 12s *JOHN BOCCABELLA* **12** *GIL McDOUGALD* **12** *YVAN COURNOYER* **12** *ERNIE WHITT* **12** *TOMMY DAVIS* **12** *DEREK HARPER*

Elite 12s

Alomar

SID ABEL: He helped Gordie Howe get Detroit's Production Line rolling, then kept his output high, both as a coach and team executive.

ROBERTO ALOMAR: He was the slick-fielding, clutch-hitting second baseman for two World Series champion Blue Jays teams.

TOM BRADY: The Montana comparisons may be premature, but he has three Super Bowl wins—with significantly less offensive talent to work with.

RANDALL CUNNINGHAM: Pre-Michael Vick, he probably was the most dangerous running/passing quarterback in NFL history. Cunningham holds the NFL career record for rushing yards by a quarterback—4,928.

Stockton

FAST FACTS

F Because longtime Yankees right fielder *Paul O'Neill* had his familiar No. 21, Roger Clemens opened his five-year New York stay in 1999 wearing No. 12. At the urging of family members, the Rocket, sporting a 4.95 ERA, switched to 22 at midseason.

F *Jim Kelly*, who grew up in East Brady, Pa., watching Pittsburgh quarterback Terry Bradshaw, chose No. 12 in his honor. He spent 11 seasons with Buffalo and led the Bills to four straight Super Bowls.

F What made *John Roach* and *Ron Widby* distinctive, digits-wise? Answer: They were the only Dallas players to wear No. 12 before the 1969 arrival of quarterback Roger Staubach.

F In nine consecutive Super Bowls—6 through 14—the winning quarterback wore No. 12.

LYNN DICKEY **12** CESAR TOVAR **12** TIM KERR **12** RON BLOMBERG **12** JOHN BRODIE **12** MIKE KEANE **12** CRAIG

BOB GRIESE: He didn't throw much, but don't let that fool you. This quarterback made key plays for the NFL's only perfect team.

JAROME IGINLA: He carries the torch offensively for Calgary but is willing to do whatever it takes to win.

KEN STABLER: The Raiders' Snake just knew how to win, baby.

JOHN STOCKTON: Forget the tiny shorts and small stature. It all boiled down to one thing: Nobody could stop this Jazzy guard on the pick and roll.

CHARLES WHITE: He was the third in USC's Tailback U. line to win the Heisman. White also was a two-time consensus All-American.

Staubach

WELCOME TO AGGIELAND

HOME OF THE 12TH MAN

Texas A&M: the 12th Man

A STORIED TRADITION, DATING TO 1922

He wears No. 12 and you can spot him as a member of the Texas A&M kickoff unit. For every rabid Aggies fan standing in anticipation, he's the focus of attention, the kamikaze walk-on who is willing to sacrifice life and limb to represent a storied tradition. He's the 12th man, an extension of every non-football player who wants to be part of another Aggies victory.

The 12th Man tradition is part of A&M's football fabric. As the story goes, E. King Gill, a basketball player who played briefly on the football team, was watching from the press box in January 1922 when A&M played Centre College in a postseason game at Dallas. As Aggie after Aggie left the game because of injury, coach Dana X. Bible sent word that he needed Gill to come down and suit up. Gill responded, donning the uniform of an injured player, but never had to go into the game.

A statue of Gill, the original 12th Man, stands outside Kyle Field. And A&M students stand throughout every game—the "12th Man" ready to jump into the fray if needed.

Kickoffs are time-honored highlights of every Aggies game. Occasionally, the 12th-man lightning even strikes. When 5-9 Robert Jordan made the tackle on the opening kickoff in A&M's 2000 game against Kansas State, Kyle Stadium exploded. "It was the loudest reaction to a football play I have heard in my 25 years here," said Aggies sports information director Alan Cannon.

Dallas' *Roger Staubach* was the winner in 6 and 12, Miami's Bob Griese in 7 and 8, Pittsburgh's Terry Bradshaw in 9, 10, 13 and 14 and Oakland's Ken Stabler in 11.

F Chicago Cubs manager *Dusty Baker* has worn 12 throughout his long playing and managerial career because that was the number worn by Dodgers outfielder Tommy Davis, his childhood hero.

Baker

REYNOLDS *12* JIM DAVENPORT *12* JOHN WATHAN *12* STAN SMYL *12* MAURICE STOKES *12* CHARLEY JOHNSON *12*

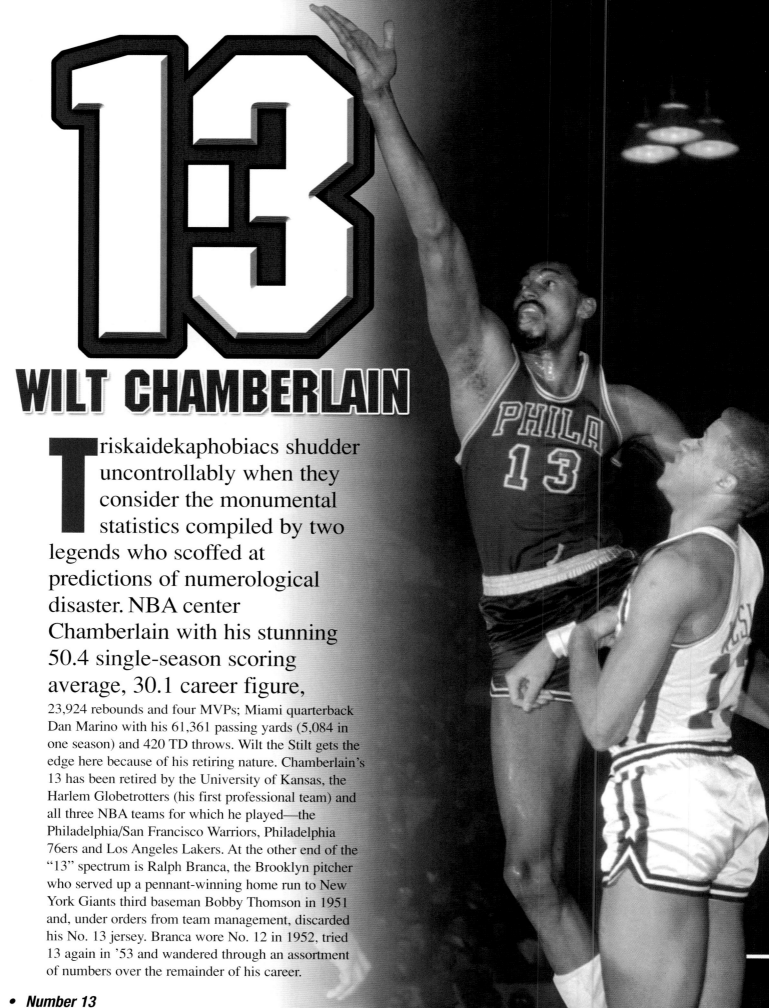

13

WILT CHAMBERLAIN

Triskaidekaphobiacs shudder uncontrollably when they consider the monumental statistics compiled by two legends who scoffed at predictions of numerological disaster. NBA center Chamberlain with his stunning 50.4 single-season scoring average, 30.1 career figure, 23,924 rebounds and four MVPs; Miami quarterback Dan Marino with his 61,361 passing yards (5,084 in one season) and 420 TD throws. Wilt the Stilt gets the edge here because of his retiring nature. Chamberlain's 13 has been retired by the University of Kansas, the Harlem Globetrotters (his first professional team) and all three NBA teams for which he played—the Philadelphia/San Francisco Warriors, Philadelphia 76ers and Los Angeles Lakers. At the other end of the "13" spectrum is Ralph Branca, the Brooklyn pitcher who served up a pennant-winning home run to New York Giants third baseman Bobby Thomson in 1951 and, under orders from team management, discarded his No. 13 jersey. Branca wore No. 12 in 1952, tried 13 again in '53 and wandered through an assortment of numbers over the remainder of his career.

LUCKY 13 PAYS OFF FOR CRAIG

When you pitch for the worst team in the modern baseball era, it doesn't really matter what kind of luck you have.

After losing 24 games for the expansion New York Mets in 1962, *Roger Craig* probably thought things couldn't get any worse. The Mets were improved in 1963; they lost only 111 games rather than 120. But things did get worse—from May 4 through August 4 of 1963, Craig lost 18 straight decisions, tying the single-season N.L. record set by Cliff Curtis in 1910. Finally, on August 9, with media attention increasing and the all-time record one loss away, Craig took drastic measures to change his luck. He switched uniform numbers, dropping his customary 38 in favor of 13.

The change paid an immediate dividend. With the Mets and Cubs tied 3-3 in the ninth inning, Craig got a break when teammate Jim Hickman hit a lazy, two-out, bases-loaded fly ball that grazed the left field scoreboard at the Polo Grounds—just as Billy Williams thought he was about to make the catch. With that not-so-grand slam, the streak was over. Craig soon switched back to 38, with which he rode out the season, but he still led the league in losses (22) for a second straight year and was rewarded with an exit from New York.

Craig ended his career with single-season stops at St. Louis, Cincinnati and Philadelphia, but he never wore 38—or 13—again as a player.

NOTABLE *13s* **BLUE MOON ODOM** *13* **STEVE BARBER** *13* **CHESTER MARCOL** *13* **MIKE PAGLIARULO** *13* **CHRIS JACKE** *13*

Elite 13s

Marino

MORT COOPER: He brought a sense of family to the Cardinals from 1940-44, pitching to catcher/brother Walker. Mort Cooper won 65 games from 1942-44 and helped St. Louis capture two World Series.

DAN MARINO: Did the Chiefs (Todd Blackledge), Patriots (Tony Eason) and Jets (Ken O'Brien) let Homer Simpson run their drafts in 1983? Why else would they pass up the NFL's future career passing leader (61,361 yards)? It wasn't the first time Marino had been passed over. His father, while coaching his Little League team, let all the other players pick their jerseys before Dan, who was left with 13. But it didn't take the young Marino long to decide the number wasn't so bad after all.

DON MAYNARD: He formed a Hall of Fame combination with Jets quarterback Joe Namath and made two TD catches in the 1968 AFL championship game leading up to Super Bowl 3. The free-spirited Texan was the game's all-time leading receiver when he retired in 1973.

STEVE NASH: NBA opponents have learned his hands are as generous as his hair is shaggy.

FAST FACTS

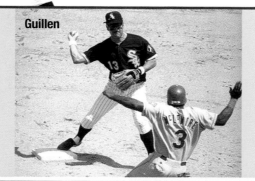

Guillen

F Major league shortstops Omar Vizquel and *Ozzie Guillen* wore 13 because Venezuelan predecessor Dave Concepcion wore it during his days with Cincinnati's Big Red Machine. Ironically, Concepcion wanted to wear Luis Aparicio's No. 11, but it was already taken by Hal McRae—so he chose 13.

F Pittsburgh's **Roberto Clemente**, who lifted No. 21 to Hall of Fame glory, wore 13 at the outset of his first major league season, 1955, before switching to 21 later in the year.

F Unlucky 13? The number was worn by three Chicago Bears Hall of Fame linemen in the 1920s, '30s and '40s—*George Trafton*, *Guy Chamberlin* and *Joe Stydahar*. No Bears player wore 13 from 1949-97.

F No. 13 has never been retired by a team in major league baseball or the NHL. But six

JAMES SILAS 13 **EDGARDO ALFONZO** 13 **CLAUDE PASSEAU** 13 **PAVEL DATSYUK** 13 **LANCE PARRISH** 13 **DAVE TWARDZIK**

KEN RILEY: The Rattler bit NFL quarterbacks for 65 interceptions from 1969-83 with the Bengals, but he's still waiting for a call from the Hall.

GLENN ROBINSON: The Big Dog filled it up in NBA arenas, but he had to—he let the guy he was guarding fill it up, too.

ALEX RODRIGUEZ: If anybody's going to be baseball's first quarter-billionaire player, it ought to be the fastest guy to hit 400 home runs. He has a legitimate chance to break Hammerin' Hank's home run record—if Barry Bonds doesn't beat him to it.

JAKE SCOTT: Marino gave the number NFL status, but this gritty Miami safety's two interceptions in Super Bowl 7 earned him two things Marino never earned: a championship ring and Super Bowl MVP award.

OMAR VIZQUEL: He picks the ball so well, it's almost unfair to let him use a glove. Not only is he a master in the field (10 Gold Gloves), he can swing the stick, too.

BILLY WAGNER: How does a pitcher so tiny (5-11) throw that hard (upper 90s)?

KURT WARNER: He's the NFL's ultimate rags-to-riches story, going from grocery bagger to Super Bowl champion and ringmaster of the Greatest Show on Turf.

Rodriguez

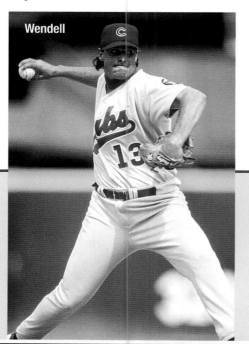

Wendell

13 AND INDY 500 ARE LIKE OIL AND WATER

Black cats and ladders are bad enough, but No. 13 and the Indianapolis 500 are like oil and water.

Thirteen's history at the 500 is about as happy (and successful) as that of the Tampa Bay Devil Rays. In 1914, George Mason became the first driver to run a 13 car at the Indianapolis Motor Speedway, finishing 23rd. In those days, numbers were assigned in the order racers entered the race; after 1914, something (or someone) always kept 13 out. Sometimes, drivers never showed; other times they withdrew. Finally, in 1926 raceway officials said, "Enough," and started skipping 13 when handing out numbers.

Louis Schneider tried over and over in the 1930s to get a 13 car entered in the Memorial Day event, but officials always made him change. In 1931, he won the race after being forced to paint over his 13. You'd think that would have convinced him to give it up—maybe the racing gods were dropping a hint? But he ignored the signs and, two years later, again had to paint over his 13. This time, however, his was the first car out of the race and he finished 42nd, the lowest in 500 history. Guess he didn't get the memo.

Greg Ray must not have gotten it, either. In 2003, Ray ran a 13 car and finished eighth. But misfortune followed him, too—the next year he dropped to 27th while driving 13, and his team disbanded after the season. Not surprisingly, the 500—again—was without a 13 in 2005.

teams in the NBA (three for Wilt Chamberlain) and two in the NFL have taken the number out of circulation.

F When the Chicago Cubs lost their 13th straight game to open the 1997 season, an error helped the New York Mets score the decisive run—the 13th unearned run given up by the Cubs during the skid. The losing pitcher was No. 13, *Turk Wendell*.

13 FRANK RYAN **13** NEIL ALLEN **13** BOBBY PHILLS **13** DAVE JENNINGS **13** BILL TUTTLE **13** GUY CHAMBERLIN **13**

Best by Number • **61**

14

OTTO GRAHAM

Pete Rose wore this number. So did pass-catching legend Don Hutson, double-double phenom Oscar Robertson and Mr. Cub Ernie Banks.

With a special deference to Boston Celtics ballhandling magician Bob Cousy and his six NBA championship rings, No. 14 honors go to Graham, the former Cleveland Browns quarterback who led his team to an amazing 10 straight championship games and seven titles in a 10-year professional career that stretched from 1946-55. Automatic Otto didn't start wearing 14 until after the NFL introduced its new numbering system in 1952, and the number switch wasn't exactly seamless. Check out Graham's uniform jersey on display at the Pro Football Hall of Fame— No. 14, superimposed over the distinct imprint of former No. 60, which apparently was ripped away in a quick changeover. A sign, perhaps, of the economic times.

FAST FACTS

F When *Lou Piniella* became manager of Cincinnati in 1990, he turned around his old Yankees No. 14 (41) out of respect for former No. 14, Reds icon Pete Rose.

F High-scoring left wing *Brendan Shanahan*, when traded to the Detroit Red Wings in 1996, opted for No. 14 because "it makes me look taller."

Shanahan

NOTABLE 14s **KENT HRBEK** 14 **HOOT EVERS** 14 **EDDIE LeBARON** 14 **PAUL KONERKO** 14 **ED PODOLAK** 14 **DAVE BERGMAN**

Elite 14s

Rose

KEN ANDERSON: Four Pro Bowls, one league MVP and 32,838 passing yards—easily the best quarterback in Cincinnati Bengals history.

ERNIE BANKS: Hey, Cubs fans, let's play two!

KEN BOYER: This Cardinals third baseman's grit—and clutch hitting—would have been a perfect fit for the old Gas House Gang, but Boyer got his own World Series title in 1964.

CYNTHIA COOPER: Where would the WNBA be without its first superstar?

BOB COUSY: He razzle-dazzled the 1950s Celtics into the championship spotlight and the NBA into our national consciousness.

LARRY DOBY: Don't forget: Jackie wasn't the only one who broke a baseball color barrier. Doby did it for the American League in 1947.

A.J. FOYT: As long as it had a steering wheel, he could win a race driving it. He's the only driver with wins in the Indy 500 (one of three four-time winners), the Daytona 500 and the 24 Hours of Le Mans.

DAN FOUTS: He put the Air in the Coryell offense but couldn't put the Super in San Diego's postseason.

GIL HODGES: The former power-hitting Dodgers first baseman later performed a miracle as manager of the 1969 New York Mets.

JEFF HORNACEK: Guile, intelligence and hard work. Nothing more needs to be said about this 14-year NBA guard.

DON HUTSON: The Green Bay pass-catching pioneer mapped a new and bolder course to the opposing team's end zone.

SAM PERKINS: The big lefty hung tough through 17 NBA seasons, but his only championship came in 1982 at North Carolina when he teamed with Michael Jordan and James Worthy.

JIM RICE: Baseball's Rodney Dangerfield never got the respect he deserved. But Boston's No. 3 all-time home run hitter still is hoping to get an invitation to the Hall.

OSCAR ROBERTSON: Was there anything he couldn't do? The Big O averaged a triple double for an entire season (1961-62) with the Cincinnati Royals and changed the way the game was played.

PETE ROSE: Charlie Hustled his way to baseball's all-time hits record—and post-career disappointment.

Y.A. TITTLE: He never quarterbacked an NFL championship team, but the Bald Eagle presided over three Giants near-misses in the early 1960s.

BUNNING GETS CURIOUS CALL OVER OTHER PHILLY 14s

It wasn't surprising when the Philadelphia Phillies announced they would retire No. 14 on opening day in 2001. What didn't make sense to many was that the honor was going to pitcher *Jim Bunning* instead of Pete Rose or Del Ennis, two other Philadelphia 14s.

Bunning won 74 games for the Phillies from 1964-67 and added 15 in a 1970-71 return to Philly that ended his career. Pre-Philadelphia, the tall righthander had posted 118 wins and pitched a no-hitter in nine seasons with the Detroit Tigers, who never got the urge to take his number out of circulation.

The Phillies explained that they retire only numbers for players who are inducted in the Hall of Fame, an honor given Bunning in 1996. Rose, who helped the Phillies reach two World Series and win their only championship in 1980, has been banned from baseball since 1989 and is not eligible for the Hall. Ennis was a slugging outfielder who topped 100 RBIs six times from 1946-56.

Bunning, who went on to become a U.S. senator from Kentucky, is well known for two other things in Philadelphia. It was Bunning who in 1964 threw 90 pitches in a perfect-game victory over the New York Mets—one of the most dominant performances in history. He also is remembered for the legendary 1971 home run he gave up to Pittsburgh's Willie Stargell—a blow that landed in the 600 level of Veterans Stadium's upper deck.

Bunning

F Pass-catching legend *Don Hutson* was the last player to wear 14 for the Green Bay Packers in 1945, but two other Hall of Famers wore it before him—founder and coach Curly Lambeau and 1920s-30s halfback John Blood McNally.

F The only No. 14 retired by an NHL team belonged to *Rene Robert*, the right wing on Buffalo's famed French Connection line.

F One-armed outfielder *Pete Gray* wore No. 14 in 1945, his only major league season. Gray batted .218 in 77 games for the St. Louis Browns with no home runs and 13 RBIs.

---

14 JON McGLOCKLIN **14** MARIO TREMBLAY **14** BILL SKOWRON **14** STEVE GROGAN **14** CLAUDE PROVOST **14** ALAN ASHBY

15
BART STARR

Yes, it's unusual for 17th-round draft picks to earn Hall of Fame distinction. And how many No. 42s blossom into 15s and lead their team to five championships?

Starr did that, and he also gained MVP honors in the first two Super Bowls and the everlasting gratitude of cheeseheads as the quarterback who made Green Bay —and Vince Lombardi—famous. Starr recalled his first day in the Packers' 1956 training camp when, fresh off the Alabama campus, he was tossed a 42 jersey for a bubble gum-card photo session. Somebody, obviously, did not think the rookie had staying power. But 16 years, 24,718 passing yards and 152 touchdown passes later, Starr was the celebrated field general of Lombardi's championship machine. And his 15 remains prominent today as one of five numbers retired by one of the game's legendary franchises.

FAST FACTS

F When pitcher *Denny Neagle* signed as a free agent with Colorado before the 2001 season, he asked for his customary No. 15, which belonged to Ben Petrick. The young catcher graciously switched numbers. It wasn't long before Petrick received a package in the mail containing a Rolex watch.

F No. 15 has been retired seven times by NBA teams, tying 22 and 32 for league honors.

Neagle

NOTABLE 15s CARMELO ANTHONY 15 DARRELL PORTER 15 CECIL COOPER 15 BABE PARILLI 15 TIM HUDSON 15 HANK SOAR

Elite 15s

DICK ALLEN: Fans who never understood this moody 1960s and '70s star needed to grasp only one fact—that he could really hit.

VINCE CARTER: OK, he's no Michael Jordan. But when healthy and motivated, he's one of the most exciting players in the NBA.

JIM EDMONDS: Those eight Gold Gloves suggest hitters should avoid hitting anything near center field; those 300-plus home runs suggest pitchers should avoid the center of the plate.

GEORGE FOSTER: He provided plenty of horsepower for the Big Red Machine, but he couldn't keep it going by himself.

HAL GREER: Wilt got credit for the 76ers' dominance in the late 1960s, but the straight-shooting Greer's steady playmaking should not be overlooked.

TOM HEINSOHN: Tommy Gun never met a shot he didn't like, but he hit enough of them to help Cousy, Russell and Co. establish the Celtics' dynasty.

VINNIE JOHNSON: You Detroit Bad Boys need some instant offense? Just put the ball in the Microwave.

DAVEY LOPES: He could steal bases and occasionally hit for power. But this second baseman's legacy is that he was part of the longest-tenured infield in baseball history.

Carter

F When *Sandy Alomar Jr.* signed a free-agent contract with the Chicago White Sox in December 2000, he had to play Let's Make a Deal with fellow catcher Josh Paul to get 15. Alomar got his number, but Paul got a computer that Alomar described as "nicer than my own."

F Lefthander *Al Jackson* lost 73 games in his four seasons (1962-65) with the New York Mets while wearing No. 15.

MEMORY OF MUNSON STILL INSPIRES YANKS

The locker stands empty with a small No. 15 placard attached to its top. Next to it, Derek Jeter goes about his daily business. Across from it, Alex Rodriguez does the same. The "15 locker" is an unpretentious shrine that has honored the memory of former New York Yankees captain *Thurman Munson* for more than 25 years.

Jeter, the current Yankees captain, is the unofficial watchman who keeps curious visitors from desecrating the stall where Munson kept his catcher's gear in the 1970s. Munson's mask, chest protector and shinguards hung there untouched for many years after his 1979 death, but finally were removed. The locker otherwise remains unattended and unchanged—an old, out-of-style, unpainted relic in the slick, remodeled clubhouse.

It's one of the many shrines that give Yankee Stadium its mystique. Munson's legacy is captured for fans by a plaque in Monument Park. The clubhouse shrine is more personal, a subtle reminder for team officials, former teammates and current players who are inspired by his memory.

Munson died tragically in 1979—his 11th season with the Yankees—while trying to land his twin-engine jet plane near his home in Canton, Ohio. The bulldog catcher with the walrus mustache and gruff, tell-it-like-it-is exterior was a seven-time All-Star and an American League MVP who led the 1977 and '78 Bronx Zoo Bombers to World Series championships.

Munson

Edmonds

TIM McCARVER: The catcher for two Cardinals World Series winners extended his career by becoming Steve Carlton's personal catcher in Philadelphia.

DICK McGUIRE: This 1950s-era Tricky Dick was so-named because he passed the ball like he had eyes in the back of his head.

EARL MONROE: Not even The Pearl knew what he was going to do with the basketball until the last possible second, which posed a serious problem for defenders.

RED RUFFING: The best six-toed pitcher (yeah, he really had only six) of all-time collected 231 wins for the great Yankees teams of the 1930s and '40s.

MILT SCHMIDT: The center of Boston's 1930s and '40s Kraut Line also served as the Bruins' captain, coach and general manager.

STEVE VAN BUREN: Philadelphia's bruising running back led the Eagles to NFL titles in 1948 and '49.

15 LARRY STEELE 15 TIM SALMON 15 NEIL LOMAX 15 LLOYD MOSEBY 15 BRAD DAVIS 15 EARL MORRALL 15 BEN SHEETS

16

JOE MONTANA

He dazzled high school fans in Pennsylvania, especially the superstitious among them, while wearing No. 13. He led Notre Dame to a national championship in 1977 while wearing No. 3, and he guided four San Francisco 49ers teams to NFL titles in the 1980s while wearing 16—the number with which he forever will be associated. So why did the three-time Super Bowl MVP opt for No. 19 when he played the final two years of his Hall of Fame career with the Kansas City Chiefs? Logic suggests a career pattern that reflects Montana's calculating side. High school No. 13 was shortened to 3 when Montana arrived at South Bend. No. 16 at San Francisco was a combination of his first two numbers: 13 plus 3. With No. 16 out of circulation in Kansas City, in honor of Chiefs Hall of Fame quarterback Len Dawson, Super Joe opted for No. 19, a combination of his last two numbers—16 and 3.

FAST FACTS

F **Brett Hull** wasn't thinking 16 when he joined Calgary full time in 1986-87. He asked for No. 15, only to learn it already was being worn by Robin Bartel. The Flames suggested 16, which Hull wore the rest of his career.

F Yankees great **Whitey Ford** didn't claim No. 16 until 1953, three years after his rookie season. Ford wore 19 in 1950 and then spent two years in military service.

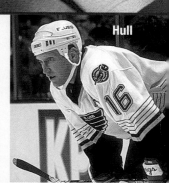

Hull

Elite 16s

THERE'S ROOM FOR ONLY ONE 16 IN NEW YORK

Lefthander Frank Viola, a 24-game winner for the Twins in 1988, was shipped to the New York Mets in July 1989 at the trade deadline. When hearing the news, Viola's first thought was to inquire about his number—the 16 he had worn for seven-plus seasons in Minnesota.

Unfortunately, he discovered, that was the same number that graced the uniform of Mets ace righthander *Dwight Gooden*, who also had a 24-win season under his belt—1985, when at age 20 he dominated National League hitters and became the youngest pitcher ever to win a Cy Young Award.

Viola made his request and Gooden listened, even expressing understanding for his feelings. But his answer was a definitive no.

"I don't care how much money he makes," Gooden said. "He can have my locker. I'll take him to all the best restaurants and show him New York. He can even have my wife. But he can't have my number. No way."

Viola switched to 26.

GEORGE BLANDA: He just kept scoring … and scoring … and scoring, both as a kicker and quarterback for 26 seasons—the longest tenure in NFL history.

BOBBY CLARKE: The captain of the Broad Street Bullies was as tough on the ice as he is now as the Flyers' general manager.

LEN DAWSON: The Chiefs' hero of Super Bowl 4 could really matriculate the ball downfield.

MARCEL DIONNE: A high-scoring center with a Kingly shot. All those goals and points and he never got to hoist

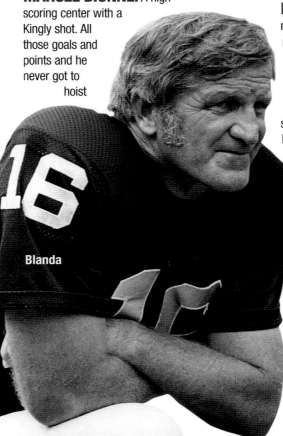

Blanda

the Stanley Cup.

WHITEY FORD: While Mantle, Maris and other Yankees bombed opponents into submission, he carved them up with his control, finesse and guile.

FRANK GIFFORD: The Giants plugged him in so many places—halfback, wide receiver, defensive back—he should have been called "the Extension Cord." Later, he was plugged into the Monday Night Football broadcast booth.

BOB LANIER: Big feet (size 22), big numbers (20.1 ppg, 10.1 rpg) and big-time respect. The only thing missing from this former center's resume is an NBA title.

TED LYONS: A 260-game winner for a White Sox team that finished in the lower half of the American League 16 times in 21 seasons (1923-42, 1946). He reached Hall of Fame heights the hard way.

HAL NEWHOUSER: No other pitcher has won back-to-back MVPs. That's pretty heady stuff for this Detroit Tigers Hall of Famer.

JIM PLUNKETT: A slow starter with a strong finishing kick. Quarterback Plunkett posted victories in the Rose Bowl as a senior at Stanford and in the Super Bowl late in his career for the Raiders.

HENRI RICHARD: You could fit him into your Pocket, but he skated like a Rocket.

PEJA STOJAKOVIC: Soft? That's hard to swallow if you're trying to keep this Pacers star from putting the ball in the basket.

Ⓕ Amazingly, well-traveled outfielder *Reggie Sanders* had been able to get No. 16 at seven of his eight major league stops heading into the 2006 season. In 2003 at Pittsburgh, he had to settle for 19.

Ⓕ When *Bobby Hull* was traded to the Hartford Whalers midway through the 1979-80 season, he had to wear 16 instead of his trademark 9. No. 9 already was being worn by new teammate Gordie Howe.

Ⓕ *Bo Jackson*, No. 34 as a Heisman Trophy-winning running back at Auburn and in the NFL with the Los Angeles Raiders, wore 16 as a left fielder for the Kansas City Royals from 1986-90.

RAMIREZ 16 TOM SANDERS 16 GARRET ANDERSON 16 JIM LONBORG 16 AL ATTLES 16 VLADIMIR KONSTANTINOV

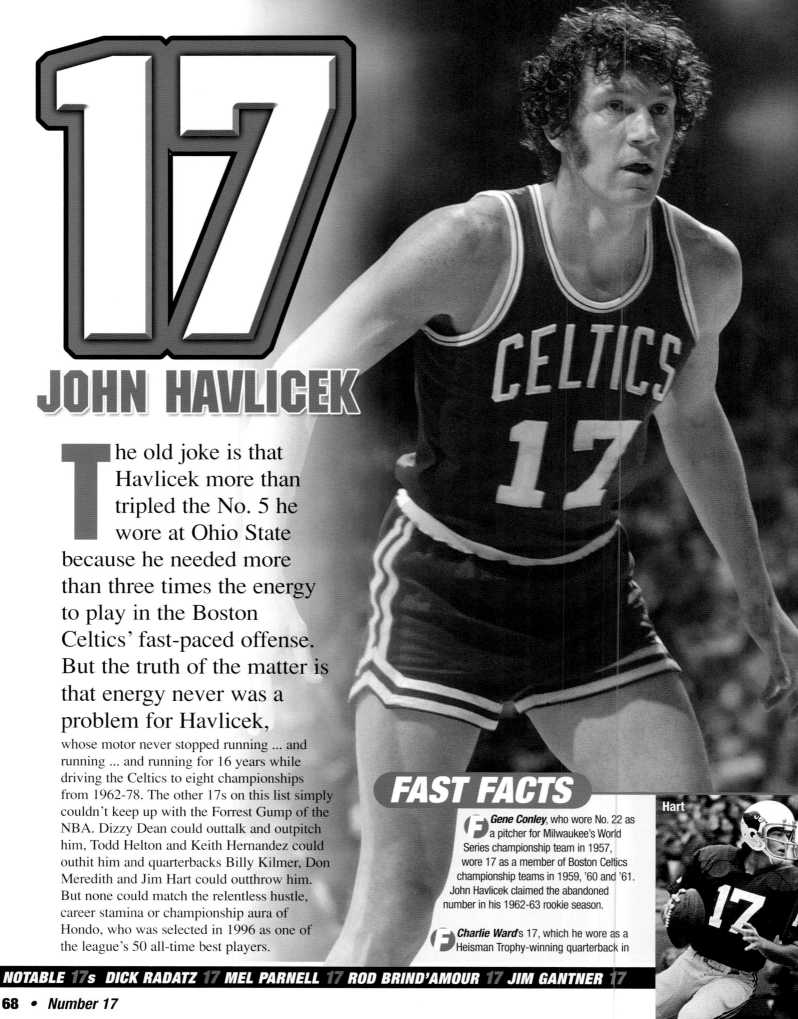

17

JOHN HAVLICEK

The old joke is that Havlicek more than tripled the No. 5 he wore at Ohio State because he needed more than three times the energy to play in the Boston Celtics' fast-paced offense. But the truth of the matter is that energy never was a problem for Havlicek, whose motor never stopped running ... and running ... and running for 16 years while driving the Celtics to eight championships from 1962-78. The other 17s on this list simply couldn't keep up with the Forrest Gump of the NBA. Dizzy Dean could outtalk and outpitch him, Todd Helton and Keith Hernandez could outhit him and quarterbacks Billy Kilmer, Don Meredith and Jim Hart could outthrow him. But none could match the relentless hustle, career stamina or championship aura of Hondo, who was selected in 1996 as one of the league's 50 all-time best players.

FAST FACTS

Gene Conley, who wore No. 22 as a pitcher for Milwaukee's World Series championship team in 1957, wore 17 as a member of Boston Celtics championship teams in 1959, '60 and '61. John Havlicek claimed the abandoned number in his 1962-63 rookie season.

Charlie Ward's 17, which he wore as a Heisman Trophy-winning quarterback in

Hart

NOTABLE 17s DICK RADATZ 17 MEL PARNELL 17 ROD BRIND'AMOUR 17 JIM GANTNER 17

Elite s

LANCE BERKMAN: Watch out for Houston's late-edition Killer B—he can sting you from both sides of the plate.

HAROLD CARMICHAEL: At 6-8 and 225, this power forward disguised as a wide receiver could outhorse any defender for the ball. That might explain why he caught passes in 127 straight games and still ranks as the best receiver in Eagles history.

DIZZY DEAN: The only things quicker than his fastball were his colorful wit and unpredictable tongue.

CARL ERSKINE: A workhorse pitcher from Brooklyn's "Dem Bums" days and a standout for all those World Series teams of the 1950s.

Kenseth

JOE GARAGIOLA: Yogi Berra's childhood buddy fell far short of matching Yogi's expertise as a catcher, but the quick-witted Garagiola made up for that in the broadcast booth.

JIM HART: Quarterback Hart and the St. Louis Cardinals were flying Air Coryell before Dan Fouts and the Chargers. They also attained the same level of playoff success—or lack thereof.

KEITH HERNANDEZ: The Cardinals (18, 37) and Mets (17) star wasn't your typical slugging first baseman, but he got on base, drove in big runs for two championship teams and defended first base like a mama bear defending her cubs.

TODD HELTON: Coors Field has something to do with his career .337 average, but no one doubts his ability to hit.

MATT KENSETH: Kenseth won't win any popularity contests, but his steady 17 car will always contend on the track.

BILLY KILMER: Can you say quarterback controversy? Kilmer was involved in one at both ends of his Redskins career—first, as the young passer trying to unseat Sonny Jurgensen, and later as the wily veteran trying to hold off brash young Joe Theismann.

DENNY McLAIN: He won 31 games for the Tigers at age 24—and only 41 through the remainder of his career. If only he could have stayed out of trouble!

DON MEREDITH: Though his playoff performances weren't always Dandy, Meredith helped build the Cowboys' winning tradition and set the stage for their dominance in the 1970s.

CHRIS MULLIN: He couldn't run or jump and looked kind of silly with that crew cut and those short shorts. But his lefty stroke was one of the smoothest in NBA history.

CHARLIE ROOT: Wouldn't you be frustrated if you posted 201 major league wins and all people wanted to talk about was whether Babe Ruth really called his shot against you in the World Series?

'CHANNEL 17' BRAINSTORM TURNS OFF N.L. BOSS

Atlanta Braves owner Ted Turner signed free-agent pitcher *Andy Messersmith* to a "lifetime contract" in April 1976, promising fans that the two-time 20-game winner "will never be traded" and "will be a Brave as long as I am." Everybody chuckled over that unlikely prospect.

Then the unpredictable Turner really got creative. He assigned Messersmith uniform No. 17, because "that is the channel of my TV station. Super 17, that's Andy." Turner was referring to WTBS, the so-called superstation whose broadcasts were carried via satellite and cable from his Atlanta base.

That's when things really got out of hand. Turner decided to nickname his big righthander "Channel" and actually had that moniker sewed on the back of his jersey instead of "Messersmith." Nobody in the National League office chuckled over the idea of a uniform advertising "Channel 17."

It didn't take long for N.L. president Chub Feeney to act. He lectured Turner about his advertising ploy and ordered him to remove "Channel" from the uniform.

Messersmith, who had compiled 20-6 and 19-14 records in the previous two seasons while wearing 47 for the Los Angeles Dodgers, posted consecutive 11-11 and 5-4 records for the Braves. After the 1977 campaign, Turner sold Messersmith's "lifetime contract" to the New York Yankees.

Messersmith

1993, is one of seven numbers retired by Florida State. Ward wore 21 through his first nine NBA seasons with the Knicks before returning to his 17 roots when he signed a free-agent contract with Houston in 2004.

F *Jim Hart* wore the same number (17) for 18 years with the St. Louis Cardinals, giving him status as dean of quarterbacks who wore a number the longest with one team.

F Former NBA star *Chris Mullin* wore No. 17 in honor of boyhood hero John Havlicek.

F When *Gordie Howe* scored his first NHL goal in 1946 for the Detroit Red Wings, he was wearing No. 17. Howe, of course, later would become synonymous with No. 9.

18

PEYTON MANNING

OK, he has a long way to go to be Dan Marino. And where's that all-important championship ring? But back off, linebacker breath, because no No. 18 has ever looked so good at the halfway point of a career, and who can argue with those 49 touchdown passes and incredible 121.1 quarterback rating Peyton placed in the NFL record books in 2004?

Charlie Joiner? Dave Cowens? Nice try, but they're not the kind of 18s who will be lovingly embraced by future generations. Mississippi fans will tell you former Rebels legend Archie Manning, Peyton's dad, was the inspiration for his number choice, but not so fast. Peyton says he wears 18 in honor of older brother Cooper, who had to stop playing football because of a spinal disorder. Peyton had to wear 16 at Tennessee but switched to 18 when drafted by the Indianapolis Colts in 1998.

FAST FACTS

F Before breaking baseball's color barrier in 1947, *Jackie Robinson* wore uniform No. 18 as a basketball star at UCLA.

F When *Bobby Labonte* drove his Pontiac to a Winston Cup championship in 2000, it marked the first victory in that series for a No. 18 car.

F In June 1989, when 22-year-old outfielder *Deion Sanders* was called up by the New

Labonte

Elite 18s

MOISES ALOU: The name ensures quality. The modern-era Alou could have been even better if injuries had not cost him his speed.

DAVE COWENS: Too small to play center? His 13.6 rebounds per game would suggest otherwise, and the Celtics star was one of the best defenders of the 1970s.

JOHNNY DAMON: This self-professed Idiot was really the savvy table-setter for Boston's 2004 World Series champion.

ROMAN GABRIEL: How did a team with the Fearsome Foursome and Gabriel, one of the best passers of the 1960s, not play in at least one Super Bowl?

TED KLUSZEWSKI: His arms were so massive, he cut off his sleeves to free up his swing. Check out those 1950s photos of the sleeveless Klu with the Reds and White Sox.

HANSONS ICON STATUS RETAINS MOVIE APPEAL

They are best remembered as the Hanson brothers, those lovable but violence-prone hockey goons who created mayhem and gained icon stature in the 1977 Paul Newman movie *Slap Shot*. Beyond that, it gets confusing. The role of *Steve Hanson* was played by Steve Carlson, *Jeff Hanson* was played by Steve's real-life brother Jeff Carlson and Jack Hanson was played by David Hanson.

For the record, the character Killer Carlson was played by Jerry Houser; Jack Carlson, the third real-life brother, missed this movie opportunity (and was replaced by David Hanson) because he had been called up by the Edmonton Oilers of the World Hockey Association. Got all that? If not, all you really need to know is that the fictional Hansons wore Nos. 16, 17 and 18 for the fictional Charlestown Chiefs of the fictional Federal League.

In fact, the Carlsons and David Hanson were not even actors—they were career minor league hockey players (they combined to play 85 NHL games between them) for the Johnstown Jets of the North American Hockey League. They were brought into the movie to give it an authentic look—and that they did. Most of the on-ice havoc they wreaked was based on antics they had employed in their real-life version of "old-time hockey."

DAVE TAYLOR: The Kings' Triple Crown line—Taylor, Marcel Dionne and Charlie Simmer—wouldn't have been effective without Taylor's defense and willingness to take on the opposing team's toughest checker.

GENE TENACE: With his combination of walks and power, Tenace was a classic A's Moneyball player—about 30 years ago.

BILL VIRDON: Getting a ball down in the Pirates outfield with Virdon and Roberto Clemente patrolling was like landing a helicopter in a hurricane. Virdon also was an outstanding manager, though his teams never seemed to have the killer instinct.

Cowens

Damon

York Yankees, he was handed uniform No. 18. Asked if he was satisfied with that, he replied, "No." When asked what number he would prefer, he answered, "Two million."

F The perfect number: New York Yankees righthander *Don Larsen* was wearing 18 when he pitched his perfect game against the Brooklyn Dodgers in Game 5 of the 1956 World Series.

18 JOHN HILLER 18 GLENN BECKERT 18 JIM LOSCUTOFF 18 TOBIN ROTE 18 BILL RUSSELL 18 GENE WASHINGTON

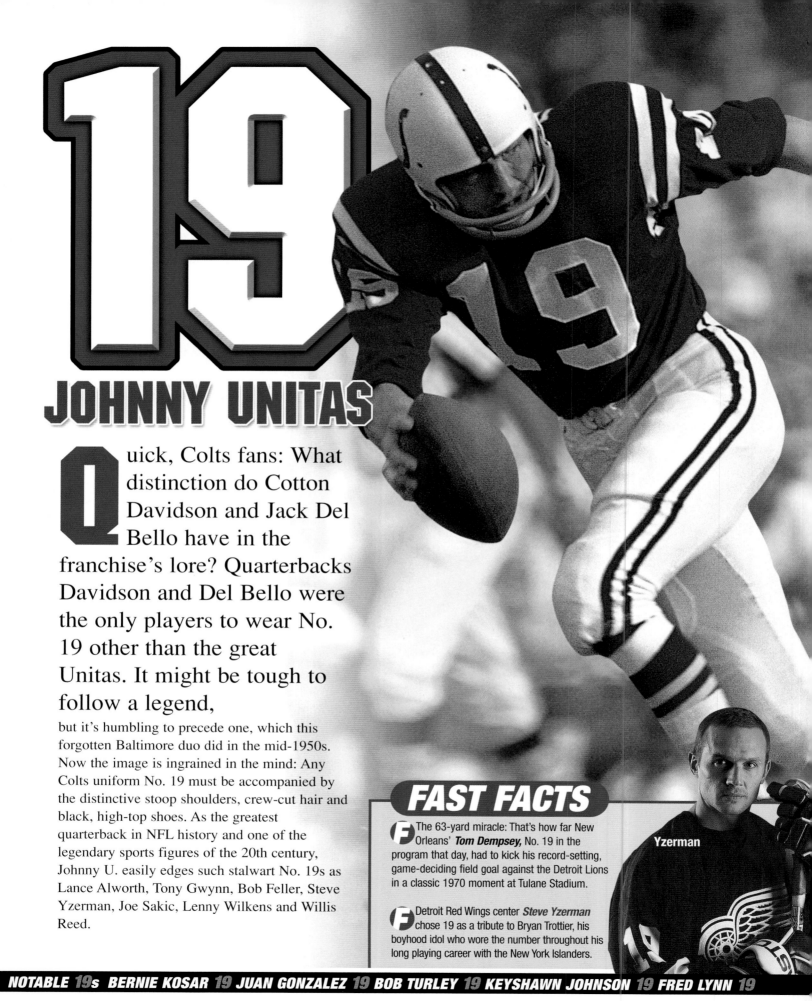

19
JOHNNY UNITAS

Quick, Colts fans: What distinction do Cotton Davidson and Jack Del Bello have in the franchise's lore? Quarterbacks Davidson and Del Bello were the only players to wear No. 19 other than the great Unitas. It might be tough to follow a legend,

but it's humbling to precede one, which this forgotten Baltimore duo did in the mid-1950s. Now the image is ingrained in the mind: Any Colts uniform No. 19 must be accompanied by the distinctive stoop shoulders, crew-cut hair and black, high-top shoes. As the greatest quarterback in NFL history and one of the legendary sports figures of the 20th century, Johnny U. easily edges such stalwart No. 19s as Lance Alworth, Tony Gwynn, Bob Feller, Steve Yzerman, Joe Sakic, Lenny Wilkens and Willis Reed.

Yzerman

FAST FACTS

F The 63-yard miracle: That's how far New Orleans' **Tom Dempsey,** No. 19 in the program that day, had to kick his record-setting, game-deciding field goal against the Detroit Lions in a classic 1970 moment at Tulane Stadium.

F Detroit Red Wings center **Steve Yzerman** chose 19 as a tribute to Bryan Trottier, his boyhood idol who wore the number throughout his long playing career with the New York Islanders.

NOTABLE 19s   BERNIE KOSAR 19 JUAN GONZALEZ 19 BOB TURLEY 19 KEYSHAWN JOHNSON 19 FRED LYNN 19

Elite 19s

BERT CAMPANERIS: The A's were fiery, competitive and very good in the early 1970s. One big reason was Campy, their speedy shortstop.

BOB FELLER: No-hitters, one-hitters, 100-mph fastballs and lots of strikeouts. This pre-Nolan Ryan brought star power to Cleveland.

JIM GILLIAM: Junior, the Dodgers' Mr. Versatility, plugged a lot of holes from 1953-66.

DAVE McNALLY: He won 181 games for the Orioles and was one of the two players who pushed baseball into the free-agency era.

DON NELSON: He's best known today as an innovative coach, but way back in the 1960s and '70s he helped the Celtics win five NBA titles.

BILLY PIERCE: The stylish lefthander never needed many runs to win a game, which is good because the White Sox didn't score many during his career.

WILLIS REED: Hobbling. Game 7. Heart. Desire. Victory. Does that ring a bell,

Feller

Knicks fans?

DAVE RIGHETTI: The New York media ripped Yogi Berra for converting Rags to a closer in 1984. So 252 saves later, who was right?

JOE SAKIC: Talk about star power! How could a team with Peter Forsberg, Patrick Roy and the high-scoring Sakic do anything but win the Stanley Cup?

BRYAN TROTTIER: The Islanders probably would not have won four consecutive Stanley Cups without Trottier's hard-nosed, two-way play.

LENNY WILKENS: Wilkens is the greatest two-way basketball Hall of Famer—15 years as a high-scoring guard, 32 more as the winningest coach (1,332 victories) in NBA history.

ROBIN YOUNT: How to make the baseball Hall of Fame in two easy steps: 1. Win MVP awards while playing two of the game's most critical defensive positions. 2. Collect 3,000-plus hits.

Young

YOUNG BEGAN, ENDED STREAK WITH NO. 19

Anthony Young's locker was filled with rabbits' feet, good-luck coins, charms and numerous letters with suggestions about how the Mets righthander might end his record-tying 23-game losing streak. Maybe Young should have just listened to his bosses before a late-June game in 1993.

They told him a story about pitcher Roger Craig, who in 1963 exchanged uniform No. 38 for 13 and immediately ended his string of 18 consecutive defeats. Why not, they asked Young, do the same thing—exchange 19 for 13—and let the "reverse luck" help him avoid setting a futility record.

No thanks, Young responded. "I started the streak with 19 and I'll end it with 19."

Young kept his promise, but not before his two-season losing skid grew to a record 27 games. His ordeal ended in a July 29 game in which Young, pitching the ninth inning against the Marlins in relief of Bret Saberhagen, surrendered a run that broke a 3-3 tie. In the bottom of the inning, however, the Mets scored twice, with Eddie Murray doubling home the winner.

Young finished 1993 at 1-16 and was 3-30 over the two seasons as both a starter and reliever. He pitched well at times and was mystified by his bad luck.

"That wasn't even a big monkey that was on my back," he said. "It was a zoo."

F *Tony Gwynn* remembers feeling gratified when he was assigned No. 19 in 1982 after being called up from Class AAA Hawaii by the San Diego Padres. Gwynn had worn 53 in the minors.

F *Lance Alworth's* No. 19, which was retired by the Chargers during the 2005 season, was worn by four players after Alworth's 1970 departure from San Diego. One was quarterback Johnny Unitas, who played his final NFL season for the Chargers in 1973.

Gwynn

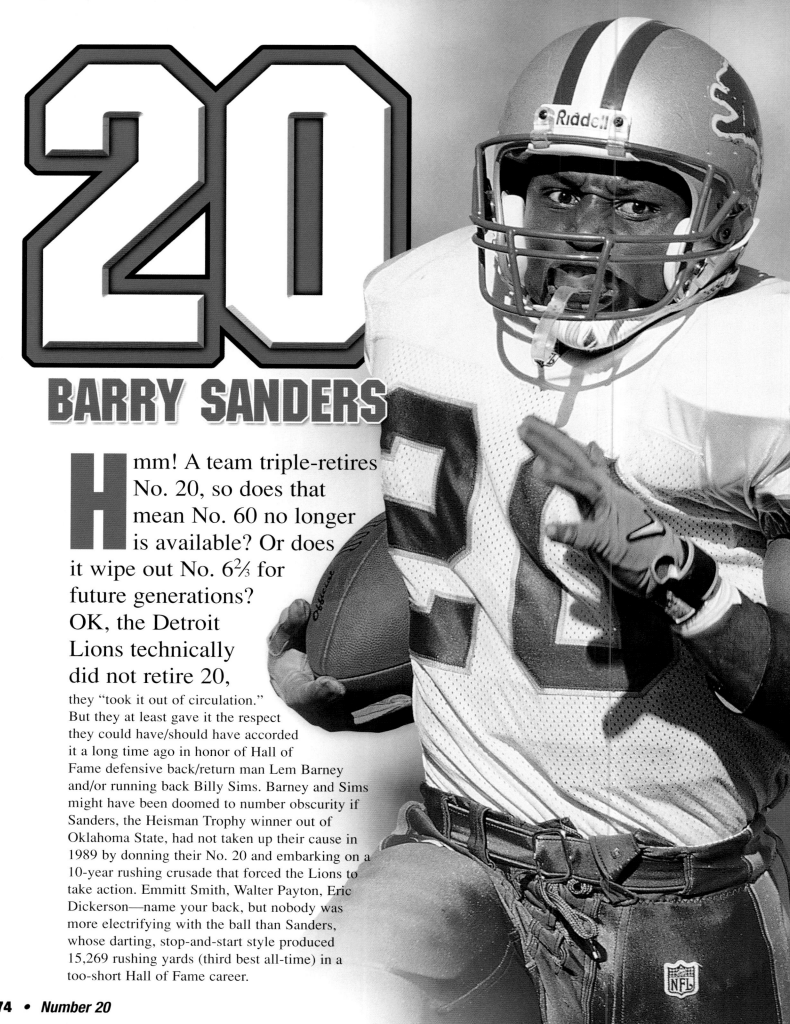

20
BARRY SANDERS

Hmm! A team triple-retires No. 20, so does that mean No. 60 no longer is available? Or does it wipe out No. 6⅔ for future generations? OK, the Detroit Lions technically did not retire 20, they "took it out of circulation." But they at least gave it the respect they could have/should have accorded it a long time ago in honor of Hall of Fame defensive back/return man Lem Barney and/or running back Billy Sims. Barney and Sims might have been doomed to number obscurity if Sanders, the Heisman Trophy winner out of Oklahoma State, had not taken up their cause in 1989 by donning their No. 20 and embarking on a 10-year rushing crusade that forced the Lions to take action. Emmitt Smith, Walter Payton, Eric Dickerson—name your back, but nobody was more electrifying with the ball than Sanders, whose darting, stop-and-start style produced 15,269 rushing yards (third best all-time) in a too-short Hall of Fame career.

5 GOOD REASONS TO KEEP A CLOSE EYE ON eBAY

Any discussion of No. 20 has to include former Phillies third baseman *Mike Schmidt*, who hit 548 homers and won 10 Gold Gloves during his Hall of Fame career. But Bryan Beban, fortunately, remembers that Schmidt once wore No. 5.

Beban is the assistant general manager of the Eugene Emeralds, a Padres Class A farm team. But in 1972, Eugene was the Phillies' Class AAA affiliate. Schmidt played second and third base for the Emeralds that season and hit 26 home runs—while wearing No. 5.

In recent years, Beban has made it a point to check eBay, looking for Emeralds-related memorabilia. Few items show up, but one that did in 2004 quickly caught his attention. It was a No. 5 jersey from '72—the one Schmidt wore before being called up by the Phillies.

Beban bid $99 and crossed his fingers that collectors would not associate the jersey with Schmidt. If they had, the price surely would have skyrocketed. No one did. Beban immediately forwarded his acquisition to a minor league baseball official for authentication.

The jersey was sent on to Schmidt, who was managing in Clearwater, Fla., at the time, with a letter promising that the Emeralds had no intention of reselling it. Schmidt added a special touch to the team's now-prized piece of memorabilia, writing on a card attached to the framed jersey, "Never will forget the Eugene Emeralds, Mike Schmidt." The jersey now hangs in the Emeralds' office.

NOTABLE 20s *GORMAN THOMAS* **20** *TOMMIE AGEE* **20** *DERON CHERRY* **20** *MANU GINOBILI* **20** *DON SUTTON* **20** *JOE MORRIS*

Elite 20s

Brock

LEM BARNEY: In his first NFL game for the Lions, Barney intercepted a Bart Starr pass and returned it for a touchdown. The rest of his Hall of Fame career was more of the same.

CLIFF BATTLES: One of the best NFL running backs of the 1930s retired because he could make more money as an assistant football coach. A sign of the times?

LOU BROCK: Every base he stole and hit he collected for the Cardinals had to rip another piece from the hearts of Cubs fans.

MONTE IRVIN: One of the last great Negro leagues players, the aging Irvin

Belfour

FAST FACTS

F Yankees shortstop **Bucky Dent** was wearing No. 20 in 1978 when he hit the stunning three-run homer at Fenway Park that decided the A.L. East Division playoff game against the Red Sox.

F Although seven major league teams have retired 20, only two teams combined in the NBA, NFL and NHL have honored the number. The Portland Trail Blazers retired it for **Maurice Lucas** and the New England Patriots for **Gino Cappelletti**.

F After leaving Chicago in 1997, goalie **Ed Belfour** began wearing No. 20 (with Dallas and Toronto) in honor of Vladislav Tretiak, the former Russian great who served as Belfour's first goaltending coach with the Blackhawks.

F Rookie righthander **Mark "The Bird" Fidrych** brought lasting fame to No. 20 in 1976 when he took baseball by storm and posted 19 wins for the Detroit Tigers. The popular Fidrych never matched

LUIS GONZALEZ 20 **RONDE BARBER** 20 **CESAR GERONIMO** 20 **MAURICE LUCAS** 20 **BRUCE BENEDICT** 20 **GINO CAPPELLETTI**

helped the Giants to two World Series and one championship.

GARY PAYTON: One of the best defenders in the NBA during his Seattle years also could put the ball in the basket.

MEL RENFRO: Making the Pro Bowl in each of his first five seasons as a Cowboys free safety earned him a switch to cornerback, where he continued to make Pro Bowls and terrorize quarterbacks.

FRANK ROBINSON: The Reds decided he was washed up at 30. So he won a Triple Crown with the Orioles and hit 179 home runs over the next six years. How many ways can you say "worst trade in baseball history"?

BILLY SIMS: Here's a thought: Barry Sanders might never have worn a Lions uniform if a knee injury had not ended this Heisman Trophy winner's career.

TONY STEWART: Why do fans and drivers have a problem with Stewart? Is it his personality or the feeling he could drive a garbage can with wheels to victory?

PIE TRAYNOR: The 1920s and '30s Pirates star might be the best third baseman not named Schmidt or Brett.

FRANK WHITE: Educated at the Royals' baseball academy, White earned a Ph.D. in fielding. You can measure his success in Gold Gloves.

CANNON STILL OWNS 20 IN BAYOU COUNTRY

Almost a half century ago, No. 20 was owned by *Billy Cannon*. He was a bona fide hero in Louisiana's Bayou country—the star for LSU's 1958 national championship team, the 1959 Heisman Trophy winner and leading man for one of the most memorable plays in college football history.

Well-known nationally, Cannon was treasured throughout the Deep South and revered in Louisiana. Kids and grown-ups were hip in their No. 20 jerseys, and parents named their children after the speedy running back, who was everybody's All-American. When his second daughter was born while he was still at LSU, a diaper bearing his No. 20 was hoisted on a flag pole at Tiger Stadium.

The Cannon legend lives on through *The Play*, the 89-yard punt return that beat rival Mississippi in 1959. In a battle of unbeatens on Halloween night, the No. 1-ranked Tigers trailed No. 3-ranked Ole Miss, 3-0, with 10 minutes remaining. Cannon fielded a punt at his own 11 and broke seven tackles on his stunning touchdown romp.

After a solid 11-year pro career, the mystique was tarnished in 1983 when Cannon was arrested in a counterfeiting scheme and eventually spent about three years in prison. But heroes die hard in Tiger country. When Cannon attended a 2003 homecoming game, he was introduced while the replay of his touchdown return played on the Jumbotron. The thunderous ovation proved that old No. 20 had been forgiven—and not forgotten.

Stewart

Kosar

that effort again in a career shortened by injuries.

F *Bernie Kosar*, who had worn 20 at the University of Miami, dropped a digit to 19 when he joined Cleveland in 1985 because of the NFL system that restricts quarterbacks to numbers ranging from 1-19.

Cannon

20 *JORGE POSADA* 20 *BOBBY BRYANT* 20

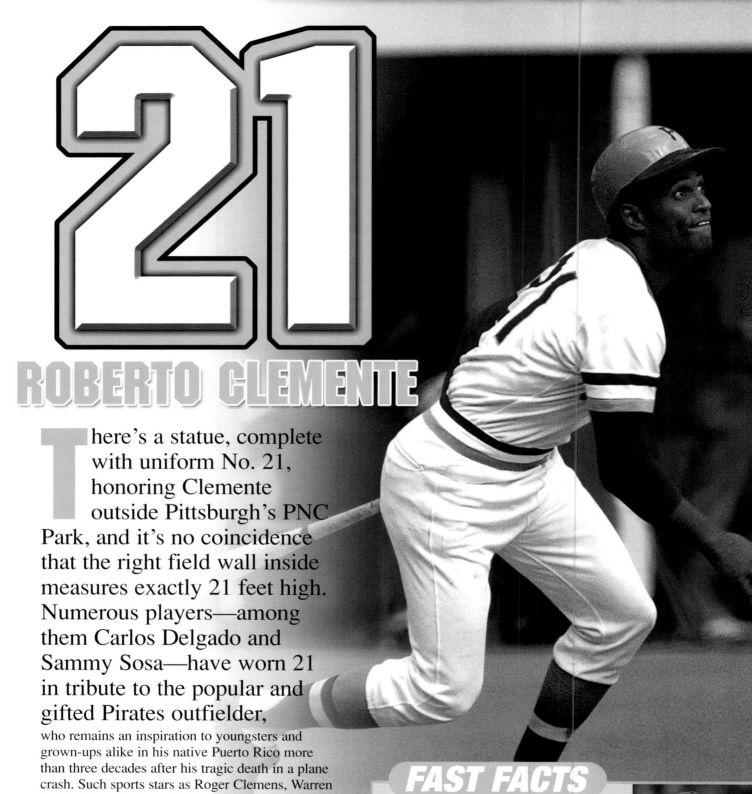

21
ROBERTO CLEMENTE

There's a statue, complete with uniform No. 21, honoring Clemente outside Pittsburgh's PNC Park, and it's no coincidence that the right field wall inside measures exactly 21 feet high. Numerous players—among them Carlos Delgado and Sammy Sosa—have worn 21 in tribute to the popular and gifted Pirates outfielder, who remains an inspiration to youngsters and grown-ups alike in his native Puerto Rico more than three decades after his tragic death in a plane crash. Such sports stars as Roger Clemens, Warren Spahn, Stan Mikita and Deion Sanders also have brought stature to the number, but none can match Clemente's on-field elegance (offensively and defensively) and legendary appeal. Roberto Clemente Walker—count the letters in his full name, which in keeping with Hispanic custom includes his mother's maiden name last, and you'll know how Clemente came up with the number 21.

FAST FACTS

F When *Roger Clemens*, the Red Sox's longtime No. 21, signed with Toronto before the 1997 season, Blue Jays first baseman Carlos Delgado graciously gave up the 21 he had worn in honor of countryman Roberto Clemente. An appreciative Clemens rewarded Delgado with a Rolex watch.

F *David Pearson,* driving the Wood Brothers' familiar 21 car from 1972-79, won 43 races, including the 1976 Daytona 500.

Clemens

NOTABLE 21S TIKI BARBER **21** PAUL O'NEILL **21** NOLAN CROMWELL **21** BOB LEMON **21** PAUL FOYTACK

Elite **21**s

Sanders

DAVE BING: The Pistons fired on all cylinders when this Hall of Fame guard got his hands on the ball in the 1960s and '70s.

CLIFF BRANCH: In the 1970s and early '80s, this Raiders receiver was "stretching the field" before the phrase became fashionable.

TIM DUNCAN: He might not be the most exciting player to watch, but his old-school style wins NBA games—and championships.

CURT FLOOD: Never mind that he was an outstanding center fielder for the Cardinals. He will be remembered for opening the door to free agency and big-money contracts.

F Good blood lines: *Terry Metcalf* (1973-77) and son *Eric Metcalf* (1998) both wore uniform No. 21 for the NFL's Arizona/St. Louis Cardinals.

F Before Roberto Clemente put on 21 during the 1955 season, the best Pittsburgh player to wear the number was shortstop *Arky Vaughan,* who had it from 1932-39.

TAYLOR EMBRACES 28 AFTER DIGITAL DETOUR

Fred Taylor is a 21 at heart, a 28 on your Sunday program. Credit former Jacksonville cornerback Aaron Beasley with the interception that changed the course of Taylor's numerological game plan.

When the talented running back was selected by the Jaguars with the ninth overall pick of the 1998 draft, he envisioned a long NFL life as 21, the number he had worn in high school and for four seasons at the University of Florida. A big contract was looming, and Taylor was willing to pay to wear his favorite number.

But when Beasley, who had been wearing 21 for two seasons with Jacksonville, was asked to set a price for his number, the response was surprising.

"He sort of jokingly said, 'Fifty Gs,' " Taylor told John Oehser of the *Florida Times-Union.* "I told him, 'That's something you can keep.' "

Beasley said the high price was a matter of principle—he was trying to establish his "own little identity" in the league. So Taylor considered his options and decided on 28, partly because he was a big fan of running back Marshall Faulk and partly because 28 did not have a notable history with the Jaguars. It does now.

Through 2005, Taylor had topped 1,000 yards rushing five times in eight seasons and scored 58 touchdowns. Beasley left Jacksonville after the 2001 season, but Taylor didn't bite, saying he had embraced life as an NFL 28.

PETER FORSBERG: Traded with five other players and two draft picks for Eric Lindros, Forsberg led the Avalanche to two Stanley Cups. Lindros led the Flyers and the NHL in concussions and unfulfilled promise.

WORLD B. FREE: With the self-induced pressure from that name, he had to fill it up in the NBA. And he did.

KEVIN GARNETT: A high schooler goes pro and shows that today's 7-footers are athletic enough to play small forward.

JIM KIICK: Where would Butch (Larry Csonka)—or the Dolphins—have been without Sundance (Kiick)?

JERRY LUCAS: He won championships at Ohio State, in the 1960 Olympic Games and with the New York Knicks. He was an NBA All-Star Game MVP, too. Enough said.

STAN MIKITA: The Blackhawks center won the Art Ross Trophy (scoring), Hart Trophy (MVP) and Lady Byng Trophy (most gentlemanly) in the same season two straight times (1966-67, 1967-68).

DEION SANDERS: He was Prime Time in football, something less in baseball—but good enough to go either way.

BILL SHARMAN: The term "pure shooter" might have been invented for this 1950s-era Celtic.

SAMMY SOSA: This former Cubs masher didn't get the single-season home run record, but he did top 60 three times. No one else has done that.

WARREN SPAHN: The winningest lefthander in baseball history won 20 games 13 times for the Braves.

DOMINIQUE WILKINS: He showed what the human body can do while providing above-the-rim special effects for the NBA highlight reel.

22

EMMITT SMITH

Close your eyes, relax and concentrate on the number 22. More than likely, the shadow sprinting through your imagination belongs to that same guy who ran through NFL defenses for 15 memorable seasons. Smith is the most visible performer in a strong cast of 22s. Thirteen years playing for America's Team ensures visibility; so do three Super Bowl rings and status as the NFL's all-time leading rusher. Pre-Emmitt, No. 22 honors might have belonged to the always popular Doug Flutie … or pitching great Jim Palmer. Sports fans with long memories might have opted for Mike Bossy, Elgin Baylor or Bobby Layne. But for today's fan, the number comes tied in a silver, blue and white ribbon. Anybody who still thinks that 2 plus 2 equals 4 obviously has not been watching football highlight reels since Mr. Durability made his NFL debut in 1990.

FIREBALL'S DAYTONA LEGACY LIVES ON

NASCAR drivers who compete in No. 22 cars still do so under the immense shadow of *Glenn "Fireball" Roberts*, the sport's first real superstar and a pioneer of the superspeedway fast tracks. And anybody competing at Daytona International Speedway knows the impact Roberts had in making the Daytona 500 the premier event of the stock car racing circuit.

Roberts, who set more than 400 racing records from 1949-64, had been a Daytona failure before 1962. He led briefly in the inaugural Daytona 500 in 1959 before suffering fuel-pump failure, dropped out quickly in 1960 with engine trouble and appeared victory bound in 1961 when his engine blew with 13 laps to go. But 1962 was a different story.

Driving Henry "Smokey" Yunick's 405-horsepower, No. 22 black-and-gold Pontiac, Roberts won the qualifying race with a blistering average speed of 156.9 mph, took the pole at an even-faster 158.7, posted the fastest qualifying time and captured the 500 by leading 144 of the 200 laps. His average time of 152.5 mph (no cautions) made him the first driver to break 150 at Daytona. The crew-cut Roberts completed his Daytona sweep with a Fourth of July win in the Firecracker 250.

Few drivers since have dominated so completely at Daytona. And few have ended careers so tragically. On May 24, 1964, Roberts suffered burns over 70 percent of his body in a multi-car crash in the World 600 at Charlotte Motor Speedway. He died 39 days later at age 35.

Roberts

NOTABLE 22s BRAD RADKE 22 BILL BUCKNER 22 MERCURY MORRIS

Elite 22s

Drexler

ELGIN BAYLOR: He never won a scoring title or NBA championship, but the high-scoring Baylor played a major role in helping the Lakers become the NBA's most popular franchise.

MIKE BOSSY: This nine-time 50-goal scorer was top gun for Islanders teams that won four straight Stanley Cups in the early 1980s.

WILL CLARK: Will wasn't always a thrill, but he never stopped competing and swinging his lethal bat.

DAVE DeBUSSCHERE: A two-sport star (basketball and baseball) who helped fuel New York Knicks championships in 1970 and '73.

CLYDE DREXLER: When the Glide joined former college teammate Hakeem Olajuwon in Houston in 1994-95, they did what they couldn't do in college—win a championship.

BOB HAYES: In 1965, the Cowboys turned the "World's Fastest Human" into a wide receiver, an idea that seemed a lot less crazy after he led the NFL in touchdowns.

BOBBY LAYNE: He partied heartily and still found time to quarterback the Lions to a pair of NFL championships in the 1950s.

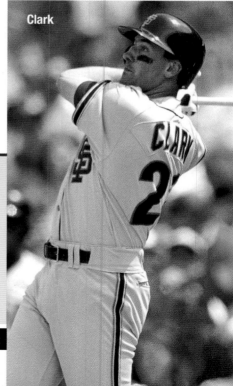

Clark

FAST FACTS

F Defenseman **Brian Leetch**, No. 2 during his 17 seasons with the Rangers, took 22 when he signed with Boston before the 2005-06 season. No. 2 (Eddie Shore) has been retired by the Bruins.

F **Willie O'Ree**, the first black player in the NHL, wore No. 22 with the Boston Bruins when he played two games in 1958 and 43 games in the 1960-61 season.

F The **Jackson brothers**, Willie Jr. (1990-93) and Terry (1995-98), were literally following in the footsteps of their father when they wore No. 22 while playing football at the University of Florida. Willie Sr. started the tradition from 1969-71.

F Vancouver left wing **Daniel Sedin** wears 22 because he was the second overall pick of the 1999 draft. Twin brother Henrik, the third overall pick in the same draft, wears 33 and plays center for the Canucks.

TAYSHAUN PRINCE 22 DAN DRIESSEN 22 ROLANDO BLACKMAN 22 VIRGIL

ED MACAULEY: There was nothing Easy about beating Macauley and the champion St. Louis Hawks in 1957-58—or Macauley's solid Celtics teams earlier.

BUCK O'NEIL: A Negro leagues star who later signed such players as Ernie Banks and Lou Brock for the Cubs.

JIM PALMER: The winningest pitcher in the 1970s and three-time Cy Young winner was manager Earl Weaver's savior—and nemesis. Their legendary bickering kept things lively in the Orioles' clubhouse.

SHERYL SWOOPES: This championship magnet helped Texas Tech to a 1993 NCAA title, three U.S. teams to Olympic gold medals and the Houston Comets of the WNBA to four titles. Nike even named a shoe line the "Air Swoopes."

Flutie

NEW ENGLANDERS STILL SAVOR FLUTIE MEMORIES

Chances are, many New Englanders still have a No. 22 Boston College jersey hanging in their closet in honor of *Doug Flutie*, who in 1984 also was recognized and admired in points beyond as college football's Little Engine That Could, the underdog who threw the miracle pass to beat Miami and who won the Heisman Trophy.

More than two decades later, Flutie still was playing football—professionally in 2005 for the New England Patriots at age 43. But he had not worn 22 since 1991 in the Canadian Football League. While the NFL's numbering system does not allow quarterbacks to wear anything over 19, no one— or system—can deny Flutie his rightful heritage.

He first wore 22 as a Pop Warner player in a Baltimore suburb and kept wearing it for his various sports teams during eight years in Florida. After his family relocated to the Boston area in the late 1970s, Flutie was so outstanding for Natick High that the school retired his 22. So did Boston College, where the 5-10 Flutie reached icon status.

Flutie, who traces his 22 love affair to former Orioles pitcher Jim Palmer and Dolphins running back Mercury Morris, wore it in 1985, his first professional season with the New Jersey Generals of the USFL. His only other pro seasons with the number were 1990 and '91, when former quarterback Joe Kapp, then general manager of the CFL's British Columbia Lions, allowed his 22 to be removed from retirement for Flutie.

Swoopes

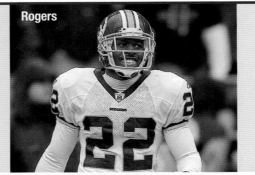

Rogers

Washington Redskins cornerback *Carlos Rogers*, the ninth overall pick in the 2005 draft, reportedly opted for No. 22 because numbers in the 30s and 40s "are ugly."

TRUCKS 22 ALLIE REYNOLDS 22 ED DANOWSKI 22 ROGER WEHRLI 22 PAUL KRAUSE 22 CHARLIE MOORE 22

23

MICHAEL JORDAN

No number has been more visibly ingrained into the international psyche and better marketed worldwide than 23, thanks to the championship script and frequent-flyer miles logged by His Airness.

Mattingly? Sandberg? LeBron James? Don't even go there! No. 23 is Jordan, whose "Be Like Mike" message echoed through the 1980s and '90s as an icon-enhancing battle cry. Kids bought into it. So did parents, fans and even Jordan's basketball and other-sport contemporaries. Englishman David Beckham, an international soccer icon who plays for Real Madrid, switched to No. 23 recently "because I'm a massive fan of Michael Jordan." Just close your eyes and visualize Chicago Bulls No. 23 with one arm extended, legs scissored and tongue wagging as he flies toward the basket, seemingly unaffected by gravity. Now say it loud, and with meaning: six NBA titles and the highest scoring average in NBA history. Case closed.

WHITTIER'S NO. 23 HAD A PASSION FOR FOOTBALL

He was nobody's All-American. In fact, *Richard M. Nixon* was barely a football player. But that did not diminish his love for the game or the passion for it that he showed while serving as president of the United States from 1969-74.

Nixon's football roots trace to the early 1930s at Whittier College, where he was a 155-pound member of the team coached by Wallace "Chief" Newman. Young Nixon was small and not very athletic, but what he lacked in skill he made up for with determination and enthusiasm. "Although sometimes taking a lacing in scrimmage," Newman once recalled, "he always came back for more."

Nixon, who wore No. 23 at Whittier, once described his football days with similar sentiment. "I was a lousy football player," he said, "but I remember Chief Newman, our coach, saying that, 'There's one thing about Nixon—he plays every scrimmage as though the championship were at stake.' "

As president, he dispensed football advice in the same manner, prematurely declaring the Texas Longhorns college football's national champions in 1969 after their late-season showdown victory over Arkansas. Coach Joe Paterno and fans of undefeated Penn State protested, but Texas indeed was voted No. 1 after defeating Notre Dame in the Cotton Bowl.

Nixon was a big fan of the Washington Redskins, perhaps because they were coached by former Whittier coach George Allen. He even suggested plays to Allen and Miami coach Don Shula. Send Paul Warfield on a down-and-out pattern against Dallas, Nixon advised Shula before Super Bowl 6. The pass was tried and broken up by the Cowboys, who defeated the Dolphins, 24-3.

NOTABLE 23s CLAUDE OSTEEN 23 TIPPY MARTINEZ 23 PATRICK SURTAIN 23 TOMMIE AARON 23 WILLIE HORTON

Elite 23s

Mattingly

KIRK GIBSON: Mr. Intensity drove the Tigers and Dodgers to World Series titles in the 1980s.

LOU HUDSON: Sweet Lou had a sweet jump shot and a sweet career for the St. Louis/Atlanta Hawks and Lakers.

PETE MARAVICH: The LSU version of Pistol Pete introduced show-stopping magic, flair and floppy-haired charisma to college basketball.

DON MATTINGLY: Though he didn't experience team success, first baseman Mattingly is one of the most popular players to wear Yankee pinstripes. His A.L. MVP, batting championship and nine Gold Gloves had something to do with that.

CALVIN MURPHY: Size didn't matter for the 5-8 Murphy, who was one of the best guards at both ends of the floor in the 1970s and '80s.

Sandberg

FAST FACTS

F Although Texas Rangers first baseman **Mark Teixeira** grew up about 20 minutes from Baltimore's Camden Yards, his favorite player was New York Yankees first baseman Don Mattingly. That's why he wears No. 23.

F Atlanta outfielder **David Justice,** after being named the National League's 1990 Rookie of the Year, on his decision to wear uniform No. 23: "I'm the (Michael) Jordan of the Braves."

F When **Ryne Sandberg** joined the Cubs in 1982, he requested 14, his old high school number. "I'd heard of Ernie Banks, I knew he was a Hall of Famer," Sandberg told the *Chicago Tribune* in 2005. "But I didn't know he wore No. 14, and I didn't know the Cubs had retired the number."

F Two of the most dramatic home runs in baseball history were hit by players wearing No. 23: **Bobby Thomson's** pennant-deciding

BOB GAINEY 23 **TROY VINCENT** 23 **MARK GUBICZA** 23 **CHAMIQUE HOLDSCLAW**

'THE NEXT MICHAEL' EVEN HAS HIS NUMBER

LeBron James, like most basketball wannabes of his generation, grew up wanting "to be like Mike." James, unlike his contemporaries, is getting his wish. From the Jordanesque athleticism and savvy maturity he displays on the court to the marketing and promotional hype that engulfs him, the Ohio-born prodigy is very much like Mike—and even dares to wear Jordan's No. 23.

Check out the James profile:

■ As a high school phenom in Akron, the 6-8, 240-pound James was a two-time consensus national player of the year, a *Parade* All-American, Ohio's Mr. Basketball and a member of three state title teams. Two of his games were broadcast by ESPN2, and others were available on pay-per-view TV in Ohio.

■ James was featured on the cover of *Sports Illustrated*—before jumping straight to the NBA from high school. "The Chosen One" was anointed by SI as the successor to Michael Jordan.

■ On the eve of the 2003 NBA draft—he was selected No. 1 overall by Cleveland—James received a $90 million endorsement contract from Nike. He later signed eye-popping beverage and trading-card deals. His first Cavaliers contract: four years, $13 million.

■ In 2003-04, James averaged 20.9 points, 5.5 rebounds and 5.9 assists for the Cavs and was named NBA Rookie of the Year. After 2004-05, his scoring average was 24.1. By Jordan standards, that's just the tip of the iceberg. But there are at least 23 good reasons to believe James will live up to his superstar destiny.

Maravich

homer for the New York Giants in 1951, and Kirk Gibson's ninth-inning shot for the Dodgers off Dennis Eckersley in Game 1 of the 1988 World Series.

James

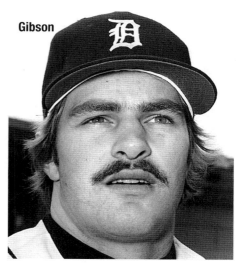
Gibson

BOB NYSTROM: The man who scored the overtime goal that clinched the New York Islanders' first Stanley Cup championship in 1980 also was a key performer in the other three—1981, '82 and '83.

CLAUDE OSTEEN: Everyone talks about Koufax and Drysdale, but lefty Osteen averaged 16 wins for the Dodgers from 1965-73.

FRANK RAMSEY: This Celtics guard turned on the NBA to the idea of the sixth man.

RYNE SANDBERG: Thank you, Phillies. Nine Gold Gloves and 282 homers after his 1982 trade to the Cubs, he's in the Hall.

TED SIMMONS: Switch hitters who hit for power and average are rare. Catchers with those qualities are coveted. Simmons filled that role for 21 years with the Cardinals, Brewers and Braves.

LUIS TIANT: Pretzel Man posted 229 wins from 1964-82—143 from 1971-80 with the Red Sox and Yankees while wearing 23.

23 *JOHNNY LOGAN* **23** *RALPH TERRY* **23** *BLAINE BISHOP* **23** *MARCUS CAMBY* **23** *OIL CAN BOYD* **23** *MARK TEIXEIRA* **23**

24

WILLIE MAYS

Aspiring young athletes beginning in the 1990s wanted to "Be Like Mike." Aspiring baseball players in the '60s, '70s and '80s wanted to be like Willie, starting with the uniform No. 24 that he showcased for 22 seasons as the greatest center fielder in history.

Ken Griffey Jr., Rickey Henderson, Barry Bonds—all have worn the number as a tribute to Mays. Former Houston center fielder Jimmy Wynn wore it, too, but only because Astros officials forced him to. They wanted him "to be Willie Mays," a goal he never quite fulfilled although he played well enough to have his "24" retired by the team. By one account, Mays was introduced to his legacy in 1951 by New York Giants manager Leo Durocher, who handed him his first uniform, pointed to the No. 24 and asked him if he liked it. Mays responded with a shrug. "All I worry about," he said, "is playing ball."

NOTABLE 24s EARLY WYNN 24 TY LAW 24 CHRIS

A DIGITAL ROAD WELL TRAVELED

Life can get complicated for a one-number guy. Just ask *Rickey Henderson,* who found that preserving his numerological karma required a combination of negotiating skills, good timing and thick skin.

Henderson began his 25-year career in 1979 wearing 35 for the A's. But when he was traded to the Yankees in 1985, Phil Niekro had that number and the speedy left fielder opted for 24 in honor of Willie Mays. He became attached to 24 during his four-plus Yankee seasons, thus beginning a digital odyssey.

The highlights:

■ Henderson wore 24 in his return to Oakland from 1989-93, but only after prying the number from Ron Hassey for golf clubs and a new suit.

■ Traded to Toronto midway through the 1993 season, Henderson had to up the ante—he paid a reported $25,000 for Turner Ward's 24—and then was dropped by the Blue Jays after the season.

■ From 1994 through '98, Henderson spent two more years with Oakland, one-plus with San Diego, part of a year with Anaheim and another with Oakland—all wearing 24.

■ At age 40, Henderson was signed by the Mets in December 1998. The deal stipulated he could wear his beloved 24, even though the number had been out of circulation (except for one brief snafu) since Willie Mays retired in 1973. Mays said late Mets owner Joan Payson had promised the number would not be reissued, and fan outcry was strong. But Henderson wore 24 until he was released in May 2000.

■ Signed by Seattle, Henderson asked for 24—and was denied. The number had belonged to Ken Griffey Jr. and would someday be retired for him. Henderson chose 35.

■ After wearing 24 in a return to San Diego in 2001, Henderson signed with Boston in 2002 and again donned 35. Manny Ramirez's 24 wasn't negotiable.

■ In 2003, his final major league season, Henderson wore 25. The Dodgers had retired 24 for manager Walter Alston.

Elite 24s

Griffey Jr.

WALTER ALSTON: After the tall, silent one choreographed the Dodgers' 1955 breakthrough, he guided them to six more pennants and three more World Series wins.

RICK BARRY: Those underhanded free throws were balanced by his deadly jump shot, maniacal drives, intensity and consistently high scoring average.

WILLIE BROWN: After introducing receivers to the bump-and-run style, this outstanding cornerback helped the Raiders reach nine AFC/AFL championship games and win a Super Bowl.

DWIGHT EVANS: It took a while for Dewey to find his groove. The durable right fielder never was the biggest star in Boston's lineup, but he ranks high in most team hitting categories.

KEN GRIFFEY JR: Injuries have betrayed this once potent Seattle star since

Bradley

FAST FACTS

F That's right, Pilgrim, Marion Morrison wore No. 24 as a tackle for USC in the 1925 and '26 seasons. Morrison went on to greater fame as an actor using the name *John Wayne*.

F Future Supreme Court justice *Byron "Whizzer" White* wore 24 in 1935, '36 and '37 as a running back at the University of Colorado.

F When NBA great *Rick Barry* signed with Houston in 1978, he couldn't wear his familiar No. 24 because it belonged to Moses Malone. Barry eased his pain by wearing 2 at home and 4 on the road.

F *Bill Bradley,* a future U.S. senator from New Jersey, wore 24 in his 10-year career with the New York Knicks. Bradley was a key performer on two NBA championship teams.

JERRY LYNCH 24 **JACK CHRISTIANSEN** 24 **BERNIE FEDERKO** 24 **MARK AGUIRRE**

24 OR 44? SUN DEVILS HAVE REGGIE'S NUMBER

The white, oval sign is permanently displayed on the right field fence at Arizona State's Packard Stadium. Beneath *Reggie Jackson's* name is a maroon "No. 44," a tribute to the longtime major league slugger who played one season, 1966, for the Sun Devils.

One problem: Jackson never wore 44 at Arizona State. He wore 24, a tribute to childhood idol Willie Mays, and hit a then-school-record 15 home runs before signing a contract with the Kansas City Athletics. Jackson wore 9 for the first half of his major league career with the A's and Orioles, 44 for the rest of it with the Yankees, Angels and A's.

Both 9 (by the A's) and 44 (by the Yankees) have been retired. So when Arizona State officials decided to retire Jackson's number, they chose to go with 44, rationalizing that's the one most associated with him during his Hall of Fame career—and that ASU's 24 eventually would be retired for Barry Bonds, which it was.

Jackson, from Wyncote, Pa., actually attended Arizona State on a football scholarship. After his freshman season, he was passing by the baseball field one day and asked coach Bobby Winkles if he could take a few batting practice swings. A couple of tape-measure home runs later, Winkles went to football coach Frank Kush and talked him into letting Jackson switch sports. In his only season, Jackson batted .327 with 65 RBIs and the Sun Devils finished 41-11.

Jackson

his move to Cincinnati. But his membership in the 500-homer club and already-stamped Hall application surely are consolation.

WHITEY HERZOG: The White Rat did his best work over his last 16 years as manager of the Royals and Cardinals—while wearing 24. Too bad he didn't discover 24-power during his forgettable playing career.

SAM JONES: Overshadowed by such contemporary guards as Oscar Robertson, Jerry West and Hal Greer, Jones took comfort in his 10 championship rings—and the Celtics banked on his clutch play.

LENNY MOORE: When Johnny U.'s Colts ran the ball or threw short, Moore was the big-play weapon of choice.

TONY PEREZ: What's a Big Red Machine without a Hall of Fame first baseman? Probably short of fuel.

MANNY RAMIREZ: Manny being Manny produces lots of offense, lots of comical moments in the outfield and lots of controversy.

CHARLES WOODSON: Injuries have slowed Woodson, but he's still one of the best cover corners in the NFL.

Gordon

F In the seven-year stretch from 1995-2001, *Jeff Gordon* won four Winston Cup Series championships driving Rick Hendrick's No. 24 Chevrolet.

24 **WILLIE WOOD** 24 **BEN OGLIVIE** 24 **BOBBY JONES** 24 **TERRY O'REILLY** 24 **JEFF MALONE** 24 **J.D. SMITH** 24

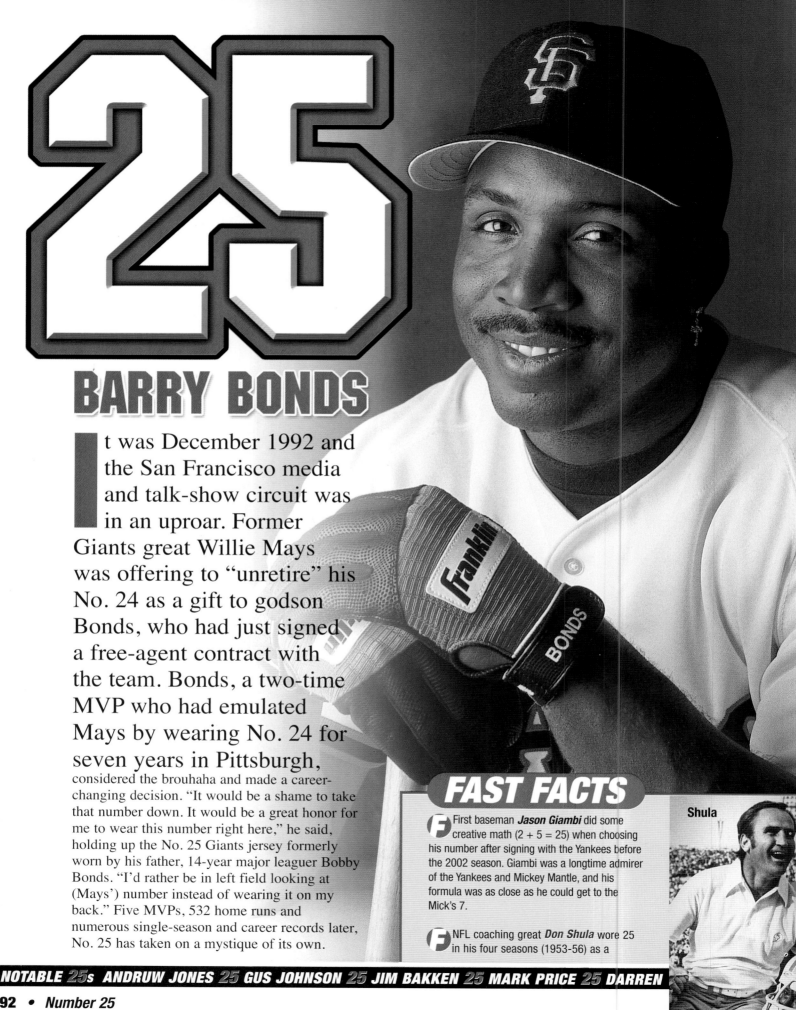

25
BARRY BONDS

It was December 1992 and the San Francisco media and talk-show circuit was in an uproar. Former Giants great Willie Mays was offering to "unretire" his No. 24 as a gift to godson Bonds, who had just signed a free-agent contract with the team. Bonds, a two-time MVP who had emulated Mays by wearing No. 24 for seven years in Pittsburgh, considered the brouhaha and made a career-changing decision. "It would be a shame to take that number down. It would be a great honor for me to wear this number right here," he said, holding up the No. 25 Giants jersey formerly worn by his father, 14-year major leaguer Bobby Bonds. "I'd rather be in left field looking at (Mays') number instead of wearing it on my back." Five MVPs, 532 home runs and numerous single-season and career records later, No. 25 has taken on a mystique of its own.

FAST FACTS

F First baseman *Jason Giambi* did some creative math (2 + 5 = 25) when choosing his number after signing with the Yankees before the 2002 season. Giambi was a longtime admirer of the Yankees and Mickey Mantle, and his formula was as close as he could get to the Mick's 7.

F NFL coaching great *Don Shula* wore 25 in his four seasons (1953-56) as a

Shula

FRED BILETNIKOFF: Hands of glue and fearless over the middle. His 589 catches rank second all-time for the Raiders.

BOBBY BONDS: This five-time 30-30 man made it cool for speedy power hitters to use their wheels.

NORM CASH: The 1961 A.L. batting champ put some bite in the offense of the 1968 World Series champion Tigers.

GAIL GOODRICH: A crafty lefthanded shooter who knew how to score—and win championships. Goodrich won twice at UCLA and once with the Lakers.

TOMMY JOHN: More impressive even than the surgery that bears his name—288 wins and 26 seasons.

K.C. JONES: Sometimes it's the company you keep. He won 10 titles in 11 seasons (two at the University of San Francisco, eight with the Celtics) as Bill Russell's teammate.

MARK McGWIRE: Big Mac gave baseball fans 583 reasons to remember his 16-year career.

RAFAEL PALMEIRO: Pre-steroids revelation, his numbers were impressive. Post-steroids revelation, they still are.

JIM THOME: He walks, hits homers and drives in runs—but looks more like Jim the barber than Jim the dedicated body builder.

Biletnikoff

DEVOTED FANS HONOR MEMORY OF TONY C.

Any Red Sox follower recognizes the date—August 18, 1967. The memory of No. 25 lying motionless in the batter's box at Fenway Park still resonates for a franchise and its legions of fans almost four decades later.

Tony Conigliaro was a 22-year-old with charisma, a sweet swing and superstar potential when his career took a detour because of a riding fastball from Angels righthander Jack Hamilton. The pitch struck Conigliaro in the face, fracturing his cheekbone, dislocating his jaw and damaging his retina. At the hospital that night, he received last rites.

Tony C., born in Revere, a Boston suburb, had taken the city by storm as a 1964 rookie outfielder when he hit 24 home runs, and he belted 32 more in 1965, becoming the youngest player (20) to win a home run title. He already had become the youngest to reach the 100-homer plateau in '67 when the beaning occurred.

After sitting out the 1968 season, Tony C. restarted his career with an opening-day home run in 1969—the beginning of a 20-homer effort that would earn him A.L. Comeback Player of the Year honors. But a 36-homer,116-RBI campaign in 1970 was followed by a shocking trade to the Angels. Deteriorating vision soon forced him out of the game. Conigliaro suffered a major heart attack in 1982, and he died in 1990 of a stroke at age 45.

Since his death, Boston fans, media and politicians have lobbied for Tony C.'s No. 25 to be retired, a movement team officials so far have resisted.

Conigliaro

defensive back for the Baltimore Colts.

F Only one 25 has been retired by a major league baseball team—in honor of Houston outfielder *Jose Cruz*.

F In 1985, lefthander *Tommy John*, making a half-season stop in Oakland before moving on to the New York Yankees, warmed up No. 25 for Mark McGwire, who arrived in '86.

F Former White Sox righthander *Monty Stratton*, who was portrayed by James Stewart in the 1949 movie *The Stratton Story*, wore 25 in three of his five big-league seasons (1936-38). The movie highlighted Stratton's courageous comeback after a hunting accident that forced amputation of his right leg.

F Former NHL defenseman *Marc Bergevin* on his long association with No. 25: "I like Christmas."

McCARTY 25 **JOSE CRUZ** 25 **TOMMY McDONALD** 25 **DON BAYLOR** 25 **VINCENT DAMPHOUSSE** 25 **JOE PEPITONE**

26

BILLY WILLIAMS

Moe, Larry and Fritzie. No, we're not talking about the Three Stooges here, although some of the Cubs teams that Moe Drabowsky, Larry Biittner and Fritzie Connally played on were comical at times.

This is about Cubs uniform No. 26, which all three players wore as warmup or in-between acts for longtime Chicago icon Williams. Drabowsky, a righthanded pitcher, was the last player to wear the number before Williams exchanged his rookie Nos. 4 and 41 for 26 in 1961. Outfielder Williams, who piled up Hall of Fame numbers for the Cubs over 16 seasons, later served three stints as a Cubs coach (1980-82, 1986-87 and 1992-2001). Biittner, a first baseman/outfielder, wore 26 from 1976-79; third baseman Connally's eight-game audition as No. 26 came in 1983. The Cubs ended the charade in 1987 by retiring Williams' number and hanging it from the right field foul pole at Wrigley Field.

FAST FACTS

F Former Tigers outfielder *Gates Brown* (1963-75), who had served time in prison, on why he wore 26: "Because they wouldn't give me my favorite number, 5081782."

F The Los Angeles Angels of Anaheim have retired No. 26 in honor of a man who never wore it. Former owner *Gene Autry* was considered the Angels' "26th man."

F No team in the NBA, NFL or NHL has retired the number 26.

NOTABLE *26*s JOE RUDI *26* WENDELL TYLER *26* GENE GARBER *26* DUSTY RHODES *26* LYDELL MITCHELL *26* DEUCE

Elite 26s

HERB ADDERLEY: The Hall of Fame cornerback blanketed receivers and made big plays for the Packers' power teams of the 1960s.

WADE BOGGS: From 1982-92 with the Red Sox, he won five batting titles and posted seven straight 200-hit seasons. But it wasn't until 1996 with the Yankees, wearing No. 12, that he won a World Series championship.

ROY FACE: He was 18-1 and saved 10 games in 1959. Face and his forkball taught Pirates fans the meaning of relief.

AMOS OTIS: The Royals' first star was a flashy center fielder with some power.

BOOG POWELL: The big first baseman looked more like a linebacker than a baseball player and provided lefthanded muscle for the 1960s and '70s Orioles.

ROD WOODSON: He was the best all-around corner in the NFL early in his career, a hard-hitting All-Pro safety later. His next move will be into the Hall of Fame.

Portis

Boggs

SUPPLY AND DEMAND: PORTIS PAYS BIG FOR 26

Call it Economics 101, supply and demand. *Clinton Portis* wanted No. 26 when he was traded by Denver to Washington before the 2004 season, and Redskins safety Ifeanyi Ohalete owned the rights to it. Negotiations were in order.

For Portis, the negotiating process might have seemed more like highway robbery once Ohalete discovered the rushing star wanted his former Broncos number very, very, very much. Portis had gained 3,099 yards wearing 26 in his first two NFL seasons, and he reportedly had endorsement opportunities tied to it. So, having just picked up a $17 million signing bonus from the Redskins, he agreed to pay Ohalete $40,000.

Portis might be the better football player, but Ohalete is a more adept businessman. He was shrewd enough, in fact, to have Redskins equipment manager Brad Berlin witness and sign the agreement. The importance of this signed document became important when Ohalete was cut by the Redskins on August 17—before the regular season started—and Portis, having already made a $20,000 payment, decided Ohalete no longer was entitled to his money.

When Portis failed to pay either the second or third installments, Ohalete sued him for the $20,000 balance plus interest and the cost of the legal action. Portis did come out better than expected, however. He settled with Ohalete out of court for a mere $18,000—bringing the total payment to $38,000.

27

JUAN MARICHAL

Sandy Koufax? Bob Gibson? Don Drysdale? Whitey Ford? Jim Bunning? In the pitching-rich decade of the 1960s, none of those Hall of Famers could come close to Marichal's win total of 191.

He was a Giant, the San Francisco variety, and the No. 27 he flashed with every high-kicking delivery made a lasting impression on hitters who never quite figured out what to expect next from the stylish Dominican righthander. Marichal couldn't match the championship-stage moments of other 27s—Carlton Fisk, Catfish Hunter and hockey's Frank Mahovlich—but there's no denying he had a flair for the dramatic. In his 1960 major league debut, he pitched a one-hit shutout; in 1963, he pitched a no-hitter. His 1965 bat-swinging assault on Dodgers catcher John Roseboro lives in infamy. A six-time 20-game winner with a five-pitch arsenal, pinpoint control and a bit of a temper … what's not to like about this Hall of Fame 27?

FAST FACTS

F Cincinnati righthander *Jose Rijo* wore No. 27 throughout his 10 seasons with the Reds—a tribute to former father-in-law *Juan Marichal.*

F *Rusty Wallace*, most often associated with the No. 2 car he drove for Team Penske from 1991 to 2005, won his only Winston Cup Series championship in 1989 driving a No. 27 Pontiac for *Raymond Beadle.*

Wallace

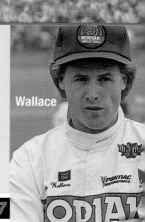

NOTABLE 27s STEVE ATWATER 27 TERRELL BUCKLEY 27 SCOTT ROLEN 27 RODNEY HAMPTON 27

Elite 27s

Houston

CARLTON FISK: Disguised in Boston as No. 27 for a decade, Fisk developed into one of the most talented—and durable—catchers in baseball history.

VLADIMIR GUERRERO: Yeah, he's an Angel, but get out of the way when baseball's premier bad-ball hitter takes a hack. Guerrero is a Triple Crown waiting to happen.

KEN HOUSTON: Big, strong, fast and good in coverage and run support, this former safety had a knack for getting his hands on the ball. Houston wore No. 29 with the Oilers in the first six years of his Hall of Fame career, No. 27 with the Redskins in the last eight.

F When safety **Kenoy Kennedy** was a Denver Broncos rookie in 2000, recently signed veteran cornerback **Terrell Buckley** approached him before the season and asked him to give up the No. 27 he had been assigned. Kennedy obliged, no strings attached, and Buckley handed him a $3,000 check two months later.

TURNER'S MANAGERIAL TEST LASTS ONE DAY

His Braves had lost 16 straight games and Atlanta owner Ted Turner decided to do something about it. So he dispatched manager Dave Bristol on "a scouting mission," appointed himself manager and slipped on a uniform for a May 11, 1977, game against Pittsburgh at Three Rivers Stadium.

Bristol, as it turned out, had been sent home (Andrews, N.C.) to relax while Turner, the 38-year-old millionaire sportsman, made plans to direct the team for 10 days—to get a feel for its problems. But the grand experiment would end after only one game.

Turner, wearing uniform No. 27, sat quietly most of the night in the Braves' dugout watching his team lose, 2-1. The Braves managed only six hits off the Pirates' John Candelaria and Goose Gossage, and all of the scoring came in the first three innings. The need for strategy was minimal.

It didn't take long for commissioner Bowie Kuhn and National League president Chub Feeney to notify Turner that anyone who owned stock in a club could not manage it. To which Turner replied, "They must have put that rule in yesterday." But, having run afoul of the league office on other matters and wanting to pick his battles, Turner stepped down and turned the team over to coach Vern Benson.

The next day, Benson and the Braves ended their losing streak with a 6-1 victory, sparking a champagne celebration. The day after that, under Bristol's direction again, the Braves were shut out by St. Louis.

Fisk

CATFISH HUNTER: He was quiet and unassuming, which meant the only thing he had in common with Oakland teammates was his ability to win. Hunter wore 27 during 10 seasons with the A's, 29 in five years with the Yankees.

FRANK MAHOVLICH: He wasn't flashy, but his effortless talent produced 533 goals, 1,103 points and six Stanley Cup titles over an 18-year career with the Maple Leafs, Red Wings and Canadiens.

PETE REISER: According to Leo Durocher, who managed Reiser and Willie Mays at the outset of their major league careers, Brooklyn's Pistol Pete could have been the better player. But Reiser's reckless style, particularly while running down balls in the outfield, resulted in injuries that kept him from fulfilling his potential.

HERB SCORE: A line drive to the eye changed the career course of this seemingly Hall-bound lefthander. Cleveland's Score could never match his previous success after he was hit by Gil McDougald's smash in 1957.

KENT TEKULVE: His unorthodox, down-under style sustained the Pirates for more than a decade and gave him status as one of baseball's premier closers.

BOB WATSON: He's a baseball trivia master's dream. Watson, the sport's first black general manager, is credited with scoring the game's one-millionth run and being the first player to hit for the cycle in both leagues. His No. 27 days were with the Astros from 1968-79.

JACK TWYMAN 27 **THOM DARDEN** 27 **KEVIN BROWN** 27 **DAL MAXVILL** 27 **WILLIE CRAWFORD** 27 **IRV CROSS** 27

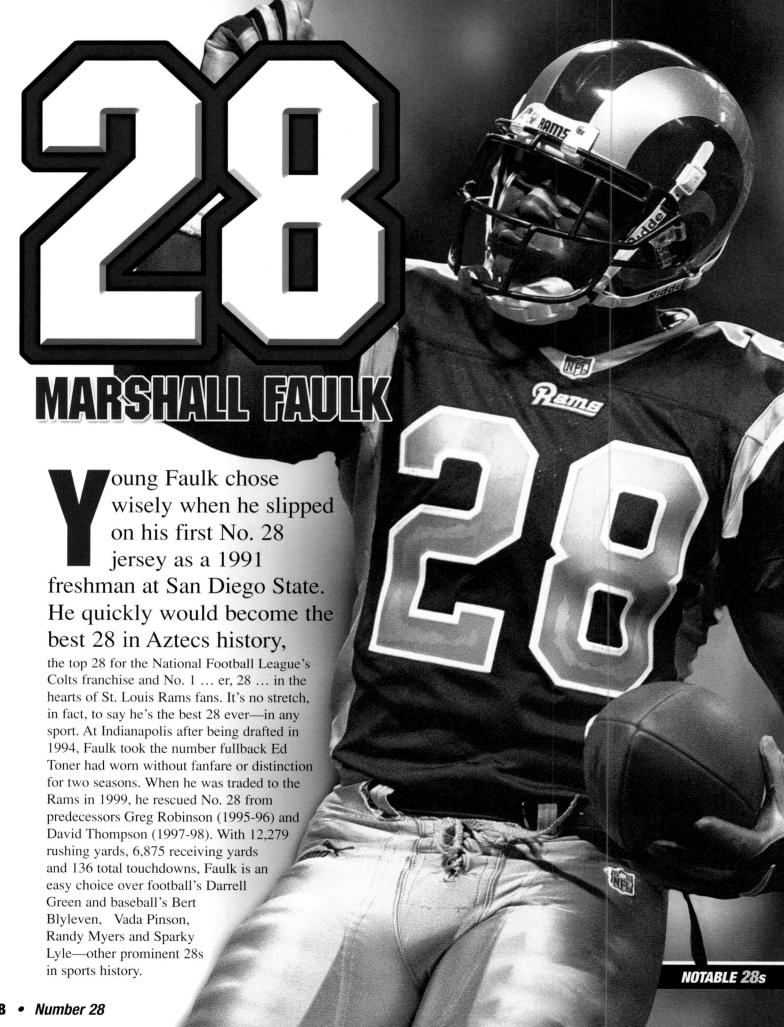

28
MARSHALL FAULK

Young Faulk chose wisely when he slipped on his first No. 28 jersey as a 1991 freshman at San Diego State. He quickly would become the best 28 in Aztecs history, the top 28 for the National Football League's Colts franchise and No. 1 … er, 28 … in the hearts of St. Louis Rams fans. It's no stretch, in fact, to say he's the best 28 ever—in any sport. At Indianapolis after being drafted in 1994, Faulk took the number fullback Ed Toner had worn without fanfare or distinction for two seasons. When he was traded to the Rams in 1999, he rescued No. 28 from predecessors Greg Robinson (1995-96) and David Thompson (1997-98). With 12,279 rushing yards, 6,875 receiving yards and 136 total touchdowns, Faulk is an easy choice over football's Darrell Green and baseball's Bert Blyleven, Vada Pinson, Randy Myers and Sparky Lyle—other prominent 28s in sports history.

NOTABLE 28s

Williams

BEER OR DING DONGS? LAID-BACK KRUK LETS WILD THING OFF EASY

One athlete paid $38,000 to get the rights to a uniform number. Others have paid smaller amounts or financed such perks as vacations, Rolex watches, jewelry, golf clubs, suits and expensive dinners. **Mitch Williams** got off easy.

Williams, the hard-throwing lefthander known as Wild Thing, was acquired by Philadelphia to be its closer in an April 1991 trade with the Chicago Cubs. He arrived to find first baseman John Kruk, the Phillies' resident flake, wearing uniform 28—the number Williams had worn throughout his five-year major league career with the Texas Rangers and Cubs. Kruk related what happened next in a 1993 appearance on the Late Night with David Letterman show:

"I saw where Rickey Henderson gave a guy $25,000 for a number," Kruk told Letterman. "Well, I got two cases of beer. So Mitch got No. 28 because his wife had a bunch of jewelry with No. 28 on it. The best part about it is he got divorced, he wears No. 99 and the two cases of beer are gone."

Kruk, who switched to 29, later admitted "I didn't even think of asking for money." Williams, discussing his negotiations with Kruk, recalled, "I knew it would be beer or Ding Dongs, I just wasn't sure which."

Williams did, indeed, switch to 99 in April 1993 after getting a divorce.

Elite 28s

Cedeno

DAVEY ALLISON: Bobby's boy was a chip off the old block. He won 19 races—15 driving car No. 28 for Robert Yates—in six-plus seasons before dying at age 32 in a helicopter crash.

BERT BLYLEVEN: Uncle Charley was Bert's best friend. Blyleven's outstanding curveball froze enough hitters to help him collect 287 wins.

CESAR CEDENO: The next Hank Aaron, Roberto Clemente and Willie Mays, all rolled into one. Cedeno didn't live up to that hype, but his career numbers for the Astros, Reds, Cardinals and Dodgers were pretty impressive.

DARRELL GREEN: Throwing deep on Green was a losing proposition for Redskins opponents for two decades. He remained one

Allison

FAST FACTS

F The number 28 has been retired by only two professional teams—both in the NFL. The Kansas City Chiefs retired it for **Abner Haynes** and the Chicago Bears for **Willie Galimore**.

F In 1995, **Curtis Martin** broke New England's single-season rushing record with 1,487 yards. In 2004, Corey Dillon broke Martin's record with 1,635. Both players wore No. 28 during their milestone seasons.

F Though 28 has been showcased by such heavyweight drivers as **Davey Allison**, **Ernie Irvan**, **Dale Jarrett**, **Ricky Rudd** and **Kenny Irwin**, no car with that number has won a NASCAR championship.

F Hank Aaron hit 385 home runs while wearing No. 44 for the Milwaukee Braves. Brother **Tommie** hit nine while wearing 28 in his three Milwaukee seasons.

28 DONALD AUDETTE 28 VADA PINSON 28 PEDRO GUERRERO 28 WILLIE GALIMORE 28 ATLEY DONALD 28 STEVE BLASS 28

of the NFL's fastest defenders into his late 30s.

ABNER HAYNES: The AFL's first Player of the Year also was the first Dallas Texans/Kansas City Chiefs player to run for 1,000 yards.

SPARKY LYLE: Don't mention this name in Boston. The Red Sox traded him and he went on to become a premier reliever and Cy Young winner—for the Yankees.

CURTIS MARTIN: Just call him Mr. 1,000. The Jets' quiet man is fourth and rising on the NFL's all-time rushing list.

RANDY MYERS: After leaving the Mets, he got downright nasty wearing No. 28 for the Reds.

PREACHER ROE: This cunning lefty's best seasons were from 1948-54 while wearing 28 for the Brooklyn Dodgers.

Martin

COLLEGE FANS HAVE DOUBLE (DIGIT) VISION

With the strong emphasis on uniform numbers among today's athletes, college football offers twice the opportunity for satisfaction. It's not unusual for fans to see two players on the same team wearing the same number on Saturdays—as long as they are on opposite sides of the ball and not in the game at the same time.

The 2004 Oklahoma Sooners made good use of that rule. They had two sets of 25, two 21s, a pair of 5s and two 28s. It was the latter number that provided one of the most potent double-number whammies in history.

Antonio Perkins, a 2003 All-American, formed the defensive and special teams half of the 28 tandem. Perkins, a speedy cornerback, was coming off a record-setting season as a punt returner, having set an NCAA single-season mark with four for TDs—three in one game against UCLA. He struggled a bit in 2004, but did return one punt for a touchdown, giving him the NCAA career record of eight.

Adrian Peterson, a 2004 All-American, was the offensive 28—literally. His 1,925-yard rushing total broke the Oklahoma single-season record and the NCAA freshman mark. Peterson also scored 15 touchdowns, topped 100 yards nine times and finished second in the Heisman Trophy balloting.

According to rules, if players wearing the same number appear on the field at the same time, a 5-yard penalty will be called for failure to wear proper equipment. If officials judge such an occurrence to be deception, the penalty will change to 15 yards for unsportsmanlike conduct.

Peterson

F *Duke Snider*, No. 4 in the hearts of Dodgers fans, hit his final four major league home runs in 1964 while wearing 28 for the San Francisco Giants. The Giants had retired 4 for Hall of Famer Mel Ott.

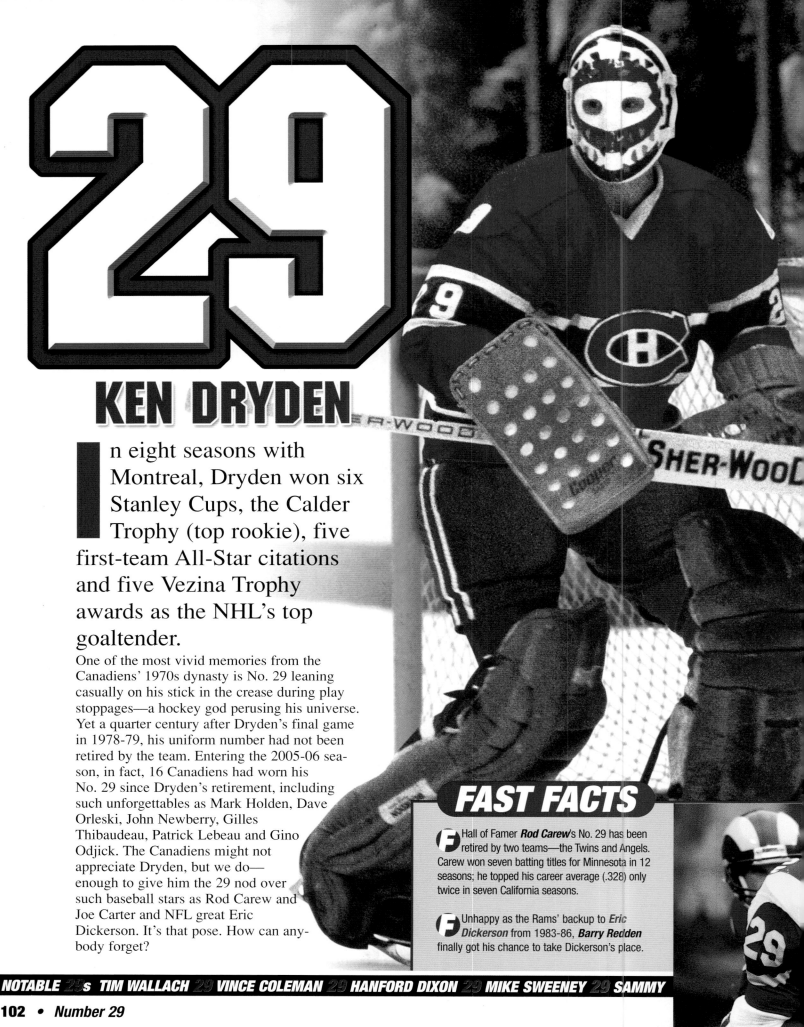

29

KEN DRYDEN

In eight seasons with Montreal, Dryden won six Stanley Cups, the Calder Trophy (top rookie), five first-team All-Star citations and five Vezina Trophy awards as the NHL's top goaltender.

One of the most vivid memories from the Canadiens' 1970s dynasty is No. 29 leaning casually on his stick in the crease during play stoppages—a hockey god perusing his universe. Yet a quarter century after Dryden's final game in 1978-79, his uniform number had not been retired by the team. Entering the 2005-06 season, in fact, 16 Canadiens had worn his No. 29 since Dryden's retirement, including such unforgettables as Mark Holden, Dave Orleski, John Newberry, Gilles Thibaudeau, Patrick Lebeau and Gino Odjick. The Canadiens might not appreciate Dryden, but we do— enough to give him the 29 nod over such baseball stars as Rod Carew and Joe Carter and NFL great Eric Dickerson. It's that pose. How can anybody forget?

FAST FACTS

F Hall of Famer **Rod Carew**'s No. 29 has been retired by two teams—the Twins and Angels. Carew won seven batting titles for Minnesota in 12 seasons; he topped his career average (.328) only twice in seven California seasons.

F Unhappy as the Rams' backup to **Eric Dickerson** from 1983-86, **Barry Redden** finally got his chance to take Dickerson's place.

NOTABLE 29s **TIM WALLACH** 29 **VINCE COLEMAN** 29 **HANFORD DIXON** 29 **MIKE SWEENEY** 29 **SAMMY**

Elite 29s

TIGERS' 29 UPSTAGES GIBSON, McLAIN

It was the Year of the Pitcher, a season headlined by Denny McLain's 31 wins and Bob Gibson's extraordinary 1.12 ERA. So it was fitting that the 1968 World Series featured the Detroit and St. Louis righthanders, both of whom would sweep their leagues' MVP and Cy Young honors. What nobody expected was this: The best pitcher in the dramatic seven-game fall classic was a paunchy Tigers lefthander wearing No. 29—*Mickey Lolich*.

McLain, baseball's first 30-game winner since Dizzy Dean in 1934, lasted only five innings in Game 1 and gave up three runs. But Gibson was virtually untouchable during a five-hit shutout in which he struck out a World Series-record 17 Tigers. Gibson pitched another five-hitter in Game 4, giving St. Louis a 3-1 Series advantage.

Lolich, a 17-game winner in the regular season, got the Tigers even in Game 2 with a six-hit victory, and kept the Tigers' victory hopes alive by winning Game 5. McLain, who had been battered in Game 4, bounced back to post a 13-1 win in Game 6 that forced a seventh game matching two-time winners Gibson and Lolich.

The climactic game was scoreless through six innings before Detroit broke through for three runs, two on a two-out triple by Jim Northrup on a ball that was misjudged by center fielder Curt Flood. Lolich finished off a 4-1 victory, his third complete-game win, and lowered his Series ERA to 1.67—the same as Gibson's.

ROD CAREW: Baseball's consummate batsman of the 1970s simply hit 'em where they ain't.

JOE CARTER: One of 13 players to drive in 100 runs 10 times, Carter wore 29 during his Toronto years. Check out those highlights of Super Joe hopping around the bases after his 1993 World Series-deciding home run.

ERIC DICKERSON: Rush, rush, rush! The man in the goggles defied injuries and controversy to rank among the NFL's all-time great runners.

KARL KASSULKE: Everybody who has seen Otis Taylor's touchdown catch-and-run for the Chiefs in Super Bowl 4 has seen Kassulke, a Vikings defensive back. He's one of the 20 or so guys Taylor knocks to the ground.

SATCHEL PAIGE: He posted a 3.29 career ERA and pitched in a World Series as a *fortysomething* major leaguer. What would the Negro leagues' best pitcher have done against big leaguers in his prime?

Carew

Smoltz

DAN QUISENBERRY: A Royal pain for hitters, this outstanding submarine closer had a big heart and a sense of humor to match.

JOHN SMOLTZ: Switching to closer late in his career—he was in that role for three full seasons—might have made him Hall-worthy. Dennis Eckersley is the only other pitcher to surpass 150 wins and 150 saves.

Dickerson

Redden, traded to San Diego in 1987, was given No. 29 and told to imitate Dickerson in a practice before the Chargers' game against Dickerson's new team—the Indianapolis Colts.

Ⓕ Unable to get 29 in 1998 because the Angels had retired it for Rod Carew, former White Sox pitcher *Jack McDowell* did what ex-Chicago batterymate Carlton Fisk once did—he turned the numbers around. After deciding on 92, McDowell had second thoughts

and switched to 72, Fisk's old number.

Ⓕ *Catfish Hunter*, who posted four 20-win seasons and earned three World Series rings while wearing 27 with the Athletics, pitched the last five years of his career (1975-79) wearing 29 for the Yankees.

Ⓕ When lefty *Tom Lasorda* appeared in eight games in 1954 and '55 for the Brooklyn Dodgers, he wore Nos. 27 and 29.

KNIGHT 29 **ALBERT LEWIS** 29 **JESSE BARFIELD** 29 **ANDRE THORNTON** 29 **ALEX WEBSTER**

30

NOLAN RYAN

No. 30 or No. 34? That always has been the question for baseball's ultimate power pitcher.

Check out the numerological travails of the record-setting Texan: When Ryan reached the majors for good with the Mets in 1968, he wanted No. 34 but deferred to veteran Cal Koonce. He settled for 30. When Ryan was traded to the California Angels in 1972, he kept 30 because Rudy May was wearing 34. In 1980, Ryan signed with Houston, discovered Jeffrey Leonard was wearing 30 and switched to 34. He remained 34 when he went to Texas in 1989 and finished with an almost equal career split between the two numbers over 27 seasons. The nod goes to 30 because of the 138 wins (second on the Angels' career list), four no-hitters (first), 40 shutouts (first) and 2,416 strikeouts (first) he posted with a halo on his hat. Ryan's numbers also were good with Houston and Texas, earning him distinction as the only major leaguer to have a number retired by three teams.

FAST FACTS

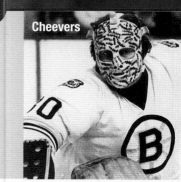

Cheevers

F The number 30 has a solid lineage with the New York Yankees. Pitcher *Mel Stottlemyre* wore it from 1964-74, and second baseman Willie Randolph had it from 1976-88.

F Goaltender *Gerry Cheevers,* wearing No. 30, backstopped the Boston Bruins to their last two Stanley Cup championships in 1970 and '72.

NOTABLE 30s KEN GRIFFEY SR. CHRIS OSGOOD TERRY PORTER KEN HOLTZMAN MARK VAN EEGHEN

'PERFECT GESTURE' HAS AN IMPERFECT TWIST

It was the perfect gesture by the near-perfect superstar center fielder who was making a triumphant return to the city of his childhood. *Ken Griffey Jr.*, acquired in a February 2000 trade from Seattle, announced he would wear uniform No. 30, the one worn by his father, Ken Sr., when he was a member of Cincinnati's Big Red Machine in the 1970s.

Choosing 30 quickly diffused a potential controversy over 24, the Willie Mays-inspired number Griffey had worn while hitting 398 home runs in 11 seasons with Seattle. No. 24 was scheduled to be retired by the Reds for former first baseman Tony Perez in a May 27 ceremony, and Perez would be inducted into the Hall of Fame later in the summer.

But everything changed after Griffey fell into a horrible slump. After the first two weeks, he was hitting under .200, hearing scattered boos and growing frustrated. So he told the Reds he wanted his old number back. The club said it was strictly up to Perez, so Griffey appealed to his father's old teammate as a member of his "extended family." He said that's the kind of thing family members do.

Perez, working for the Marlins as a special assistant, was shocked. "The number is going to be retired and I want it retired," he said. "A number isn't going to make you a better hitter."

The Reds retired No. 24 as planned. Griffey went on to hit 40 homers and drive in 118 runs in his first season as No. 30.

Davis

Griffey Jr.

MARTIN BRODEUR: Has any goalie ever handled the puck better than this two-time New Jersey Stanley Cup winner?

ORLANDO CEPEDA: His dad, Pedro, was known as the "Babe Ruth of the Caribbean," but the Baby Bull is the only Cepeda in baseball's Hall of Fame.

GERRY CHEEVERS: It wasn't uncommon to see goalies with stitch marks on their face in the early NHL, but Bruins goalie Cheevers was the only one with stitches on his face mask.

TERRELL DAVIS: John Elway couldn't win the big one until yard-grinder Davis and the Mile High Salute showed up.

CLARKE HINKLE: Green Bay's kamikaze fullback/linebacker is remembered for his legendary battles with Chicago bruiser Bronko Nagurski.

BERNARD KING: A devastating knee injury forced King to miss two years and change his style of play, but he still averaged 22.5 points over an impressive NBA career.

TIM RAINES: The Rock, who added speed to Montreal's offense, was one of four Expos to have his number retired.

BILL WILLIS: One of the trailblazers of integration in modern pro football, he made the Browns' middle guard position famous and earned a spot in the Hall of Fame.

MAURY WILLS: The Dodgers shortstop, the first man in the 20th century to steal 100 bases, ushered in a new era of speed baseball in 1962.

F **George McGinnis,** a former Indiana Mr. Basketball, played at Indiana University and for Indiana of the ABA and NBA. It's only fitting the Pacers retired No. 30 for this bruising forward.

F The Cleveland Indians' decision to retire former pitcher Bob Lemon's No. 21 in 1998 forced manager *Mike Hargrove,* who had worn 21 through most of his baseball career, to make a change. He switched to 30.

WILLIE RANDOLPH 30 LAWRENCE McCUTCHEON 30 ICKEY WOODS 30 MOOSE HAAS

31
GREG MADDUX

It wasn't supposed to be a long-term relationship. Maddux knew in September 1986, when he made his first appearance for the Chicago Cubs, that the No. 31 on his back might not be there for long. He figured, understandably, that the Cubs would retire the former number of Ferguson Jenkins, a future Hall of Famer who won 284 major league games—167 for Chicago, including six straight 20-win seasons from 1967-72. Not so. And now Maddux, four Cy Young Awards and an 11-year detour through Atlanta later, is back in Chicago and still wearing the number, now as a certified member of baseball's 300-win club. The rise to elite status has not changed the feelings of Maddux, who maintains a healthy respect for his elders. When asked why he chose to wear No. 31 in the first place, he answered quickly: "Fergie Jenkins had it."

FAST FACTS

F In **Dave Winfield**'s final major league season at Cleveland, 1995, he wore his familiar 31—but not without serious consideration. The number had not been worn since pitcher Steve Olin had been killed two years earlier in a boating accident. The Indians checked with Olin's wife before issuing the number.

F **Jim Taylor** rushed for 8,207 yards and posted five straight 1,000-yard seasons for Green Bay and helped the Packers win four NFL championships, including a Super

Smith

NOTABLE 31s JIM PERRY 31 NED GARVER 31 LaMARR HOYT 31 WILBERT MONTGOMERY 31 BOB FORSCH 31 DUANE

Elite 31s

WILLIAM ANDREWS: A knee injury clipped the wings of this gifted Falcons back.

JOHN FRANCO: 424 career saves. What a screwball!

PRIEST HOLMES: This spiritual leader gave his best sermons in the end zone while scoring 66 TDs for the Chiefs from 2002-2004.

FERGUSON JENKINS: This seven-time 20-game winner is one of two pitchers to register 3,000 strikeouts with fewer than 1,000 walks.

Holmes

JIM PERRY: He kept it all in the family with brother Gaylord—their 5,110 strikeouts are more than any other brother tandem, and they're the only siblings to claim Cy Young Awards.

MIKE PIAZZA: Maybe he's not the best defensive catcher of all-time, but he might be the position's most consistent all-around hitter.

DONNIE SHELL: Anybody trying to part the Steel Curtain had to watch out for this hard-hitting safety, the last layer of defense.

BILLY SMITH: He didn't talk much to the media—if he had, his ranking among all-time goalies might be higher—but he was a stone wall for the Islanders in the playoffs.

DAVE WINFIELD: The athletic Winfield was a Gold Glove outfielder who could hit for average and power. His career numbers would have satisfied anyone except George Steinbrenner, who apparently expected Ruthian production and Jacksonesque dramatics.

IT'S 'MILLERS' TIME WHEN 31 IS DISCUSSED

As siblings go, they were not unusual. Basketball games in the back yard, elbows flying, bodies crashing and tongues wagging—always spewing forth trash talk. Only thing is, they were brother and sister. Check out the resumes of the greatest brother-sister act in hoops history, *Cheryl* and *Reggie Miller*:

Cheryl Miller

Cheryl: At Riverside (Calif.) Poly High, she was the first four-time Parade All-American (male or female) in history and once scored 105 points in a game. At USC, she powered the Trojans to two NCAA championships, averaged 23.6 points and 12 rebounds and was the first four-time All-American. Cheryl also led the 1984 U.S. women's Olympic team to a gold medal and coached USC and Phoenix of the WNBA.

Reggie: The fourth all-time leading scorer in UCLA history was the 11th overall draft pick by Indiana in 1987 and went on to become the Pacers' all-time leading scorer (25,279 points) in an 18-year career. Reggie, who led the 1996 men's Olympic team to a gold medal, is one of the most accomplished 3-point marksmen in history. He compiled a .439 percentage at UCLA and holds the NBA career record for 3-point field goals made. Cheryl, a year and a half older than Reggie, one-upped her brother on several counts. She is a member of the basketball Hall of Fame and her number was the first ever retired by the USC basketball program. That number—31—was worn by both Cheryl and Reggie throughout their illustrious basketball careers.

Bowl, but the team never retired his No. 31. Taylor played one season for New Orleans and rushed for 390 yards. The Saints did retire his 31.

F *Billy Smith*, who backstopped the New York Islanders' four straight Stanley Cup titles from 1980-83, is one of two 31s retired by NHL teams. The other is goalie Grant Fuhr, who helped Edmonton to four Cup titles in a five-year span from 1984-88.

F The Buffalo Bills' first logo in 1960 pictured a player wearing 31—a "neutral" number that wouldn't promote a specific player—in front of a buffalo. Only *Preston Ridlehuber* (by accident briefly in 1969) wore that number before 1990.

F On May 26, 1959, when Pittsburgh lefty *Harvey Haddix* pitched 12 perfect innings against Milwaukee before losing in the 13th, he was wearing 13 reversed—unlucky 31.

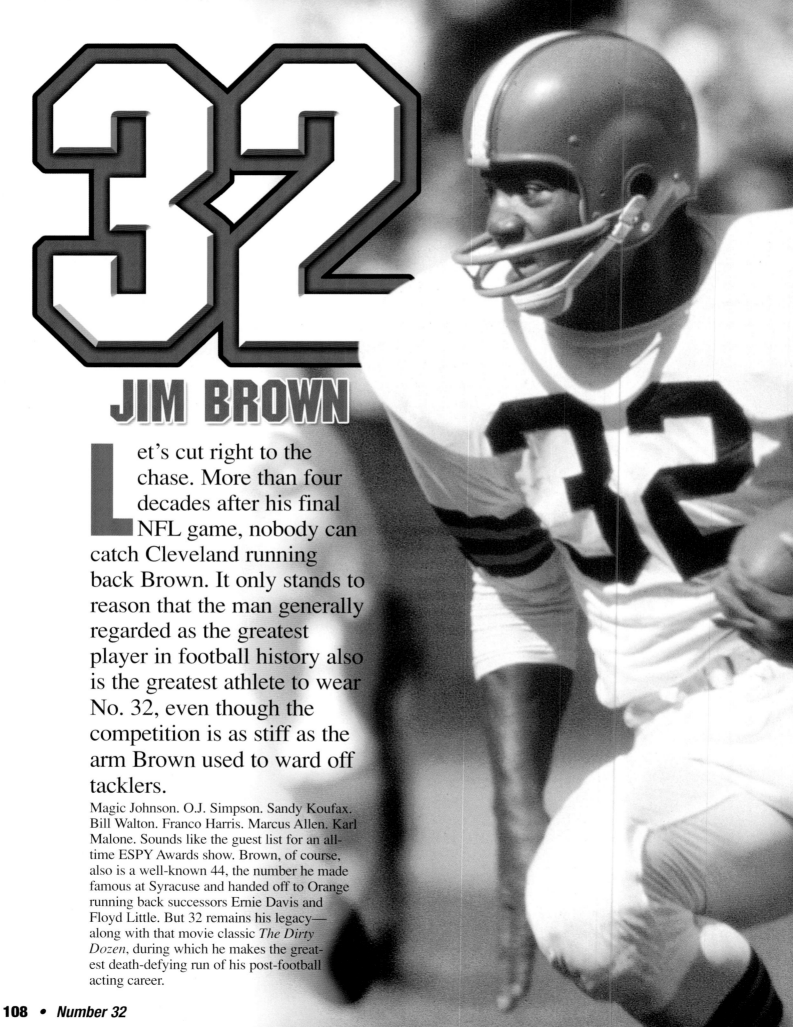

32

JIM BROWN

Let's cut right to the chase. More than four decades after his final NFL game, nobody can catch Cleveland running back Brown. It only stands to reason that the man generally regarded as the greatest player in football history also is the greatest athlete to wear No. 32, even though the competition is as stiff as the arm Brown used to ward off tacklers.

Magic Johnson. O.J. Simpson. Sandy Koufax. Bill Walton. Franco Harris. Marcus Allen. Karl Malone. Sounds like the guest list for an all-time ESPY Awards show. Brown, of course, also is a well-known 44, the number he made famous at Syracuse and handed off to Orange running back successors Ernie Davis and Floyd Little. But 32 remains his legacy—along with that movie classic *The Dirty Dozen*, during which he makes the greatest death-defying run of his post-football acting career.

Carlton

'RESPECTFUL' GLADDEN JUST SAYS NO

When the San Francisco Giants signed veteran lefthander *Steve Carlton* on July 4, 1986, Giants outfielder Dan Gladden faced a problem. He could keep the No. 32 he had worn in his first three full major league seasons, or he could show respect for a 300-game winner and switch numbers, letting Carlton have the 32 he had worn for seven years in St. Louis and 15 in Philadelphia.

Gladden took the high road and switched to 10, which he wore the rest of the season. When he was traded to Minnesota the next spring, the Twins issued him his old 32, putting his career back on track. Carlton lasted a month with the Giants, was picked up by the Chicago White Sox and opened the 1987 season with Cleveland—wearing 32 at each stop.

Then it was deju vu all over again. Carlton was traded to Minnesota on July 31, 1987, and Gladden again faced the 32 dilemma. This time, however, he simply said no. "I already had given it to him once," Gladden said, "and he didn't hold onto it very long."

Carlton switched to No. 38 for his final year and a half—the only seasons of his 24-year career when he wore a number other than 32. Gladden kept 32 for five seasons with the Twins and two more with Detroit.

NOTABLE 32s RICKY WATTERS *32* FRED BROWN *32* JACK PARDEE *32* TOM BROWNING

Elite 32s

MARCUS ALLEN: With the fate of the world hinging on fourth-and-goal from the 1, is there anybody you'd rather see get the ball?

BILLY CUNNINGHAM: White men can't jump? Then why did they call this 76ers Hall of Famer the Kangaroo Kid? He succeeded at every level.

FRANCO HARRIS: Four Super Bowl rings, nine Pro Bowls, 12,120 rushing yards. Any questions?

ELSTON HOWARD: It figures that the guy who integrated the Yankees also integrated the American League MVP fraternity.

MAGIC JOHNSON: Truly Magic. Some

Johnson

Walton

Simpson

FAST FACTS

When *Julius Erving* arrived in Philadelphia before the 1976-77 season, he wanted the 32 he had worn in the ABA with the Virginia Squires and New York Nets. Since plans were in the works to retire 32 for *Billy Cunningham*, the man who soon would become his coach, he switched to 6.

Tough guy winger *Rob Ray* reportedly wore No. 32 throughout his 15 NHL seasons with Buffalo and Ottawa because he was a plus-3 and scored 2 points in his first NHL game in 1989.

Karl Malone couldn't wear his longtime No. 32 when he signed with the Lakers in 2003-04 because it was retired for Magic Johnson. So he opted for 11, the number he wore as a member of the Dream Team in the 1992 Olympic Games.

Dave Winfield, traded by the Yankees to the California Angels in 1990, also traded his

'63 WAS A VERY GOOD YEAR FOR NO. 32s

The 1963 sports year was good for the number 32. Both of baseball's Most Valuable Player awards went to No. 32s, as did the National Football League's MVP.

Los Angeles Dodgers lefthander *Sandy Koufax* won National League MVP honors after posting a 25-5 record, a sparkling 1.88 ERA and 306 strikeouts. He also earned the first of three Cy Young Awards he would claim in a four-year span.

American League MVP honors went to New York Yankees catcher Elston Howard, who batted .287, hit 28 homers and drove in 85 runs. Howard's Yankees won 104 games and the A.L. pennant, setting up a World Series showdown against the Dodgers. But Koufax won twice in the fall classic as Los Angeles pulled off a shocking four-game sweep.

The 32 uprising was completed by Cleveland running back Jim Brown, who rushed for 1,863 yards and 12 touchdowns while averaging a whopping 6.4 yards per carry. Brown's totals, achieved in a 14-game schedule, helped the Browns post a 10-4 record that fell one game short of the New York Giants in the NFL's Eastern Conference.

For the record: 1963 MVP honors went to Bill Russell (6) in the National Basketball Association, Gordie Howe (9) in the National Hockey League and Lance Alworth (19) in the American Football League. The Heisman Trophy was claimed by Navy's Roger Staubach (12).

athletes are so special, they change the way their sport is played. Johnson made big guards and behind-the-back and no-look passes acceptable. And his smile and showmanship were perfect fits for L.A.

SANDY KOUFAX: If this artful Dodger hadn't retired at age 30, nobody would debate the greatest lefthanded pitcher of all time.

JOHNNY LUJACK: Irish eyes smiled on this 1947 Heisman-winning quarterback, who was a four-sport wonder.

KARL MALONE: His rim-rattling dunks and fadeaway jumpers came special delivery after John Stockton passes.

KEVIN McHALE: The former Celtics power forward had more moves than the world's best pickup artist.

O.J. SIMPSON: Both famous and infamous, he was a marquee player at USC and with the Buffalo Bills ... and starred in the 1973 NFL classic, *2003: A Rushing Odyssey*.

BILL WALTON: The center of everyone's dreams scored, passed and defended while winning college and NBA championships at UCLA, Portland and Boston.

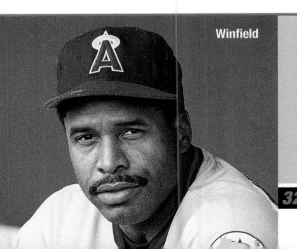

Winfield

Koufax

longtime 31 uniform for a 32. Angels pitcher *Chuck Finley* had No. 31.

F When *Clarence "Bevo" Francis* scored an NCAA record (all divisions) of 113 points for Rio Grande in a game against Hillsdale on February 2, 1954, he was wearing No. 32—reportedly because that's the number of points his coach, Newt Oliver, expected him to average.

32 JERRY LUCAS **32** MIKE CURTIS **32** JAMES WILDER **32** JACK TATUM **32**

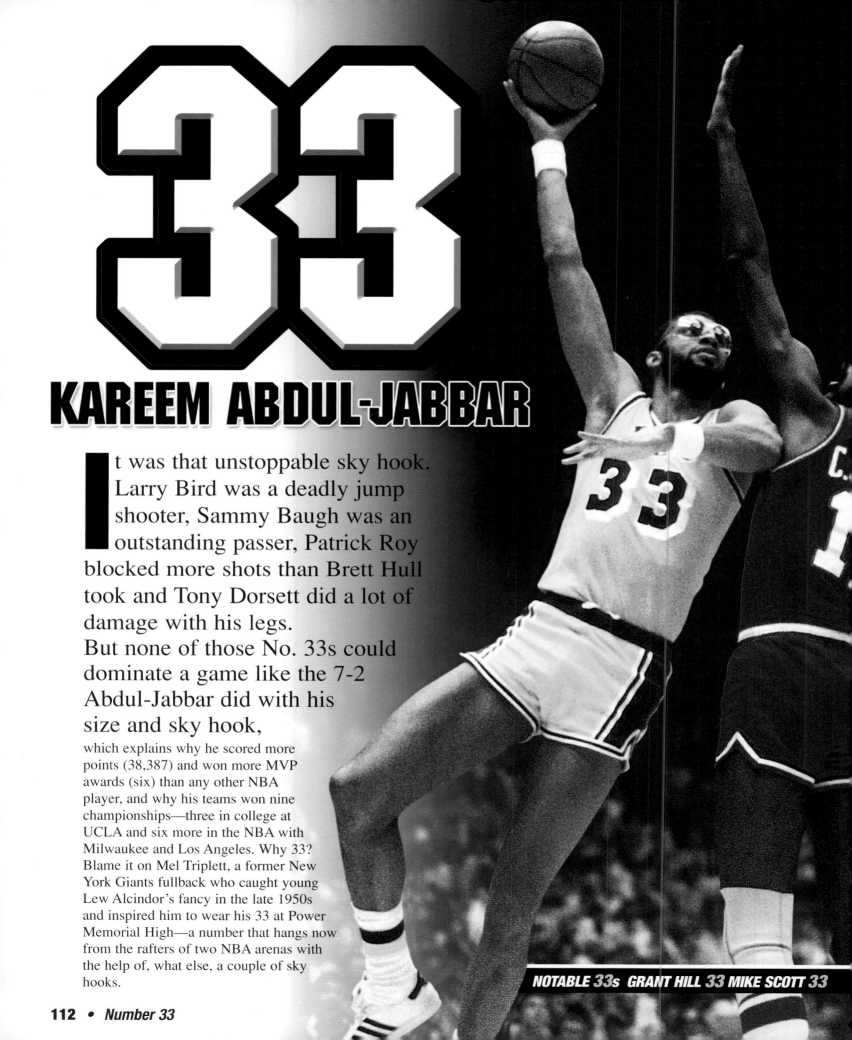

33

KAREEM ABDUL-JABBAR

It was that unstoppable sky hook. Larry Bird was a deadly jump shooter, Sammy Baugh was an outstanding passer, Patrick Roy blocked more shots than Brett Hull took and Tony Dorsett did a lot of damage with his legs.

But none of those No. 33s could dominate a game like the 7-2 Abdul-Jabbar did with his size and sky hook,

which explains why he scored more points (38,387) and won more MVP awards (six) than any other NBA player, and why his teams won nine championships—three in college at UCLA and six more in the NBA with Milwaukee and Los Angeles. Why 33? Blame it on Mel Triplett, a former New York Giants fullback who caught young Lew Alcindor's fancy in the late 1950s and inspired him to wear his 33 at Power Memorial High—a number that hangs now from the rafters of two NBA arenas with the help of, what else, a couple of sky hooks.

NOTABLE 33s GRANT HILL 33 MIKE SCOTT 33

WHETHER 33, 32 OR 34, SHAQ DOMINATES

Shaquille O'Neal is not superstitious. That's probably a good thing because he's not very lucky with numbers. The 7-1, 315-pound center gained legendary status in three seasons at LSU wearing uniform 33. Everybody assumed he would take that number to great heights in the NBA, including the Orlando Magic, the team that drafted him with the first overall pick in 1992 after his junior season. On draft day, the Magic presented Shaq with a No. 33 jersey with his name on the back.

The team assumed forward Terry Catledge was willing to give up his number. He wasn't. Catledge said the Magic had approached him about switching numbers, but he had promised only to consider the request.

Catledge was adamant about keeping 33, which he had been wearing for five years, including all three seasons of Orlando's existence. O'Neal said, "No problem," and took No. 32, which he wore to distinction through four seasons in Orlando.

When O'Neal signed a free-agent contract with the Los Angeles Lakers after the 1995-96 campaign, he couldn't take 33 because it was retired for Kareem Abdul-Jabbar, and he couldn't wear 32 because it was retired for Magic Johnson. So he opted for 34, which he wore for eight seasons—three of which produced championships.

Shaq was traded to Miami after the 2003-04 season and returned to his No. 32 jersey—presumably because 33 belonged to longtime Heat star Alonzo Mourning.

Elite 33s

Dorsett

SALVAN ADAMS: In his 1975-76 debut season, this mobile 6-9 center led the Suns to the NBA Finals and won the Rookie of the Year honors.

SAMMY BAUGH: Slingin' Sammy slung college football into the forward-pass era, then did the same for pro football. The multi-talented Baugh, a Washington fan favorite during the 1930s and '40s, led the NFL in passing, punting and interceptions at various points of his legendary career.

LARRY BIRD: How does a Hick from French Lick become a Legend? Here's the checklist: A nemesis of similar skill and fame? Check. Flair for the dramatic? Check. Unmatched standard of excellence? Check. Playing for a storied franchise? Double check.

TONY DORSETT: How did a 190-pound running back last long enough to gain 6,082

Roy

FAST FACTS

F No. 33 in his two fabulous seasons at Michigan State, *Magic Johnson* switched to 32 when he joined the Lakers because Kareem Abdul-Jabbar already had 33.

F *Hot Rod Hundley*, the colorful former Minneapolis/Los Angeles Lakers star, was the subject of a 1970 book written by Bill Libby entitled, *Clown: Number 33 in Your Program, Number 1 in Your Heart.*

F Cincinnati lefty *Johnny Vander Meer* threw his consecutive no-hitters in 1938 while wearing double 3s.

F *Harry Gant*, NASCAR's original Skoal Bandit, is remembered for an incredible run in September 1991 when, at age 51, he drove Leo Jackson's No. 33 Chevrolet to four consecutive victories on the Winston Cup circuit, earning the nickname Mr. September.

MARTY PATTIN 33 **AARON ROWAND** 33 **JOSE CANSECO** 33 **OTIS THORPE**

yards in college and 12,739 more in the NFL? Not even Touchdown Tony or the Dallas Cowboys know the answer to that question.

PATRICK EWING: Has there ever been a more intimidating college center? The Georgetown giant also dominated the middle for the Knicks, but never brought home an NBA championship.

ALONZO MOURNING: What is it about Georgetown, the No. 33 and defensive centers who make opponents lose their lunch? Mourning knows how to turn up the Heat.

EDDIE MURRAY: Steady Eddie, one of four players to amass 500 homers and 3,000 hits, did not have a lot of truly spectacular seasons for the Orioles. But he sure had a lot of really good ones.

Bird

SCOTTIE PIPPEN: Playing second fiddle isn't that bad when it gets you six championship rings.

PATRICK ROY: Pressure? Roy thrived on it. The winningest goalie of all-time lifted the Stanley Cup four times for the Canadiens and Avalanche.

F San Francisco quarterback Joe Montana had Jerry Rice, but he also had No. 33 *Roger Craig*, a standout running back and the first player to record 1,000 yards rushing and receiving in the same season.

JORDAN HITS FOR CYCLE WITH THANK YOU GIFT

There are "gestures" and then there are "grand gestures." The one *Brian Jordan* made after his 2005 return to Atlanta was well beyond either.

The 38-year-old outfielder, who was signed in January, had hoped to get the No. 33 he had worn from 1999-2001 with the Braves and from 2002-04 with the Los Angeles Dodgers and Texas Rangers. Jordan requested the number because "it is important to me. It's the way people in Atlanta recognize me." He was pleasantly surprised when third base coach Fredi Gonzalez gave it to him without any demands.

Jordan, however, decided compensation was in order. And he asked hitting coach Terry Pendleton to help him pick out a present and deliver it to Gonzalez. Surprise!

"It's like winning the lottery," Gonzalez told *Atlanta Journal-Constitution* writer David O'Brien after checking out the $40,000 customized Bourget "Fat Daddy" motorcycle that was parked outside the clubhouse door before an April 9 game against the New York Mets. "Brian shouldn't have done it. It's too nice."

Pendleton, a motorcycle enthusiast like Gonzalez, had tricked his friend into providing information about color and model and then passed the word on to Jordan, who wrote the check. After surprising Gonzalez, Jordan capped off his grand gesture with a grand slam against the Mets, the key blow in Atlanta's 6-3 victory.

DAVID THOMPSON: Pre-Jordan, the most spectacular skywalker to come out of the North Carolina basketball factory was Thompson, who helped N.C. State win a national championship and then wowed Denver fans with his high-flying act.

Murray

Jordan

34

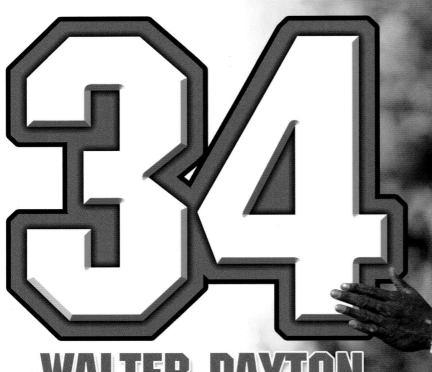

WALTER PAYTON

You'd better walk softly around these heavyweights. Shaquille O'Neal, Charles Barkley and Hakeem Olajuwon wore this number. So did Nolan Ryan, Bo Jackson, Kirby Puckett and Fernando Valenzuela. If that's not enough body mass, check out Earl Campbell, the human cannonball who rolled over NFL defenders for 10 black-and-blue seasons.

Leave it to a 5-10, 200-pound running back nicknamed "Sweetness" to steal their thunder. Payton was to 34 what Michael Jordan was to 23. The intense work ethic, room-brightening smile and NFL rushing record he once held validated the popularity that lifted him to a higher pedestal among sports celebrities. And to think the number connection almost didn't happen. Payton had worn 34 through four seasons at Jackson State, but the number belonged to Bears defensive back Norm Hodgins in 1974. Payton, the untested rookie, got it when Hodgins was not invited back in '75.

FAST FACTS

F **Thurman Thomas'** 34 jersey is one of three retired by Oklahoma State. Thomas, the Cowboys' all-time leading rusher, finished his college career in 1987—as sophomore Barry Sanders waited his turn.

F Chicago Cubs righthander **Kerry Wood**, who grew up idolizing Nolan Ryan, copied his motion, powerful leg kick and power-pitching style. Not surprisingly, Wood wears Ryan's familiar No. 34.

NOTABLE 34s BO JACKSON 34 CHARLES OAKLEY 34 PAUL SPLITTORFF 34 MEL DANIELS 34 ANDY

Elite 34s

RAY ALLEN: One glimpse of that sweet jump shot tells NBA followers he's got game.

CHARLES BARKLEY: He wasn't a role model, but his all-around game was something to emulate. Although he was a half-foot shorter than many players at his position, his versatility and tenacity more than made up for his lack of height.

AUSTIN CARR: A great collegiate scorer at Notre Dame—he once scored 61 points in an NCAA Tournament game—Carr also made an impact with the NBA's Cavaliers.

ROLLIE FINGERS: Two teams retired his No. 34, which is almost as impressive as his handlebar mustache and 341 career saves.

JOE PERRY: He was the NFL's all-time leading rusher before Jim Brown and the first runner to post back-to-back 1,000-yard seasons. Perry was known by 49ers fans as The Jet.

KIRBY PUCKETT: This no-neck, round little center fielder was the "Looks Can Be Deceiving" poster boy. He made Twins baseball fun to watch in the 1980s and '90s.

THURMAN THOMAS: Without this outstanding all-purpose running back, the Bills never could have lost four straight Super Bowls.

FERNANDO VALENZUELA: Fernandomania was all the rage in 1981, when this rotund Dodgers lefty became the first pitcher to win Rookie of the Year and Cy Young honors in the same season.

HERSCHEL WALKER: The three-time consensus All-American was dominant during a 33-3 career at Georgia, less so in his itinerant career in the NFL.

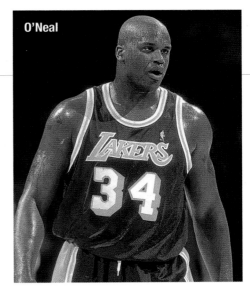

O'Neal

YES, HOUSTON, 34 IS A FINE NUMBER

Houston has this thing about the number 34—and understandably so. Just try to name a city with three sports franchises that have retired the same number. Debate over Houston's best No. 34 can be intense. Former Oilers running back Earl Campbell and former Astros pitcher Nolan Ryan both were born in Texas, and Campbell was a 1977 Heisman Trophy-winning running back at the University of Texas before playing in the NFL. Former Rockets center *Hakeem Olajuwon* was born and raised in Nigeria, but he played college basketball at the University of Houston and starred for Guy Lewis' Phi Slama Jama teams of the early 1980s.

All three were dominant in their sports. The 5-11, 232-pound Campbell was a three-time NFL rushing champion who averaged 1,383 yards over his first six seasons and helped the Oilers reach two AFC championship games. Both times they lost to the eventual Super Bowl champion Pittsburgh Steelers. Ryan struck out a major league-record 5,714 batters, fired a record seven no-hitters and won 324 games over his 27 seasons, nine of them in an Astros uniform. Ryan's best years, arguably, were in the American League.

Olajuwon spent 17 of his 18 NBA seasons with the Rockets and posted 26,946 career points and 13,748 rebounds. The 7-foot center blocked more shots than any player in NBA history, and he has another distinction that gives him a leg up on the other Houston favorites: The Dream was the centerpiece for two championships—the Rockets'1994 and '95 NBA crowns.

Wood

F During the *Bo Jackson* craze in 1990, Chicagoland Processing Corp. issued 15,000 limited-edition silver coins with Bo wearing Kansas City's No. 16 baseball uniform on one side and Oakland's No. 34 football uniform on the other. It required an unusual joint licensing agreement between MLB and the NFL.

F In 1962, *Cookie Gilchrist*, wearing 34 for the Buffalo Bills, became the American Football League's first 1,000-yard rusher.

F Super *Joe Charboneau*, the colorful Cleveland outfielder who won 1980 A.L. Rookie of the Year honors before free-falling into oblivion, had a small role in the 1984 movie *The Natural* playing one of Roy Hobbs' teammates. Charboneau wore 34 in his three big-league seasons.

RUSSELL 34 CHET LEMON 34 DAVE STEWART 34 PEDRO BORBON 34 DALE CARTER

35

PHIL NIEKRO

The Atlanta Braves had the right idea when they retired Niekro's No. 35 and erected a statue outside Turner Field to honor him in 1984. But in retrospect, they probably got a little ahead of themselves.

In 1985, they watched baseball's winningest knuckleballer record his 300th career victory while wearing the pinstripes of the New York Yankees in his 22nd big-league season; near the end of 1987, 50 wins after Niekro's last pitch for the Braves, Atlanta re-signed him and "unretired" the number for one game—a 15-6 loss to San Francisco in which Knucksie made his career farewell appearance (and, mercifully, was not charged with the loss). Niekro remembers being handed a uniform No. 35 without fanfare, discussion or explanation when he was called up by the Milwaukee Braves in 1964. And he vaguely recalls somebody warning him that previous players wearing that number kept getting sent to the minors. Fortunately, he didn't listen.

FAST FACTS

F Who's that 35? In 1947, it was rookie catcher *Yogi Berra*, who was destined for Hall of Fame glory wearing uniform No. 8 for the Yankees.

F Baltimore Colts running back *Alan Ameche* was wearing No. 35 when he scored the sudden-death touchdown in the 1958 NFL championship game against the New York Giants.

Ameche

NOTABLE 35s **AENEAS WILLIAMS** 35 **SAL MAGLIE** 35 **JOHN HENRY JOHNSON** 35 **CHRISTIAN OKOYE** 35 **MIKE RICHTER**

118 • *Number 35*

Elite 35s

HOUK MANAGED JUST FINE WEARING NO. 35

New York Yankees fans remember him fondly as No. 35. So do fans in Detroit and Boston, where *Ralph Houk* completed less-successful—but always entertaining—stints in a 20-year managerial career.

Houk, of course, will always be saluted by New Yorkers as the mastermind behind three straight American League pennants and two World Series championships after taking over for Casey Stengel in 1961. Houk's 35 was highly visible in his rookie managerial campaign as Roger Maris and Mickey Mantle waged a memorable home run derby and the Yankees rolled to 109 regular-season wins and a five-game World Series victory over Cincinnati.

During his 11 Yankees seasons, five with Detroit and four with the Red Sox, the Major also impressed with his theatrical flair. No less an authority than Baltimore manager Earl Weaver once saluted him as king of the umpire baiters, and stories abound about Houk's sharp tongued, dirt-kicking, hat-throwing arguments.

Houk, who as a backup catcher appeared in only 91 games for the Yankees from 1947-54, might have become associated with another uniform number if not for a quirk of fate. Another catcher made his major league debut in 1955, taking Houk's number.

"I wore No. 32 as a player," Houk recalled, "but when I rejoined the Yankees (as a coach in 1958), Elston Howard had that number. Ellie wanted to give it back, but I told him a player was more important than a coach."

Howard repaid Houk's respect by winning A.L. MVP honors for his pennant-winning Yankees in 1963.

MIKE CUELLAR: A key member of Baltimore's deep rotation from 1969-76, this crafty lefthander won 20 games four times and shared a Cy Young Award. He also beat Cincinnati in the finale of the Orioles' 1970 five-game World Series win.

TONY ESPOSITO: Three Vezina Trophies and Hall of Fame election suggest this longtime Blackhawks goalie had no problems living in the shadow of his big brother.

DARRELL GRIFFITH: Dr. Dunkenstein, the high-flying former Louisville star, made NBA life bearable for

Utah fans in the early 1980s.

REGGIE LEWIS: The post-Larry Bird hangover meant tough times for the Boston Celtics, and Lewis' tragic death in 1993 of a heart ailment further speeded the team's descent.

MIKE MUSSINA: From Baltimore to New York, this workhorse righthander has been one of the most productive and durable pitchers of his era.

FRANK THOMAS: The Big Hurt could have been even more hurtful in his White Sox days if not for foot problems and assorted other injuries.

Thomas

F Yankee *Don Larsen* might have been perfect, but Brooklyn's Sal Maglie wasn't too shabby himself in Game 5 of the 1956 World Series. Maglie, wearing 35, gave up five hits in a 2-0 loss.

F The Pittsburgh Steelers, one of the NFL's forlorn franchises from 1933 through the 1960s, boasted five future Hall of Famers who wore No. 35 during that span: *John Blood McNally* (1934), *Cal Hubbard* (1936), *Walt Kiesling* (1937),

Bill Dudley (1942, '45-46) and *John Henry Johnson* (1960-65).

F Longtime White Sox first baseman *Frank Thomas* chose 35 by combining his high school football (3) and baseball (5) numbers.

36

MEADOWLARK LEMON

With all due respect to baseball Hall of Famers Gaylord Perry and Robin Roberts and NFL bulldozer Jerome Bettis—none of whom ever made a halfcourt hook shot for adoring fans— this number belongs to the Clown Prince of Basketball.

Lemon, who was born Meadow George Lemon III in 1935, not only was the best-known No. 36 during his 24-year career (1954-79) with the Harlem Globetrotters, he was one of the most recognizable athletes in the world. As the vocal centerpiece of the clowning Trotters, Lemon performed in 94 countries and 1,500 North American cities; his clowning routines also entertained millions of children via Saturday morning cartoon shows. Lemon, who was awarded the Naismith Memorial Basketball Hall of Fame's Lifetime Achievement Award, is one of three Globetrotters to have a uniform number retired since the team organized in 1926.

FAST FACTS

F First baseman **Eddie Waitkus,** the inspiration for Roy Hobbs in *The Natural* (a 1952 book made into a movie in 1984), was shot in a Chicago hotel room in 1949 by obsessed fan Ruth Ann Steinhagen. Waitkus had worn No. 36 in 1946, '47 and '48 with the Cubs when he was a favorite of Steinhagen, a Chicagoan. He was making a return visit to the city as a member of the Philadelphia Phillies.

F **Rasheed Wallace,** acquired by Atlanta in a trade with Portland on February 9, 2004, played one game for the Hawks,

NOTABLE 36s **JOE NIEKRO** 36 **MERTON HANKS** 36 **CLEM DANIELS** 36 **MARIO SOTO** 36 **MATTHEW BARNABY** 36 **JOE**

120 • *Number 36*

Elite 36s

STEPHEN KING STORY TIES GORDON TO 36

Few players can claim a more personal tie to a number than pitcher *Tom Gordon.*

Gordon, the righthander with the big curveball, recorded 46 saves for the Red Sox in 1998 and apparently inspired one notable Red Sox fan, who wrote a novella with Gordon as a central character.

In Stephen King's 1999 story entitled, *The Girl Who Loved Tom Gordon*, 9-year-old Trisha McFarland idolizes the reliever and is wearing a Red Sox practice jersey with "36 GORDON" on the back when she wanders off in the woods and becomes lost. Carrying only a radio, Trisha tunes in Red Sox games on her nine-day odyssey, listening as her hero—"the handsomest man alive"—blows away opponents. Gordon becomes her imaginary companion, helping her escape danger, real and perceived.

"He said he needed a guy (for the story) and liked the way I carried myself," Gordon said, referring to King. "It was greatly appreciated."

Gordon has tried hard to keep the No. 36 he first wore through most of his eight years as a starter for Kansas City. After injury-plagued seasons in 1999 and 2000 and then stints with the Cubs and Astros, he negotiated for the number when he signed in 2003 with the White Sox. He also got it when he rebounded in 2004 and '05 as a key figure in the Yankees' bullpen.

That success whetted Gordon's desire to be a closer again—a longing he satisfied by signing a free-agent contract with Philadelphia before the 2006 season. But satisfaction came with a price—No. 36 has long been retired by the Phillies for Hall of Famer Robin Roberts.

JEROME BETTIS: The wheels on the Bus kept going 'round and 'round—right on up the NFL rushing charts.

LeROY BUTLER: Favre quarterbacked the offense, but Butler was the Packers' defensive quarterback during their double Super Bowl run in the 1990s.

Bettis

scored 20 points and was traded to Detroit. Wallace wore 36 in that game, becoming the first Atlanta player ever to wear that number.

F In the one game he played in 1949 for the Brooklyn Dodgers, future actor *Chuck Connors,* aka *The Rifleman*, wore uniform No. 36.

F *Jackie Jensen,* the first athlete to play in both the Rose Bowl and a World Series, wore

DAVID CONE: Strikeout titles, World Series rings, a Cy Young Award, two 20-win seasons and a perfect game. What more could devoted Coneheads want?

JIM KAAT: What's most impressive—25 years in the big leagues, 283 career wins or 16 Gold Gloves?

JERRY KOOSMAN: The skilled lefty was a two-time 20-game winner in a 19-year career, but nothing could top the miracle he helped work for the 1969 Mets.

DON NEWCOMBE: He struggled in big games, but Newk still was a multiple 20-game winner for the Brooklyn Dodgers and the first man to win Cy Young and MVP awards in the same season.

GAYLORD PERRY: Everyone knew he threw the spitter, but nobody could prove it. Talent and psychology added up to 314 wins and 3,534 strikeouts.

ROBIN ROBERTS: His fastball and durability were legendary in the 1950s, when he exceeded 300 innings in six consecutive seasons. His career victory total was a robust 286.

Perry

36 as a running back at the University of California. He wore No. 4 through most of his career as a right fielder for the Boston Red Sox.

37
CASEY STENGEL

Always a thirtysomething kind of guy, the Old Professor wandered aimlessly from uniform No. 31 to 36 back to 31 and finally to 32 in a meandering managerial career with the Brooklyn Dodgers and Boston Braves in the 1930s and '40s. It wasn't until Stengel was handed uniform No. 37 by the Yankees in 1949 that he became empowered with the vision, insight and wisdom that helped him reach championship heights. Stengel inherited the number from his predecessor, Bucky Harris, who had led the Yankees to a World Series title in 1947, his first of two seasons at the helm. Which means that No. 37-adorned Yankees managers produced 1,340 wins, 11 pennants and eight Series crowns in 14 years before the number was retired in honor of Stengel. Conversely, Stengel's No. 37, sans Yankees pinstripes, worked a different kind of magic from 1962-65. The not-so-Amazin' Mets stumbled to a 175-404 record under the lovable Casey, who was punished by having his number retired a second time.

Elite 37s

SHAUN ALEXANDER: A big-time runner who scores touchdowns about as often as it rains in Seattle. Alexander scored 28 in 2005, an NFL single-season record.

ERIC DESJARDINS: The steady defenseman has displayed his work ethic as No. 37 since 1996-97, his second full season with the Flyers.

LESTER HAYES: He stuck to receivers like glue. Maybe there was a secret to the Oakland cornerback's success.

JIMMY JOHNSON: This Hall of Fame corner wasn't the best athlete in his family. That honor went to brother Rafer, a world decathlon champion. Coordinators plotting against the 49ers still made it a point not to test this gifted defender.

FAST FACTS

F After a three-year retirement, cornerback **Deion Sanders** returned to the field for a September 12, 2004, game at Cleveland wearing No. 37—his age. Sanders reportedly told teammates he wanted to make sure every receiver didn't forget how old he was.

F Nobody has worn Chiefs uniform No. 37 since the death of **Joe Delaney**, the 24-year-old running back who drowned in 1983 while trying to rescue three boys in a Monroe, La., pond. Delaney ran for 1,121 yards in 1981, the first of his two NFL seasons.

F California Angels reliever **Donnie Moore** was wearing 37 when Boston's **Dave Henderson** hit the dramatic ninth-inning homer that kept the Red Sox alive in Game 5 of the 1986 A.L. Championship Series.

NOTABLE 37s BILL LEE 37 LARRY CENTERS 37 RODNEY HARRISON 37 DAVE STIEB 37 PAT FISCHER 37 DOAK WALKER

3·8
CURT SCHILLING

It's that bloody sock. Yeah, fans in Philadelphia loved big No. 38 way back in the 1990s. And Arizona Diamondbacks followers swooned over the big righthander as he helped their team procure a World Series championship in 2001. But it wasn't until 2004, when desperate Red Sox fans watched Schilling win 21 games and bleed all over the damn Yankees' American League Championship Series parade, that 38 became a replica-jersey phenomenon. Boston fans certainly won't forget his gut-wrenching ALCS effort that helped them end an 86-year World Series title jinx. Or the wonderful pain he caused those unfriendly neighbors who always seem to be ahead of their beloved Sox in the A.L. East standings. And lest Boston fans forget, Schilling easily trumps a long list of less-than-illustrious Red Sox 38s that includes Gene Stephens, Tom Umphlett, Don Gile, Jim Willoughby, Charlie Mitchell, Todd Benzinger and Jeff Gray.

FAST FACTS

F Wearing 38 is a special honor at the University of Mississippi. It is given at the beginning of each season to the team's top senior defender in memory of **Chucky Mullins**, who died May 6, 1991, after being paralyzed in the Rebels' 1989 homecoming game.

F No team in major league baseball, the National Football League, the National Basketball Association or the National Hockey League has retired uniform No. 38.

F Two non-related Venezuelan righthanders, **Victor Zambrano** of the Mets and **Carlos Zambrano** of the Cubs, both were wearing No. 38 when they faced each other in August 2005.

Elite 38s

ERIC GAGNE: If great closers are expected to intimidate, Gagne has it covered. He's a hulking, bearded, goggled, admitted former hockey goon with nasty heat and a devastating changeup. His Dodgers record—160 saves in 166 chances through 2005—says it all.

GEORGE ROGERS: From Heisman glory at South Carolina to four 1,000-yard NFL seasons with the Saints and Redskins. Not bad for a poor kid from Duluth, Ga.

TODD WORRELL: You have to wonder what kind of numbers this Cardinals closer might have posted if not for major elbow and shoulder problems during his prime.

NOTABLE 38s ARNIE HERBER 38 KIMBLE ANDERS 38 CLYDE WRIGHT 38 ANTONIO LANGHAM 38 RICK AGUILERA

39

ROY CAMPANELLA

Ray Lucas wore it for two games in 1933. John Corriden was wearing it in 1946 when he made his lone appearance as a pinch runner. Pitcher Ed Chandler wore No. 39 for 15 games in 1947.

The athletic genius of Campanella is that he took a nondescript Brooklyn Dodgers uniform number and made it special. Campy's off-field genius was measured in good will and spirit, qualities he exhibited for 35 years while confined to a wheel chair after a near-fatal car crash in 1958. There is no clever numerological explanation for the player/number association. Campy, sometime during his first major league season with Brooklyn in 1948, was handed a new jersey bearing the No. 39, which he would wear throughout his 10-year Hall of Fame career. Campanella was the first black catcher in modern major league history and a three-time National League MVP.

FAST FACTS

F Perfect harmony: Hall of Famer *Larry Csonka*'s No. 39 was retired by Miami in 2002 as part of the Dolphins' 30th anniversary celebration of their 17-0 season.

F Comedian and television sitcom star *Bill Cosby* wore No. 39 in the early 1960s when he played running back for Temple.

NOTABLE 39s *DOUG WEIGHT* 39 *LEN BARKER* 39 *BOB VEALE* 39 *KERMIT ALEXANDER* 39 *JOE NUXHALL* 39

Elite 39s

LARRY CSONKA: The prototypical power runner for Don Shula's run-first Dolphins of the 1970s plowed a path right into the Hall of Fame.

MIKE GREENWELL: The long shadows in which he played were not cast by Fenway's Green Monster. A .303 career average while trying to live up to Boston predecessors Ted Williams, Carl Yastrzemski and Jim Rice is pretty impressive.

AL HRABOSKY: He was the Mad Hungarian, and "mad" didn't necessarily mean angry. Just try standing in against some guy with a blazing fastball who stomps around behind the mound, pounding his glove and acting as if he wants to chew glass. Go ahead and scoff, but Hrabosky was a top-notch reliever in the late 1970s.

HUGH McELHENNY: The owner of the 49ers called him the savior of the franchise. Knee injuries were the only thing that ever really

contained this electrifying runner in the 1950s.

DAVE PARKER: Pirates fans never really embraced Roberto Clemente's followup act, but the big right fielder had similar tools. Injuries and off-field problems kept him from living up to Clemente's Hall of Fame example in a career that eventually took him to six big-league cities.

Hrabosky

Csonka

NO FILIBUSTER NEEDED; SENATOR GIVES UP 39

Jason Spezza has this thing about 9. It's a goal-scorer's number, and like any good Canadian kid he wanted to be like Rocket, Gordie, the Golden Jet and, of course, old double-9, Wayne Gretzky. Spezza's dad wanted that, too, which is why he handed him a No. 9 sweater when he was a boy.

All of which explains how Spezza ended up as 39 for the Ottawa Senators—well, kind of. Blocked from wearing 9 (Martin Havlat) and 19 (Petr Schastlivy) when he was called up from the AHL by the Senators in 2002-03, Spezza opted for 39 because it had the coveted 9 plus 3, a multiple of 9. Spezza quickly became a fan favorite, scoring seven goals in his 33-game trial and 22 more in 2003-04.

Just as No. 39 sweaters were springing up in Ottawa, the Senators signed veteran goalie Dominik Hasek before the 2004-05 season and asked rising star Spezza to give up his 39 to a superstar.

"The guy is going to be a Hall of Famer," Spezza said at a news conference introducing Hasek. "That's a number he's been wearing his whole career and it means a lot to him. I don't mind wearing No. 19. I always liked Steve Yzerman as a kid growing up."

The door opened for 19 when Schastlivy was traded to Anaheim. As it turned out, it all became a nonissue when the NHL canceled its 2004-05 season because of a labor dispute. When the 2005-06 campaign opened, however, Hasek was wearing his familiar 39 and the 22-year-old Spezza had that Yzerman look as Ottawa's top-line center.

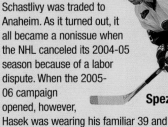

Spezza

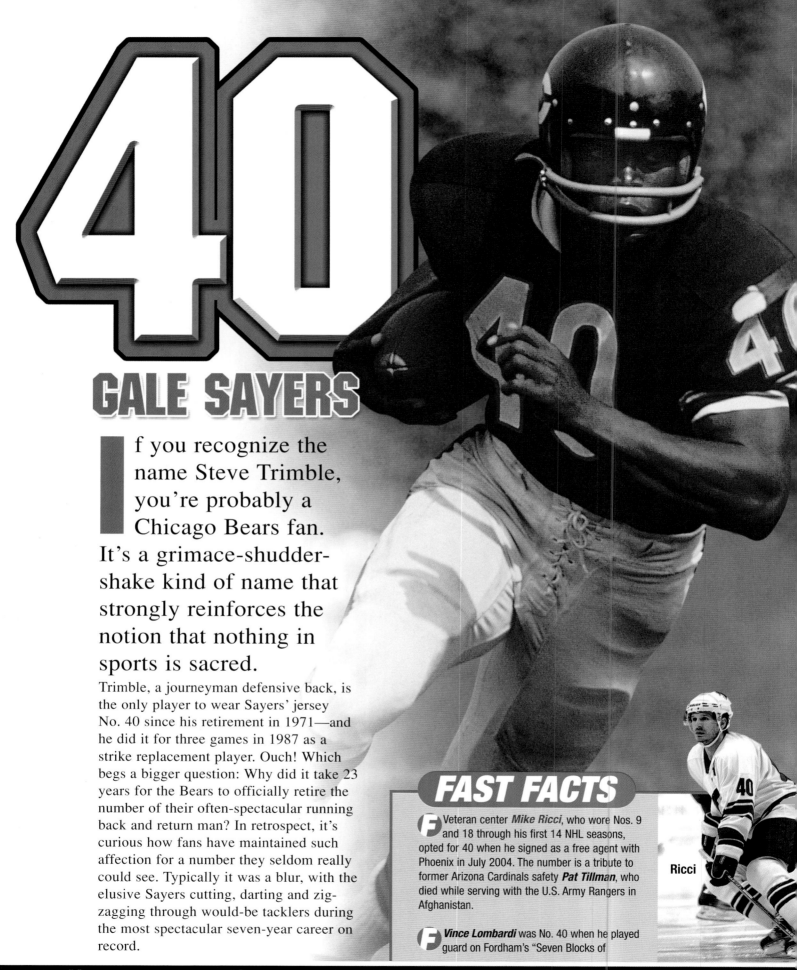

40

GALE SAYERS

If you recognize the name Steve Trimble, you're probably a Chicago Bears fan. It's a grimace-shudder-shake kind of name that strongly reinforces the notion that nothing in sports is sacred.

Trimble, a journeyman defensive back, is the only player to wear Sayers' jersey No. 40 since his retirement in 1971—and he did it for three games in 1987 as a strike replacement player. Ouch! Which begs a bigger question: Why did it take 23 years for the Bears to officially retire the number of their often-spectacular running back and return man? In retrospect, it's curious how fans have maintained such affection for a number they seldom really could see. Typically it was a blur, with the elusive Sayers cutting, darting and zig-zagging through would-be tacklers during the most spectacular seven-year career on record.

FAST FACTS

F Veteran center *Mike Ricci*, who wore Nos. 9 and 18 through his first 14 NHL seasons, opted for 40 when he signed as a free agent with Phoenix in July 2004. The number is a tribute to former Arizona Cardinals safety *Pat Tillman*, who died while serving with the U.S. Army Rangers in Afghanistan.

F *Vince Lombardi* was No. 40 when he played guard on Fordham's "Seven Blocks of

Ricci

NOTABLE 40s TOM BROOKSHIER 40 BARTOLO COLON 40 BOBBY JOE CONRAD 40 JAMES HASTY 40 STEVE BUSBY

Elite 40s

Kemp

to happen, whether running or catching the ball, for powerful Rams teams in the 1950s.

SHAWN KEMP: There haven't been too many NBA power forwards with more natural ability. Too bad about all that off-court stuff.

BILL LAIMBEER: The biggest, nastiest Bad Boy kept things lively for Pistons fans in the 1980s.

JOE MORRISON: The New York Giants' Mr. Versatility from 1959-72 played six positions well enough to get his number retired.

DANNY MURTAUGH: He managed the Pirates to 1,115 wins and two World Series titles. Only Fred Clarke can top the win total.

RICK SUTCLIFFE: Wearing No. 40 for the first time in 1984 after a midseason trade to the Cubs, he posted a 16-1 record and carried his new team into the playoffs. But his before-and-after numbers were not as impressive.

DON WILSON: The only pitcher to throw two no-hitters for the Astros was a double-figure winner for eight straight seasons in the late 1960s and early '70s.

MIKE ALSTOTT: Bucs fans appreciate big fullback Alstott, one of the best clock-eaters in the game.

ELROY HIRSCH: It was those legs—those "crazy legs." He was a big play waiting

DETERMINED PLUMMER HONORS 'A FRIEND'

It was a little decal, about the size of a quarter, that displayed the number 40 on the back of a Denver helmet. But in the eyes of NFL officials, it screamed defiance.

The problem: Any punishment levied against Broncos quarterback *Jake Plummer* for wearing the decal in honor of Pat Tillman, a longtime friend and former Arizona State and Arizona Cardinals teammate, would be a public relations nightmare. Tillman, the safety who had given up his lucrative career to fight for his country, died in the spring of 2004 while serving in Afghanistan with the U.S. Army Rangers.

The league had honored Tillman in its games of September 19 and 20, 2004. Players on all 32 teams wore the helmet decal, and Tillman's former team, the Cardinals, retired his No. 40. Only the Cardinals were allowed to keep wearing the decal, which meant that Plummer was violating the NFL's dress code when he attached it to the back of his helmet for a September 26 game against San Diego.

The NFL fined him $10,000 and threatened to double that if he wore it the next week. Plummer didn't wear it October 3, but he did October 10. "I'm just trying to honor a close friend of mine," Plummer said.

League officials negotiated a solution with the quarterback: Plummer would not be fined but would stop wearing the decal. He would film a public service announcement honoring Tillman and other veterans that would be played at Denver games throughout the season and at every NFL stadium the weekend after Veterans Day. And a No. 40 decal would be placed on the north end zone wall at Denver's Invesco Field.

Mark it down as a TD pass for Jake the Snake.

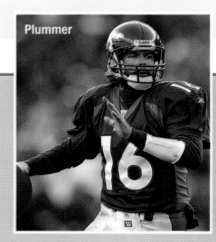

Plummer

Granite" offensive line in 1936 and '37.

F *Chuck Connors*, television's fast-shooting Rifleman, was a light-hitting first baseman who wore No. 40 and batted .239 in 1951, his only season with the Chicago Cubs.

F When Boston backup center fielder *Dave Henderson* delivered a two-out, ninth-inning, season-extending two-run homer off

California closer *Donnie Moore* in Game 5 of the 1986 A.L. Championship Series, he was wearing No. 40.

F Because of a mandatory numbering system in the short-lived AAFC, *Elroy Hirsch* wore No. 80 from 1946-48 with the Chicago Rockets. But the superstitious "Crazy Legs" had his more familiar 40 (University of Wisconsin and later the NFL's Rams) stitched on the inside of his jersey.

---

40 *DICK ANDERSON* **40** *FRANK FILCHOCK* **40** *WAYNE MILLNER* **40** *KEN WILLARD* **40** *DON WILSON* **40** *CALBERT CHEANEY*

41

TOM SEAVER

He wore 13 in Little League, 11 as a baseball and basketball star in high school and No. 37 at USC. Numbers never meant much to the strong righthander, who told a New York Newsday writer in 1988 how he got his first professional uniform. "I wore 21 at (Class AAA) Jacksonville and that was a funny story," Seaver said. "I was just a green rookie and we had a lot of veteran players. They rolled the uniforms in on a rack like you see on Seventh Avenue and everybody made a mad dash for them. There was one left when I got there." The acquisition of No. 41 was even less romantic. In his spring audition with the New York Mets in 1967, Seaver arrived at St. Petersburg, Fla., and found a uniform hanging in his locker. Two decades, 311 wins, three Cy Youngs and 3,640 strikeouts later, Tom Terrific had given the previously nondescript 41 a special niche in baseball lore.

FAST FACTS

Piccolo

F On May 8, 1999, Cardinals fans—accustomed to seeing slugger **Mark McGwire** in uniform No. 25—did a double take when No. 41 was retired in his honor by USA Baseball before a game against the Pirates at Busch Stadium. That's the number Big Mac wore as a member of the 1984 U.S. Olympic team.

F No. 41 has not been worn by a Chicago Bears player since 1969, *Brian Piccolo*'s last year

NOTABLE *41s* **GLEN RICE** *41* **PHIL VILLAPIANO** *41* **ELDEN CAMPBELL** *41* **PAT HENTGEN** *41* **CHARLES NAGY** *41* **MATT**

Elite 41s

RETRO RAVE SWEEPS UP OLD-SCHOOL UNSELD

Not unlike the Hula Hoop, the Slinky and the Pet Rock of generations past, the retro jersey became all the rave for the hip-hop generation in the early 2000s—equal parts sports, memorabilia, fashion and cool. And right there in the center of this throwback craze was Mr. Old School himself, former Washington Bullets star and coach *Wes Unseld*.

Not Unseld himself exactly, but his old red, white and blue No. 41 jersey, the one he wore in 1978 when he led the Washington franchise (predecessor of today's Wizards) to its only NBA championship. In the spring of 2004, there it was, listed at $430, the highest-priced retro jersey on a fast-growing market.

Unseld, who at 6-7 and 245 pounds was the epitome of power basketball and dedication to his craft, seemed mystified by his return to prominence. But two factors drove the popularity of Unseld's 41. First, rapper Sean "P. Diddy" Combs wore the jersey when he appeared on NBC's *Last Call With Carson Daly* in 2002. Then phenom basketball star LeBron James briefly lost his high school eligibility in 2003 after accepting two throwback jerseys from a Cleveland store worth $845— Unseld's 41 and Chicago Bears running back Gale Sayers' 40.

A fashion frenzy ensued, pushing Unseld's jersey into the $400-plus stratosphere and inspiring this response from one of the NBA's most grounded enforcers: "I think they're nuts."

Nowitzki

GLENN DAVIS: Mr. Outside was half of the most famous running duo in college football history and Army's 1946 Heisman Trophy winner.

EDDIE MATHEWS: A slugger, a gamer and a fighter. Third baseman Mathews and Hank Aaron pounded away in the 1950s and '60s, giving the Braves one of the top 1-2 home run punches in history.

TOM MATTE: This popular Colts running back is best remembered for his two-game emergency stint at quarterback when Johnny Unitas and Gary Cuozzo were injured near the end of the 1965 season. A quarterback wearing 41 was strange enough. But Matte, using plays written on his wristband, led the Colts to victory over the Rams before losing a Western Conference play-off thriller to Green Bay in overtime.

DIRK NOWITZKI: A 7-footer who can move, shoot from anywhere and rebound is an NBA coach's dream—or his worst nightmare.

GLEN RICE: His picture should be next to the word sniper in the dictionary. After gunning Michigan to the NCAA championship with a tournament-record 184 points in 1989, he became one of the NBA's top marksmen.

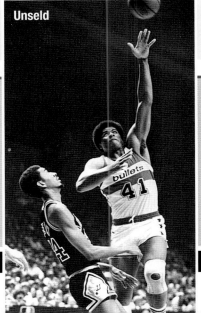

Unseld

with the team before his death in 1970 of embryonal cell carcinoma. Piccolo's relationship with Hall of Famer Gale Sayers was the subject of the 1971 made-for-television movie *Brian's Song*.

F Englishman *Roger Bannister*, with entry No. 41 pinned to his chest, ran the first sub 4-minute mile on May 6, 1954, finishing in 3:59.4 at a small meet in Oxford, England.

F Rumor has it that former lefthander *Jerry Reuss* selected his Dodgers No. 41 because he found it appealing when he saw it on a highway sign.

SNELL 41   CHARLIE WATERS 41   CHRIS SHORT 41   EUGENE ROBINSON 41   JIM SLATON 41

42

JACKIE ROBINSON

And then there was one. The grandfatherly beneficence of Major League Baseball has almost run its course with the retirement of Mo Vaughn after the 2003 season and only New York Yankees relief ace Mariano Rivera left to wear the game's "universal number."

When Robinson's Brooklyn Dodgers No. 42 was retired "in perpetuity" in 1997 by commissioner Bud Selig on the 50th anniversary of Robinson's Brooklyn debut, the 12 major leaguers already wearing 42 were allowed to keep it for the rest of their careers. Some gave it up voluntarily in honor of the man who broke baseball's modern color barrier; others retired or were denied the number when they changed teams. Vaughn was the last African-American player to wear the number. Rivera, who like Robinson has spent his entire career in New York, could become the last Hall of Famer.

FAST FACTS

F **Ronnie Lott**, who earned his Hall of Fame stripes as a cornerback and safety for the Joe Montana-era San Francisco 49ers, began wearing No. 42 as a high school wide receiver because he wanted to emulate NFL greats **Paul Warfield** and **Charley Taylor**.

F Leland High School in San Jose and Arizona State University have retired **Pat Tillman**'s No. 42. Tillman's 40 jersey was retired by the NFL's Arizona Cardinals after he died while serving his country in Afghanistan in 2004.

NOTABLE 42s CHUCK MUNCIE 42 VIN BAKER 42 MO VAUGHN 42 JOHN BROCKINGTON 42 DAVID LEE 42 JERRY

Elite 42s

PETTY LEGACY STARTED WITH 1959 DAYTONA WIN

He's the patriarch of NASCAR's first family, a pioneer who helped speed his sport away from the dusty dirt tracks of yesteryear. Well before Petty Enterprises became inexorably tied to No. 43 and the winning legacy of King Richard, father *Lee* was a driving force in his No. 42 racers.

Lee, who didn't start driving until age 35, won 54 NASCAR races and three Winston Cup titles, far short of Richard's 200 and seven. But it was his win in the inaugural 1959 Daytona 500, NASCAR's first major league race, that put the sport on the road to respectability. Driving his 42 Oldsmobile on the 2½-mile asphalt track at new Daytona International Speedway, the elder Petty outdueled Johnny Beauchamp's Thunderbird in a grueling race that didn't yield a winner until three days later.

With 15 laps remaining, Petty and Beauchamp began a bumper-to-bumper battle that became even more intense when the cars pulled side by side with three laps to go. They ran that way the rest of the race.

As they hit the finish line, it was too close to call—but NASCAR president Bill France tried anyway. He declared Beauchamp the winner, a decision that would be reversed after more than two days of checking still pictures and movies. Petty, 44, finally was awarded the $19,000 first prize and credited with an average speed of 135.521.

More important, NASCAR suddenly was knocking on the door of big-time status, and the first of four generations of Petty drivers was in the winner's circle.

Lee Petty

ELTON BRAND: Call it poetic justice, but it can't be easy starring at Duke, the best program in college basketball, and then playing in the NBA for Bulls teams that finished 17-65 and 15-67.

CHARLEY CONERLY: They didn't call him Chuckin' Charley for nothing. He flung the ball with maximum skill—first at Ole Miss, then with the Giants in the NFL.

CONNIE HAWKINS: Before there was Dr. J. or Michael, the Hawk soared into our basketball imagination. One of the original rim walkers, he was one of the superstar players to bolt from the ABA to the NBA.

WALT HAZZARD: His NBA career wasn't spectacular, but he helped prove that a coach and school—John Wooden and UCLA—belonged among the basketball elite. Hazzard starred for Wooden's first championship team in 1964.

RONNIE LOTT: Talk about toughness: Lott had the tip of his pinkie finger amputated rather than undergo surgery and miss the 1985 playoffs. And that's only part of the reason he gained recognition, first as one of the game's outstanding cornerbacks, then as its premier safety.

SID LUCKMAN: Everyone went to the new T-

Worthy

formation after Bears quarterback Luckman showed 'em how it was done in the 1940 title game. Bears 73, Redskins 0.

BRUCE SUTTER: Batters still confounded by the split-finger fastball can blame relief ace Sutter for popularizing it in the 1970s.

CHARLEY TAYLOR: From running back wannabe to pass-catching genius, Taylor became a big-play machine for quarterback Sonny Jurgensen and the Redskins.

NATE THURMOND: He wasn't as good defensively as Bill Russell, and he couldn't score like Wilt Chamberlain, but he might have been a better all-around center than either. He was truly a warrior.

PAUL WARFIELD: Can you imagine having a Hall of Fame receiver and never getting him more than 52 receptions in a season? Welcome to the old-school NFL.

JAMES WORTHY: Magic was great, but did anybody finish the Showtime fast break better than Worthy?

Tillman

Magnum, 42: Actor *Tom Selleck*, known to millions of television watchers for his TV role as Thomas Magnum, wore No. 42 while playing 10 basketball games for USC in the 1965-66 and 1966-67 seasons. He scored four points.

When *Kevin Willis* began his NBA career with the Atlanta Hawks in 1984-85, he never would have guessed he'd be wearing his same No. 42 for the same Hawks (second time around) more than two decades later (in 2004-05)—at age 42.

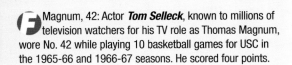

43

RICHARD PETTY

Kings and heroes want to go out in a blaze of glory. King Richard simply went out in a blaze. In his final NASCAR appearance, Petty parked his flaming No. 43 car next to a fire truck and watched helplessly as it was extinguished.

Though he eventually finished the race, there was no Hollywood ending for a career that reads like a movie script, complete with taskmaster father Lee, who once bumped his son into the wall when they were racing against each other, a hometown sweetheart who became his wife and those Petty trademarks, which were accidents of fate (Petty blue was created when he mixed cans of blue and white paint so he would have enough to cover his first car, and No. 43 was chosen because dad's car was 42). Add a Hollywood smile to the Hollywood story, and it's easy to see why they called him King. Those 200 wins and status as NASCAR's first $1 million career winner might have something to do with it, too.

Elite 43s

DENNIS ECKERSLEY: Starter or closer? The Eck provided the best of both worlds in a Hall of Fame career that produced 197 wins and 390 saves.

KEN FORSCH: Half of baseball's only no-hit brother tandem posted a 114-113 record from 1970-86 with the Astros and Angels.

MEL HARDER: He won 223 games for the Indians wearing No. 18 but was just as valuable wearing No. 43 as the team's pitching coach for 15 years. Just ask Early Wynn, Bob Lemon, Mike Garcia and Herb Score, four of the many elite pitchers he helped develop.

FAST FACTS

F Future Heisman winner **Herschel Walker**, No. 43 during his superstar career in high school, reversed the digits (34) at the University of Georgia because 43 belonged to veteran linebacker Keith Middleton.

F **Craig Kilborn**, the former host of CBS' *The Late Late Show*, wore No. 43 during his three-year career as a guard/forward at Montana State.

NOTABLE 43s **LARRY BROWN** 43 **MIKE PRUITT** 43 **GRANT LONG** 43 **DAVE HAMPTON** 43 **PATRICE BRISEBOIS** 43

FASCINATION FOR PETTY DRIVES DAUGHERTY

Daugherty

What does a 7-foot African-American NBA All-Star have in common with a good-old-boy NASCAR driver from North Carolina? For starters, the number 43. *Brad Daugherty*, also from North Carolina, has been a huge Richard Petty fan since childhood. His fascination with The King goes back to about age 10 when his dad took him to a race at a nearby track. After the race, young Brad spotted Petty packing his gear on the infield and yelled his name, waving.

Petty looked over, strolled toward Brad, stopped and talked to him. Then he took off his cap, autographed it and handed it to the startled youngster. Daugherty never forgot the gesture, which he repaid by wearing No. 43 in high school and for eight years with the NBA's Cleveland Cavaliers. He would have worn it in college at North Carolina, too, but he lost a coin flip with fellow freshman Curtis Hunter for 43 and settled for 42.

Daugherty's emotional tie to Petty was well known. When the Cavs retired his number in a 1997 ceremony, the players gave him a golf cart painted in Petty's traditional electric-blue with No. 43 on the sides.

When his career ended after the 1994-95 season, Daugherty became part owner of a Craftsman Truck team—the sport's first African-American owner since NASCAR's inception in 1948. No longer an owner, Daugherty now dabbles in projects to help bring diversity to NASCAR while marketing the sport to minorities.

CLIFF HARRIS: The fearless Cowboys safety earned six Pro Bowl citations, two Super Bowl rings and distinction as a member of the NFL All-Decade Team in the 1970s.

CARL LOCKHART: The Spider gave Giants opponents arachnophobia from 1965-75, gobbling up passes after luring them into his web.

DON PERKINS: The six-time Pro Bowler can't match the flashy rushing totals of New Agers Emmitt Smith and Tony Dorsett, but he can claim distinction as the first Cowboys back to run for 6,000 yards.

JACK SIKMA: His tall, pale frame and curly blond hair gave him a docile look, but his 9.8 career rebounding average and 15.6 scoring mark shot down that misconception. He was a steadying force in Seattle's paint for nine seasons, in Milwaukee's for five more.

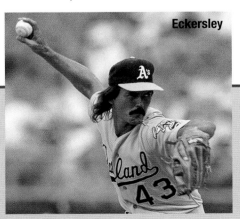

Eckersley

F *Raul Mondesi*, emotionally attached to 43, pleaded with pitcher Miguel Batista to give him the number when he was traded to Arizona in July 2003. Batista, swayed by Mondesi's disclosure that he has tattoos of "43" all over his body, switched to 25 and got a Rolex watch in return.

F When veteran closer *Dennis Eckersley* signed with Boston prior to the 1998 season, the Red Sox gave him his familiar 43 (matching his age) and forced young pitcher Derek Lowe to switch numbers.

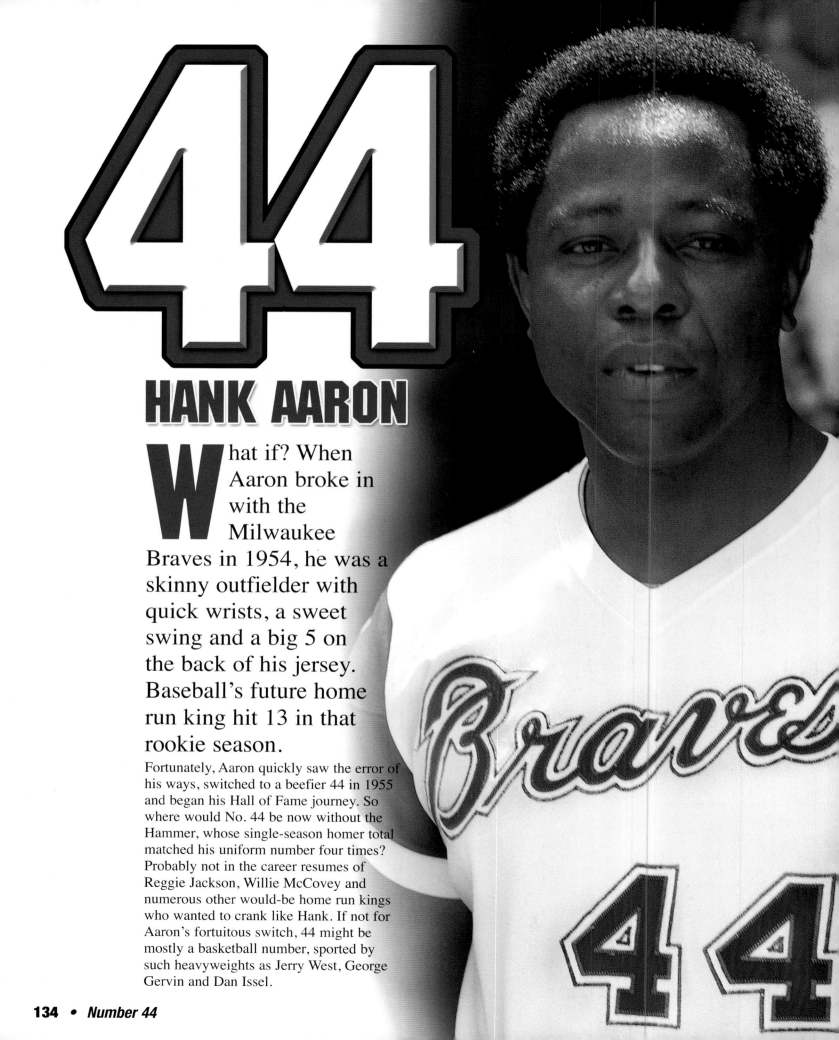

44

HANK AARON

What if? When Aaron broke in with the Milwaukee Braves in 1954, he was a skinny outfielder with quick wrists, a sweet swing and a big 5 on the back of his jersey. Baseball's future home run king hit 13 in that rookie season.

Fortunately, Aaron quickly saw the error of his ways, switched to a beefier 44 in 1955 and began his Hall of Fame journey. So where would No. 44 be now without the Hammer, whose single-season homer total matched his uniform number four times? Probably not in the career resumes of Reggie Jackson, Willie McCovey and numerous other would-be home run kings who wanted to crank like Hank. If not for Aaron's fortuitous switch, 44 might be mostly a basketball number, sported by such heavyweights as Jerry West, George Gervin and Dan Issel.

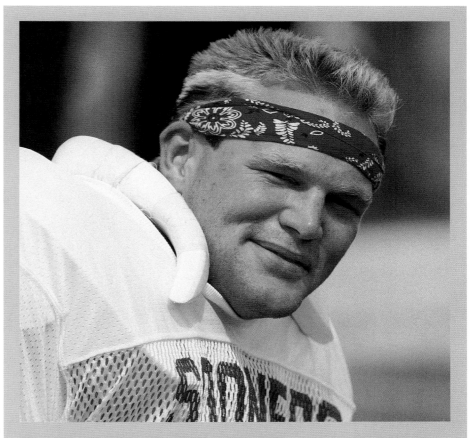

WITHOUT 44, THE BOZ JUST ISN'T THE BOZ

Brian Bosworth was colorful, outrageous and brimming with bravado as an Oklahoma Sooner. Everybody's All-American was hip and famous—and talented enough to merit a 10-year, $11 million contract with the NFL's Seattle Seahawks in 1987.

Unfortunately, he also was No. 44. NFL rules stipulate that linebackers must wear numbers in the 50s or 90s, thus blocking The Boz from being The Boz. After an extensive holdout, he signed and was handed No. 55, setting off a controversial chain reaction.

Bosworth, claiming the Seahawks had promised to get him special dispensation to wear 44, wore the number in three exhibition games in '87. But with NFL officials watching closely, he played the season opener against Denver wearing 55—with 44 painted on his shoes.

Bosworth's agent hired a Seattle attorney, who obtained a one-game restraining order from a Seattle District Court judge that allowed Bosworth to wear 44 against Kansas City. "The number thing may not be a big deal to anybody else," Bosworth said, "but it is a big deal to me."

Claiming that barring 44 had an unfair economic impact on his client, the agent pointed to his corporation, 44-Boz Inc., which made sunglasses (44 Blues) and blue jeans (Seattle 44 Blues). He also cited a "Land of Boz" poster that pictured No. 44 Bosworth with a Playboy playmate. A King County Superior Court judge sided with the NFL and denied the request for a preliminary injunction.

Whatever the effect of the number hassle, Bosworth spent only three seasons (wearing 55) in Seattle, playing 24 of 48 games. He never appeared in the NFL again.

NOTABLE **s** KYLE ROTE   ROB NIEDERMAYER   HANK GATHERS   ELROD HENDRICKS   RAY WASHBURN

Elite 44s

Labonte

CHUCK FOREMAN: This versatile Vikings back played in three Super Bowls in the 1970s, all losers.

GEORGE GERVIN: Opponents couldn't melt down the Spurs as long as the Iceman was around.

DAN ISSEL: He wasn't smooth, extremely athletic, big or strong. He was, however, consistent, hard-working and Hall-worthy.

REGGIE JACKSON: His best all-around years might have been with the A's, but say "Reggie" and people think pinstripes, playoffs, home runs—Mr. October.

LEROY KELLY: How can you lose Jim Brown, the best running back in NFL history, and not miss a beat? Cleveland simply turned to backup Kelly, who recorded three straight

Pronger

FAST FACTS

F Braves fans were seeing double on April 8, 1974, when **Hank Aaron**, wearing No. 44, hit his record-breaking 715th home run off Dodgers lefthander **Al Downing**, who also was wearing 44.

F **Ed Marinaro** and **Michael Warren**, both of whom played police officers in the hit 1980s television series Hill Street Blues, wore No. 44 as outstanding college athletes. Marinaro, a running back at Cornell, was runner-up to Pat Sullivan for the

1971 Heisman Trophy. Warren was a starting guard on UCLA's 1967 and '68 NCAA championship teams.

F Edmonton defenseman **Chris Pronger**, who wanted **Bobby Orr**'s No. 4 when he reached the NHL, couldn't get it, so he "added a four, double the pleasure" to become 44.

F Former power forward **Kevin McHale**, who wore No. 44 at the University of Minnesota,

1,000-yard seasons and won two NFL rushing titles to jump-start a career that would take him all the way to Canton.

TERRY LABONTE: If NASCAR greatness is measured by consistency, Labonte definitely qualifies. He has finished in the top 10 in points 17 times and won two Cup championships—one in his familiar 44.

WILLIE McCOVEY: First and second basemen held their breath when this San Francisco Giant stepped to the plate. One of baseball's most feared mashers hit 521 home runs.

CHRIS PRONGER: Big, mean and talented. How can anyone be sure he's a real person and not some "perfect defenseman" robot?

JOHN RIGGINS: The Redskins and Jets

West

broke the mold with Riggins. When was the last time NFL teams were brutalized by a head-cracking, 1,000-yard-rushing fullback?

JERRY WEST: This hard-working, jump-shooting perfectionist once said he expected every shot to go in—and almost half of them did. The longtime Los Angeles superstar would later have a hand in building two Lakers dynasties.

PAUL WESTPHAL: Getting traded from Boston, the NBA's best franchise, might have seemed like a raw deal at the time, but things worked out OK. Westphal became a star with the Suns, first as a player, then as a coach.

AT SYRACUSE, 44 IS A POWERFUL SYMBOL

To fully comprehend the legend of 44, you have to be there—at Syracuse University. Over a 13-year period, that number was worn by three of the greatest running backs in college history—*Jim Brown* (1954-56), *Ernie Davis* (1959-61) and *Floyd Little* (1964-66).

It's not a stretch to say 44 is to Syracuse what pinstripes are to the New York Yankees and the Golden Dome is to Notre Dame. It is an all-powerful symbol of excellence and held in great esteem by Orange fans.

Consider that the university had its zip code changed from 13210 to 13244 and its telephone prefix from 423 to 443. When the school finally retired No. 44—the number was considered a huge recruiting tool by former coach Ben Schwartzwalder—in 2005, the ceremony came 44 years after Davis won the school's only Heisman Trophy.

Gifford Zimmerman was the first of 25 players to wear No. 44 in 1921, Rob Konrad the last in 1998. But it was Brown who brought it national attention. He scored 43 points (six TDs, seven PATs) in one college game and went on to glory with the Cleveland Browns.

Davis led the Orange to the 1959 national title and was selected No. 1 overall by the Redskins in the 1962 draft. His rights were traded to the Browns, but Davis died of leukemia at age 23 before ever playing in the same backfield with Brown. Little was an electrifying runner and punt returner who went on to NFL fame with Denver.

A 16-foot replica jersey No. 44 is displayed near the roof in one end zone of Syracuse's Carrier Dome.

Brown

switched to 32 with the NBA's Celtics because a guard named Pete Maravich had 44 when he got to Boston. McHale's 32 now is retired.

F Before outfielder *Eric Davis* made his big-league debut with Cincinnati in 1984, he was handed a No. 44 jersey by Reds equipment manager *Bernie Stowe*. Davis apparently reminded Stowe of another 44 outfielder with super quick wrists.

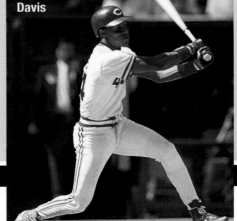
Davis

MARV HUBBARD 44 *JASON ISRINGHAUSEN*

DICK LeBEAU 44 *KEN PHELPS*

45
BOB GIBSON

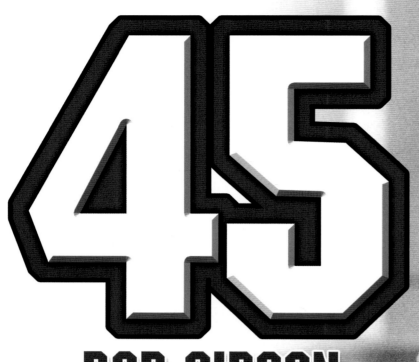

Officially, lefthander Dean Stone can claim distinction as the last St. Louis Cardinals player to wear uniform No. 45 before that growling, scowling pitching monster arrived from Omaha, Neb.

Unofficially, righthander Jim Donohue claims bragging rights as the opening act for the hard-throwing Gibson. "I was the last player cut by the team in the spring of 1960," recalled Donohue, who never pitched in a regular-season game for the Cardinals. "I wore 45 that spring. Gibby wore 31. That number was just given to me for spring training. Numbers really didn't mean anything in those days. We were just glad to be in the big leagues." For the record: The five pitchers who wore No. 45 before Gibson (Gordon Jones, Dick Littlefield, Von McDaniel, Bill Wight and Stone) combined for a 15-18 record for the Cardinals. Gibson was 248-169 wearing No. 45.

NOTABLE 45s **CECIL FIELDER** 45 **GARY FENCIK** 45 **JIM BEATTIE**

JORDAN REMOVES HIS DISGUISE, SOARS AGAIN

After 17 games late in the 1994-95 season, four more against Charlotte in the first round of the playoffs and one against Orlando in the Eastern Conference semifinals, Superman finally pulled off his disguise. *Michael Jordan* discarded the No. 45 he had been wearing, reclaimed his 23 and soared back into the penthouse of his NBA universe.

Chicago fans, who had watched him score only 19 points and commit eight turnovers wearing 45 in the semifinals opener, loved it. Magic fans, who watched No. 23 erupt for 38 points in Game 2, hated it. So did NBA officials, who fined the Bulls $25,000 for the "unauthorized" number switch and threatened more fines if Jordan continued to wear 23 in the playoffs.

Jordan, who had retired after the 1992-93 season to try his hand at baseball, wore 45 as a mediocre minor league player. When he came out of basketball retirement in March 1995, he kept 45, saying he wouldn't wear 23—the number he had worn for nine previous NBA seasons—because that was his number before his father, James, was murdered in 1993. But a struggling Jordan relented: "No. 23 is me, so why try to be something else?"

Despite the NBA's threat, Jordan—with the support of his team—played the rest of the series wearing 23. Orlando, led by Shaquille O'Neal, eliminated the Bulls in six games and the league, as promised, hit the club with a $100,000 fine. But Superman was back, and so was the seed that would blossom into another three-year Bulls championship run.

JOHN CANDELARIA 45 **STEVE ROGERS** 45 **KENNY EASLEY** 45 **SPEEDY DUNCAN** 45 **STEVE BALBONI** 45 **RAEF LaFRENTZ**

Elite 45s

Green

A.C. GREEN: The Cal Ripken of the NBA played in a record 1,192 consecutive games from 1986 to 2001 for the Lakers, Suns, Mavericks and Heat.

PEDRO MARTINEZ: The excitable Dominican knows how to pitch—and win. In 2004, he and his Red Sox teammates even figured out how to beat the Yankees.

TUG McGRAW: You had to believe when McGraw took the mound in a close game. The 1969 and '73 Mets certainly did. So did the '80 Phillies.

RIK SMITS: The jump-shooting 7-4 Dutchman with shaggy blond hair wore No. 45 for the last eight seasons of his 12-year NBA career.

RUDY TOMJANOVICH: As an

FAST FACTS

When pitcher **Terry Mulholland** signed with Minnesota in April 2004, coach Scott Ullger gave him the shirt off his back—literally. For his No. 45 jersey, Ullger got a new set of golf clubs.

For his six NBA seasons in the 1970s, long-range shooter **Geoff Petrie** was

Podres

the face for the expansion Portland Trail Blazers. His 45 was the second number retired by the franchise.

Dodgers lefthander **Johnny Podres**

was wearing 45 in 1955 when he secured Brooklyn's first and last championship by shutting out the New York Yankees in Game 7 of the World Series.

The Cleveland Browns retired 45, the number former Syracuse Heisman Trophy winner **Ernie Davis** would have worn in his rookie 1962 season. Davis, who wore 44 in college, was diagnosed with leukemia and died in 1963 without ever playing in the NFL.

KELVIM ESCOBAR   **CARLOS LEE**   **JIM BERTELSEN**   **TIM WORRELL**

Martinez

Davis

All-Star power forward in the 1970s, Rudy T is best remembered for picking himself up and coming back from the most vicious on-court attack in NBA history. As a coach, he is revered for those two championships he brought to Houston in the 1990s.

EMLEN TUNNELL: Emlen the Gremlin was an interception waiting to happen. He had 79 in 14 NFL seasons, and is credited with developing many of the pass-coverage techniques for the safety position. Tunnell was the first black to play for the Giants in the post-World War II era, and the first to be inducted into the Hall of Fame.

GRIFFIN'S 45, OTHER OHIO STATE NUMBERS FINALLY GET CLOSURE

For most of its history, Ohio State refused to retire numbers. Some were "unofficially" taken out of circulation, but no number was declared off limits ad infinitum. Not even 45, which was worn by Mr. Buckeye himself, *Archie Griffin*.

Such a loophole helped the Buckeyes recruit Andy Katzenmoyer in the mid-1990s. A Parade All-American and one of the most coveted linebackers to come out of Ohio in years, Katzenmoyer asked if he could wear the number he had worn since the seventh grade, 45. The Buckeyes said yes.

There was some outcry from fans, who had not seen a Buckeyes 45 since 1975, when Griffin rushed for the last of his 5,589 yards and became the only player to win the Heisman Trophy in back-to-back years. Griffin, OSU's associate athletic director when Katzenmoyer arrived, said he didn't care, as long as he "wears it pretty doggone well."

Katzenmoyer did. He was the Butkus Award winner (the nation's outstanding linebacker) in 1997 and leader of a defense that helped 11-1 Ohio State to a No. 2 Associated Press final ranking in 1998. Katzenmoyer declared for the NFL draft after his junior season and was picked 28th overall by New England.

After Katzenmoyer's departure, OSU did an about-face and announced it would retire the numbers of its Heisman winners. Griffin was first, at halftime of an Iowa-Ohio State game on October 30, 1999. It was an emotional ceremony for the man who only three years earlier had said he didn't care.

Tomjanovich

46

LEE SMITH

For an under-50 number, 46 lacks marquee value. Only one professional team has retired it, and that was to honor a player killed in an offseason construction accident.

Don Mattingly could have owned 46, but the New York Yankees first baseman wore it for two years and then challenged Michael Jordan for 23 supremacy. Bad decision. Cleveland Browns kicker/offensive lineman Lou Groza discarded his 46 and lifted 76 to Hall of Fame glory. Smith, baseball's all-time saves leader, is the best of the 46s—at least he was for eight very productive seasons with the Chicago Cubs. But even this scowling, hard-throwing righthander tried other numbers—47, 48 and 49— during his late-career wanderlust. Smith gets the 46 nod over Houston lefthander Andy Pettitte and two former NFL players—Oakland Raiders tight end Todd Christensen and Cincinnati Bengals running back Pete Johnson.

FAST FACTS

F **Todd Christensen** was a numerological anomaly in the NFL. Listed as a running back when he joined the Raiders in 1979, he wore No. 46. Christensen kept that number for 10 years, even though he played eight of those as a tight end—a position that normally requires a number in the 80s under the NFL's numbering system.

F Lefthander **Andy Pettitte**, who always will be No. 46 in the hearts of Yankees fans,

Trachsel

NOTABLE 46s **JIM MALONEY** 46 **GARY LAVELLE** 46 **MIKE MAROTH** 46 **DANNY ABRAMOWICZ** 46

Elite 46s

TODD CHRISTENSEN: This pass-catching tight end was just one of those wild and crazy Raiders from 1979-88.

MIKE FLANAGAN: There was nothing flaky about this lefthander, who won 23 games for the pennant-winning Orioles in 1979 and was a Baltimore rotation mainstay for 11 of his 18 big-league seasons.

DON FLEMING: The young safety started in his only three seasons {1960-62} for the Cleveland Browns before he was electrocuted in 1963 while working an offseason construction job in Orlando, Fla. Fleming is the only player from the four major professional sports to have his No. 46 retired.

Christensen

PETE JOHNSON: The Bengals' third-leading career rusher did most of his ball-toting as a fullback from 1977-83.

TIM McDONALD: The early 1990s 49ers are best remembered for their offense, but a defense that included safety McDonald was not too shabby, either

ANDY PETTITTE: Pinstripes and 46 worked well for the lefty with a postseason flair.

switched to 21 as a tribute to former New York team-mate *Roger Clemens* when he signed with his hometown Houston Astros before the 2004 season.

(F) When Cardinals first baseman *Mark McGwire* broke *Roger Maris'* single-season home run mark on September 8,

1998, his record-breaking No. 62 came off No. 46— Cubs righthander *Steve Trachsel*.

(F) For 13 seasons from 1977-89, Red Sox fans associated No. 46 with righthander *Bob Stanley*. The starter/reliever won 115 games and saved 132 more over that span.

BEARS' DOUG PLANK IS A NUMBER, NOT A NAME

Most players would be honored to have their coach name a defense after them. But what if that honor was accorded because a coach couldn't remember that player's name? That's what happened to Chicago Bears strong safety *Doug Plank* in the early 1980s.

Bears defensive coordinator Buddy Ryan introduced his new defensive scheme, which used the strong safety (Plank) as an extra linebacker and allowed the other linebackers to blitz at will, as the "46 defense"—Plank's number. It caused big problems for quarterbacks.

It didn't really surprise Plank when Ryan couldn't think of his name—Ryan always had a hard time with such details. But what Ryan did think of—a lot—was ways to make life uncomfortable for opposing quarterbacks. The idea of the new scheme was to pressure them into premature throws and mental mistakes by hitting them, over and over. Ryan liked to boast, "We'll find out who the second-team quarterback is."

That often was the case. By 1984, the Bears and their 46 defense were dominating opponents. In 1985, they held 14 regular-season and postseason opponents to 10 or fewer points en route to an 18-1 overall record and victory in Super Bowl 20.

Unfortunately, Plank wasn't around to enjoy the fruits of his namesake. An injury forced him to retire after the 1982 season. But he watched the scheme become popular later in Philadelphia and Arizona (Ryan head coaching stops) as well as at Tennessee, where Ryan protege Jeff Fisher has coached since 1994.

Plank

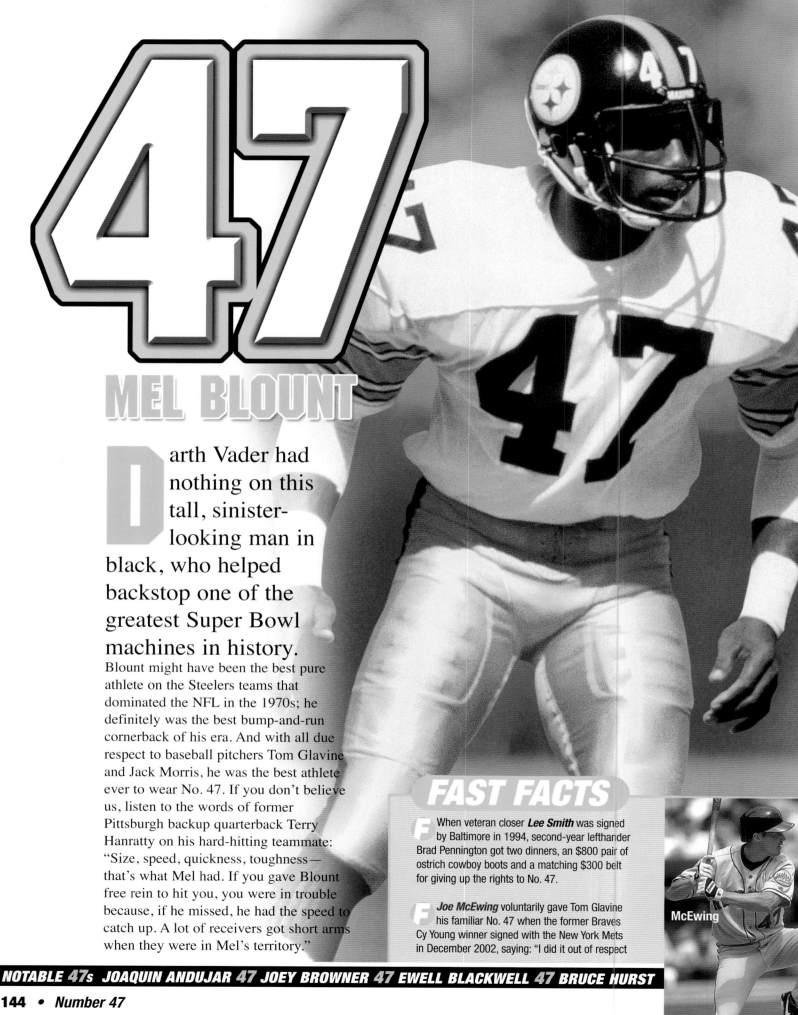

47

MEL BLOUNT

Darth Vader had nothing on this tall, sinister-looking man in black, who helped backstop one of the greatest Super Bowl machines in history. Blount might have been the best pure athlete on the Steelers teams that dominated the NFL in the 1970s; he definitely was the best bump-and-run cornerback of his era. And with all due respect to baseball pitchers Tom Glavine and Jack Morris, he was the best athlete ever to wear No. 47. If you don't believe us, listen to the words of former Pittsburgh backup quarterback Terry Hanratty on his hard-hitting teammate: "Size, speed, quickness, toughness— that's what Mel had. If you gave Blount free rein to hit you, you were in trouble because, if he missed, he had the speed to catch up. A lot of receivers got short arms when they were in Mel's territory."

FAST FACTS

When veteran closer **Lee Smith** was signed by Baltimore in 1994, second-year lefthander Brad Pennington got two dinners, an $800 pair of ostrich cowboy boots and a matching $300 belt for giving up the rights to No. 47.

Joe McEwing voluntarily gave Tom Glavine his familiar No. 47 when the former Braves Cy Young winner signed with the New York Mets in December 2002, saying: "I did it out of respect

McEwing

NOTABLE 47s JOAQUIN ANDUJAR 47 JOEY BROWNER 47 EWELL BLACKWELL 47 BRUCE HURST

Elite 47s

Glavine

ROD BECK: Intimidating, no. But consistency and hard work earned the stocky righthander with the big mustache 286 career saves.

TOM GLAVINE: He lives on the outside corner, which is a pretty exclusive neighborhood. Two Cy Youngs and 275 wins suggest this artistic lefthander controls his own fate.

JOHN LYNCH: Tough, mean and savvy. After 11 solid seasons at Tampa Bay, Lynch is putting on a safety clinic for Denver fans.

JACK MORRIS: Though a Tiger at heart,

Morris also is remembered for his 1991 performance with the Twins—an 18-12 record and a gutty 10-inning shutout in Game 7 of the World Series. He had ups and downs in his 18-year career, but his 254-186 record and four World Series rings are impressive.

JESSE OROSCO: So you don't believe the baseball adage that a lefty pitcher can hang around forever? People's exhibit A: Jesse Orosco.

ILLEGAL TACKLER WAS 'TOO FULL OF ALABAMA'

There he was, No. 47, streaking down the right sideline en route to an apparent 95-yard touchdown run. Suddenly, as Rice's *Dicky Moegle* crossed the 50-yard line near the Alabama bench, a Crimson Tide player bolted onto the field and smashed him to the turf. Fans watching the 1954 Cotton Bowl in Dallas sat in stunned disbelief, not totally sure what they had just seen.

Referee Cliff Shaw was sure and flagged Alabama's Tommy Lewis, awarding the touchdown to Moegle. One of the most shocking plays in college bowl game history occurred in the second quarter with Rice leading, 7-6. The Owls, who had trailed 6-0 in the opening period, went on to post an easy 28-6 victory.

"I kept telling myself I didn't do it. I didn't do it. But I knew I had," a penitent Lewis said of his stunning entry onto the field of play. "I guess I'm too full of Alabama."

Moegle also was full of Alabama after feasting on the Crimson Tide for 265 yards on 11 carries (24.1 per attempt). In addition to his 95-yard run, Moegle also broke free on TD bursts of 79 and 34 yards. Ironically, Alabama's only touchdown was scored on a 1-yard run by fullback Lewis.

Moegle, whose spectacular bowl game performance was forever overshadowed by the illegal tackle, went on to play seven years in the NFL with San Francisco, Pittsburgh and Dallas. He wore 47 at all three stops.

for Tommy." Out of respect for Joe, Glavine reciprocated by financing a baby nursery in McEwing's home.

F Running back *Chic Harley,* the first real Ohio State gate attraction during the World War I era, had his No. 47 retired at halftime of a 2004 Buckeyes-Penn State game. Harley's popularity often is credited as the impetus to building Ohio Stadium ("the house that Harley built") in 1922.

LEWIS (A)   MOEGLE (R)

47 LeROY IRVIN **47** JOEY JAY **47** RICH PILON **47** JOHNNY SAMPLE **47** RYAN McNEIL **47** JESSE WHITTENTON

48

JIMMIE JOHNSON

Give him points for consistency, just a few, and J.J. might have a couple of NEXTEL Cup titles under his belt. Through the 2005 NASCAR season, Johnson's No. 48 Lowe's Chevrolet had been spotted in the points-standing top 10 for 139 of his 144 weeks as a full-time driver and in the victory circle after 18 races.

Kurt Busch certainly knows what it's like being drafted by the relentless Johnson. Apparently running on cruise control in the 2004 points chase, Busch watched Johnson win three straight races and four of the final six to pull within an eyelash of catching him. Busch held on by a measly eight points, but Johnson claimed the consolation prize with a season-best eight wins. The longer this determined Californian races, the better he gets. In 2005, he became the first driver to win three straight 600-mile events. And in 2006, he added the Daytona 500 to his impressive victory-circle resume.

Elite 48s

DARYL JOHNSTON: The Moose cleared running lanes for Emmitt Smith from 1990-99, and he helped lead the Cowboys to three Super Bowl wins.

RAMON MARTINEZ: For a while, younger brother Pedro was the lesser-known pitcher in this family. Ramon's 135-88 career record falls short of Pedro now, but it isn't too shabby.

SAM McDOWELL: The most feared fastball of the 1960s belonged to Cleveland's "Sudden Sam," the dominating lefty in the American League. McDowell, who often was compared to Sandy Koufax, fell short of elite status in 15 big-league seasons, partly because he tried to trick hitters rather than overpower them.

FAST FACTS

F Pre-NFL and the Chicago Bears, *Gale Sayers* was doing his zigging and zagging and TD bragging in a No. 48 jersey for the Kansas Jayhawks. It's one of three football numbers retired by the school.

F *Angelo Bertelli*, the first of Notre Dame's seven Heisman Trophy winners, wore No. 48 while leading the Irish to the 1943 national championship.

F *Karl Spooner*, the Brooklyn lefthander who pitched shutouts in his first two big-league games after being called up from the

NOTABLE 48s ANDY PAFKO 48 ROOSEVELT LEAKS 48 TORII HUNTER 48 RICK REUSCHEL 48 KEN ELLIS 48 TRAVIS

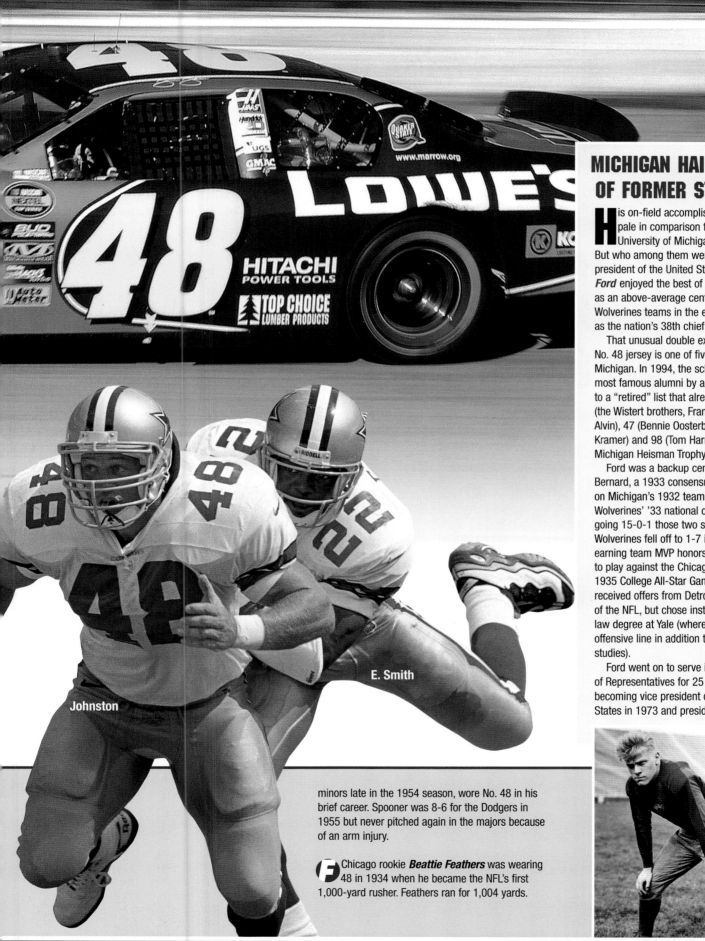

MICHIGAN HAILS NO. 48 OF FORMER STAR FORD

His on-field accomplishments might pale in comparison to many University of Michigan football greats. But who among them went on to become president of the United States? *Gerald Ford* enjoyed the best of both worlds, first as an above-average center/linebacker for Wolverines teams in the early 1930s, later as the nation's 38th chief executive.

That unusual double explains why Ford's No. 48 jersey is one of five retired by Michigan. In 1994, the school honored its most famous alumni by adding his number to a "retired" list that already included 11 (the Wistert brothers, Francis, Albert and Alvin), 47 (Bennie Oosterbaan), 87 (Ron Kramer) and 98 (Tom Harmon, one of three Michigan Heisman Trophy winners).

Ford was a backup center to Chuck Bernard, a 1933 consensus All-American, on Michigan's 1932 team and the Wolverines' '33 national champions. After going 15-0-1 those two seasons, the Wolverines fell off to 1-7 in 1934 with Ford earning team MVP honors and an invitation to play against the Chicago Bears in the 1935 College All-Star Game. He even received offers from Detroit and Green Bay of the NFL, but chose instead to pursue a law degree at Yale (where he coached the offensive line in addition to focusing on his studies).

Ford went on to serve in the U.S. House of Representatives for 25 years before becoming vice president of the United States in 1973 and president in 1974.

E. Smith

Johnston

minors late in the 1954 season, wore No. 48 in his brief career. Spooner was 8-6 for the Dodgers in 1955 but never pitched again in the majors because of an arm injury.

F Chicago rookie *Beattie Feathers* was wearing 48 in 1934 when he became the NFL's first 1,000-yard rusher. Feathers ran for 1,004 yards.

Ford

HAFNER *48* **SCOTT YOUNG** *48* **STEPHEN DAVIS** *48* **OLIVER PEREZ** *48* **RALPH GARR** *48* **TIM FOX** *48* **JEREMY AFFELDT**

Best by Number • **147**

49

RON GUIDRY

25-3

... 1.74 ERA ... nine shutouts ... 248 strikeouts. Such theatrics leave lasting imprints, especially when performed by a skinny 160-pound lefthander on baseball's biggest stage.

Throw in a colorful nickname, a big heart and the nastiest slider this side of Cooperstown and you end up with Louisiana Lightning, No. 49 if you're keeping a scorecard. Guidry's best Cy Young impression came in 1978, but he also reached the 20-win plateau in 1983 and '85 and helped pitch the New York Yankees to two World Series championships. The number 49? That came courtesy of veteran Yankees clubhouse attendant Pete Sheehy when Guidry made his big-league debut in 1975. Sheehy handed the youngster his new uniform, along with a challenge: No Yankee had been able to make 49 famous. Three decades later, the number has been retired by baseball's most celebrated franchise and a Guidry plaque hangs proudly in Yankee Stadium's Monument Park.

FAST FACTS

F During his first of three seasons with the St. Louis Browns (1951), former Negro leagues great *Satchel Paige* wore 22 and 49. He switched to 29 in 1952.

F *Carl Weathers*, best known for his recurring role as Apollo Creed in the Rocky movies, wore No. 49 as a linebacker for the Oakland Raiders in 1970, No. 51 in 1971.

NOTABLE 49s ROB DIBBLE 49 TOM NIEDENFUER 49 MIKE SIANI 49 DENNIS SMITH 49 WARREN CROMARTIE 49

Elite 49s

Paige

Mitchell

LARRY DIERKER: From righthanded pitcher to broadcaster to manager: No. 49 won 137 games for the Astros on the mound, 448 in the dugout. He also was the first Houston pitcher to win 20.

TOM LANDRY: Everybody knows about Tom Landry, coach of the Dallas Cowboys. But what about Landry the defensive back/defensive coordinator for the Giants in the 1950s? The 4-3 and flex defenses and the spread offense were among Landry's innovations.

BOBBY MITCHELL: Overshadowed as a running back by Jim Brown in Cleveland, Mr. Versatility blossomed in Washington as a big-play receiver and return man. The first black player in Redskins history lists among his career exploits a 232-yard rushing game, a 218-yard receiving effort, 98- and 92-yard kickoff returns, a 90-yard touchdown run, a 99-yard pass play and a 78-yard punt return.

KNUCKLEBALLERS ALL AFLUTTER OVER 49

In the spring of 1992, before *Tim Wakefield* made his major league debut with Pittsburgh, he got the opportunity to meet and work briefly with fellow knuckleballer Charlie Hough, a veteran of 22 big-league seasons. When Wakefield finally auditioned with the Pirates, he was wearing Hough's No. 49.

Make that Hough's 49, Tom Candiotti's 49 and Hoyt Wilhelm's 49. "When I first got to the big leagues with the Pirates," explained Wakefield, a Red Sox pitcher for more than a decade, "I wanted to wear 49 in honor of Charlie Hough and Tom Candiotti. I worked with Charlie Hough that spring before I got called up to the big leagues, so I wanted to keep the (knuckleballers) fraternity thing with the number going."

Wilhelm, who pitched 21 major league seasons, wore 49 for his first five (1952-56) with the New York Giants. Candiotti wore it throughout a 16-year career with five teams and Hough kept it for 25 years in a career that took him to four cities. Through 2005, Wakefield had posted 144 wins, all but 14 with the Boston Red Sox.

Like Hough, Wakefield was a minor league infielder who fooled around with the knuckleball and soon discovered that it was his ticket to the majors. But why did all these guys wear 49? Some suspect it's symbolic of the speed with which the fluttering, darting and dipping pitch gets to the plate.

Wakefield

50

DAVID ROBINSON

There are Twin Towers in basketball. And then there are TWIN TOWERS. Ralph Sampson, a 7-4 skyscraper, was a member of the former; the 7-1 Admiral was part of the latter. Which is something of an irony because Sampson, the fomer Virginia center who was drafted in 1983 by the NBA's Houston Rockets, was Robinson's favorite player, the reason he chose No. 50 at the U.S. Naval Academy and later with the San Antonio Spurs. But whereas Sampson's career gradually fizzled after working in tandem with 7-0 Hakeem Olajuwon for four seasons, Robinson was paired late in his outstanding 14-year career with 7-0 Tim Duncan—and the Spurs won two NBA championships with those two giants as teammates. It seemed only fitting in 1996 when No. 50 was named one of the 50 best NBA players of all-time and a member of the league's 50th Anniversary All-Time Team.

Elite 50s

JAMIE MOYER: The ultimate crafty, soft-throwing lefthander has survived 19 seasons and carved out 205 big-league wins through 2005—139 since converting to No. 50 with the Red Sox and Mariners.

J.R. RICHARD: Fate saved N.L. hitters from Houston's big No. 50. Richard, poised to join baseball's elite strikeout fraternity, was felled by a stroke in 1980 and ended his 10-year career with 107 wins and 1,493 Ks.

MIKE SINGLETARY: Those eyes—intense, focused, never-blinking—provided an uneasy sense that one of the game's outstanding middle linebackers was ready to strike again for the Bears.

GOOSE TATUM: This early "Clown Prince" developed many of the comedy routines the Harlem Globetrotters still use today.

FAST FACTS

F *Dick Butkus*, who made 51 the most-feared number in the NFL from 1965-73, actually wore No. 50 in his All-American career at Illinois.

F Two Hawaiian-born players, pitcher *Sid Fernandez* (1983-97) and outfielder *Benny Agbayani* (1998-2002), wore 50 because they were from the "50th state." There was, however, a twist to Agbayani's 50 devotion. He reportedly was a big fan of the 1970s television show *Hawaii Five-O.*

F In 1998, New York Yankees bench coach *Don Zimmer* celebrated his 50th season in baseball by switching to uniform No. 50. The team rewarded him with a World Series ring.

NOTABLE 50s MIKE TIMLIN 50 BRYANT REEVES 50 TOM HENKE 50 COREY MAGGETTE 50 REBECCA LOBO 50

DICK BUTKUS

Mel Rogers. Doug Becker. Bruce Herron. Kelvin Atkins. Mark Rodenhauser. Jim Morrissey. It's enough to make you growl, spit, scowl and deliver a hard forearm to the jaw of anybody who looks cross-eyed at you. How, in the name of Dick Butkus, could any Chicago Bears player dare to wear jersey No. 51, which is soaked in the legend of the greatest middle linebacker in NFL history? All six of the aforementioned players did in the 20-year span from Butkus' retirement to 1994, when his number was officially retired—finally. Why the delay? Team officials blamed it on a numbers game: The Bears already had retired more numbers than any other NFL team and were afraid there wouldn't be enough left for current players. To which Butkus growled, "They only play with 45 players, and they have 100 numbers."

FAST FACTS

F Linebacker *Bryan Cox* played 12 NFL seasons for five teams. In 10 of those seasons, he wore No. 51 and his teams posted records of .500 or better. In the other two, he wore 52 and his teams had losing marks. Cox wore 52 in 1996 and '97 for the Bears because 51 had been retired for Dick Butkus.

F In the 1990 Daytona 500, *Bobby Hamilton* drove the first 41 laps in a Mello Yello No. 51 movie car as the stunt double for actor Tom Cruise, who played driver Cole Trickle in the NASCAR-themed movie *Days of Thunder*. Hamilton drove near the back of the pack so that footage could be shot for the film.

F In the long history of the St. Louis Cardinals, only one player wore 51 before *Willie McGee* claimed it as his signature number in 1982. Neil Fiala wore it for three games in 1981.

Elite 51s

RANDY CROSS: Joe Montana's center set the bar high with three Pro Bowl appearances and three Super Bowl rings. He'll have trouble matching that success as a broadcaster.

TREVOR HOFFMAN: The Padres' closing statement: Turn out the lights, pack up and go home—the game is over.

RANDY JOHNSON: Facing the Big Unit is as nasty as it gets—even when he's wearing that pinstriped No. 41.

ICHIRO SUZUKI: Ichiro knows at least three English words: hit, hit, hit.

BERNIE WILLIAMS: This speedy switch-hitting, power-hitting center fielder was a key cog in the Yankees' winning machine of the 1990s and 2000s.

NOTABLE 51s SAM MILLS 51 JIM LYNCH 51 TERRY FORSTER 51 BRODERICK THOMAS 51 MICHAEL DOLEAC

52

RAY LEWIS

No. 52 is to the current NFL what No. 56 was to the 1980s. When Baltimore interior linebacker Lewis steps on the field to play defense, the eyes of every man, woman and child focus on the chiseled form of a football machine. "When you go into a game against (the Ravens), the first thing you look at for the game plan is where Ray Lewis is and how to block him," said Pittsburgh coach Bill Cowher. Much the same as former New York Giants linebacker Lawrence Taylor, Lewis, a Super Bowl MVP and seven-time Pro Bowl selection, plays with a driving passion and intensity that demand constant attention. And like Taylor, there's always that disturbing off-field baggage. But the bottom line is Lewis' magnetic game presence—anybody who takes his eyes off No. 52 probably will regret it.

Elite 52s

ADAM FOOTE: Big Foote left a big imprint in his 13 seasons in Quebec and Colorado. Patrick Roy got a lot of credit for the Avs' Cup crusade, but Foote anchored a defense that kept the heat off him.

MIKE WEBSTER: The ultimate blue-collar workhorse for four Pittsburgh Super Bowl champions. The nine-time Pro Bowl center played in 177 consecutive games in his 17-year career.

BUCK WILLIAMS: How does somebody 6-8 average double digits in rebounds over a 17-year career in the 1980s and '90s? Discipline, technique and lots of hard work.

FAST FACTS

F Outfielder *Chin-feng Chen*, who became the first Taiwan-born player to reach the major leagues when called up by the Los Angeles Dodgers in 2002, wore No. 52 in 2004 and '05 stints with Las Vegas of the Pacific Coast League. In other words, he was 52 for a team called the 51s.

F No St. Louis Cardinals player wore No. 52 before pitcher *Rheal Cormier*, who wore it from 1991-94 before switching to 34.

F Linebacker *Pepper Johnson*, denied his familiar No. 52 when signed by Detroit in 1996 because it belonged to *Scott Kowalkowski*, played that season wearing 99.

NOTABLE 52s C.C. SABATHIA **52** ROBERT BRAZILE **52** HAPPY HAIRSTON **52** MIKE BODDICKER **52** JOSE CONTRERAS

DON DRYSDALE

I t's a hard, in-your-face number. Youngsters begged their coaches for it in the 1950s and '60s so they could pitch nasty and mean, just like Double D. The number bleeds Dodger blue. It is tough, intense and unrelenting, not unlike a 95-mph fastball under the chin. Drysdale's "make-my-day" attitude provided the perfect righty complement to lefthander and fellow intimidator Sandy Koufax from 1959-65 when Nos. 53 and 32 led the Dodgers to three World Series championships. The number has its soft side, too. Millions of movie viewers have noted that 53 is the number that adorned Herbie the Love Bug in all five flicks about the adventurous Volkswagen Beetle. Why 53? Because Bill Walsh, the producer of the 1969 original, *The Love Bug*, was a Don Drysdale and Los Angeles Dodgers fan.

Elite 53s

HARRY CARSON: This Hall of Fame linebacker was a Giant, from beginning to end, and carried the team until Bill Parcells and Lawrence Taylor helped him deliver a Super Bowl championship.

ARTIS GILMORE: An ABA icon and NBA intimidator. Gilmore's name often is missing in discussions of basketball big men, but big No. 53 was a warrior.

RANDY GRADISHAR: From 1974-83, the path to the Broncos' end zone passed through the fiercest, angriest and most talented middle linebacker west of the Mississippi.

BILL ROMANOWSKI: This controversial, boundary-testing linebacker was a key member of four Super Bowl champs.

MICK TINGELHOFF: This career-long Viking, the NFL's best center pre-Mike Webster, is still waiting for his Hall of Fame invitation.

FAST FACTS

Rookie free-agent linebacker **Bobby Abrams** wore No. 53 in the 1990 New York Giants training camp, but switched to 51 before the season. "I didn't want to be known as the guy wearing **Harry Carson's** number," he explained.

Goaltender **Nikolai Khabibulin**, who wore 35 in earlier career stops at Phoenix and Tampa Bay, reversed the digits (53) when he signed in 2005 with Chicago. The Blackhawks have retired 35 in honor of **Tony Esposito**.

Former Cardinals pitcher (1986-90) **Greg Mathews** wore No. 53 because he was a big Walt Disney fan and identified with Herbie the Love Bug, another 53. "We're both used to getting out of a lot of tough jams," he said.

NOTABLE 53s JEFF BOSTIC 53 MARK EATON 53 BOBBY ABREU 53 DARRYL DAWKINS 53 HUGH DOUGLAS 53

54

GOOSE GOSSAGE

OK,

Hall of Fame defensive tackle Randy White can make a legitimate claim to this working-class number. But let's be honest. The lasting image of 54 is the round-faced, body-contorting, ever-menacing Goose,

flailing around near the pitching mound after unleashing another 98-mph heater for the New York Yankees and eight other teams over a 22-year major league career. The guy was big, fun and colorful. And he was borderline superstitious. "I just loved that number," he said, equating its magic to his football mentality. There also was pride over Gossage's ability to take a number usually associated with baseball wannabes and give it status befitting one of the game's all-time best closers. It was enough to make your Fu Manchu twitch.

FAST FACTS

F Two Dallas Cowboys who played different positions and never stepped on the field at the same time won Super Bowl MVP awards wearing the same No. 54: linebacker **Chuck Howley** in Super Bowl 5 and defensive tackle **Randy White** (co-MVP with teammate Harvey Martin) in Super Bowl 12.

F When the Orlando Magic courted forward **Horace Grant** before signing him in 1994, the Magic rented two limousines and Michael Eisner's suite at Disney World. One limo dropped Magic center **Shaquille O'Neal** off at the hotel. The other brought Grant,

NOTABLE 54s CHRIS SPIELMAN 54 BRAD LIDGE 54 CHUCK HOWLEY 54 E.J. JUNIOR 54 MIKE MacDOUGAL 54 FRED

Elite 54s

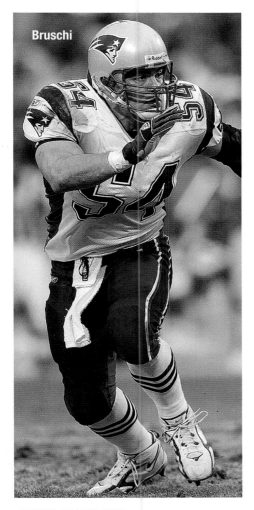

Bruschi

TEDY BRUSCHI: He was a crucial part of New England's three Super Bowl titles in four years—like the heart is a crucial part of the human body.

HORACE GRANT: Forget the goggles and think about the three rings he earned as a frontcourt warrior for the Michael

Jordan-era Bulls.

LUCIOUS JACKSON: Big Luke worked in the trenches for one of the great NBA teams of all time—the 1966-67 76ers featuring Wilt Chamberlain, Billy Cunningham, Hal Greer and Wali Jones.

MARQUES JOHNSON: This ultra-smooth No. 54 was the driving force behind UCLA's 1975 NCAA basketball championship—the Bruins' last until 1995.

ZACH THOMAS: When drawing up an offensive game plan against the Dolphins, be sure to account for linebacker Thomas.

BRIAN URLACHER: From super popular to controversial, ultra-linebacker Urlacher remains the middle man of Chicago's football universe.

RANDY WHITE: This Doomsday Cowboy was strong, super quick and intense. Few defensive tackles could destroy blockers and game plans with more impunity than White, who missed one game in 14 seasons and earned nine Pro Bowl invitations.

Mazzone

who opened the door to the suite and found O'Neal there holding Grant's No. 54 Magic jersey.

Ⓕ Quarterbacks and other skill-position players usually dominate jersey sales, but NFLshop.com reported that Bears middle linebacker *Brian Urlacher*'s No. 54 was the leagues top seller nationally from April 2001 through March 2002.

NEW TEAM, BUT SAME NUMBER AND WISDOM

Typically, *Leo Mazzone* is visible only when trouble is brewing. He pops out of the dugout, saunters to the mound for a brief conference with the pitcher and returns to the bench, having imparted his calming words of wisdom. Mazzone has perfected this routine, which became a vital element of his job description when Bobby Cox took over the Braves' managerial reins in 1990 and turned his pitching staff over to No. 54. Like Cox, Mazzone had become an Atlanta institution.

Or so Braves fans thought. Things suddenly changed after the 2005 season when Mazzone signed on as pitching coach of the Orioles under manager Sam Perlozzo, a longtime friend. As in Atlanta, Mazzone is teaching, molding a young staff and imparting wisdom. And he's still wearing 54.

Over the last decade and a half, Mazzone has built a reputation as perhaps one of the best pitching coaches ever. Pitching was the backbone of Braves teams that won 14 division championships (and one World Series) from 1991-2005, missing only in 1994 when a strike ended the season prematurely. Atlanta's Greg Maddux (three), Tom Glavine (two) and John Smoltz (one) won six Cy Young Awards during that span, and Mazzone's staffs finished either first or second in ERA among all major league teams every season from 1992 through 2002.

Mazzone's results—starting in the Braves' minor league system in 1979—have been amazing. Considering Baltimore's struggles in recent years, the Orioles are hoping his mastery continues.

Urlacher

55
OREL HERSHISER

So how does a football number worn by such bangers as Lee Roy Jordan and Junior Seau become a baseball institution? Spite. Hershiser, a pitching long shot when he was called up by the Los Angeles Dodgers in 1983, was assigned 55 because "they didn't think I was going to make the club." He did, and soon the Dodgers offered to lower his number. Hershiser declined, choosing to rock with the digits that got him to the dance. Hershiser and his 55 were front and center during a magical 1988 season in which the righthander won 23 games, set a big-league record with 59 consecutive scoreless innings, won the Cy Young Award and captured MVP honors in the World Series. Hershiser, who spent 13 of his 18 seasons with the Dodgers, grew fond of a number that adorned his wife's jewelry, a swimming pool, various pieces of engraved glass and some crystal. Hershiser reportedly even built a room in his house shaped like the number 55.

FAST FACTS

F Two numbers have been "unretired" at the University of Florida. When 1966 Heisman Trophy winner **Steve Spurrier** took over as Florida coach in 1990, he pulled his own No. 11 out of retirement and also asked former linebacker Scot Brantley to do the same with his 55. Brantley agreed.

F **Bob Grim**, the last American League rookie to win 20 games, wore No. 55 when he fashioned a 20-6 record for the 1954 Yankees.

NOTABLE 55s **KEITH PRIMEAU** 55 **E.J. HOLUB** 55 **CHRIS HANBURGER** 55 **MAXIE BAUGHAN** 55 **ERIC DAZE** 55 **DOUG**

Elite 55s

DERRICK BROOKS: Florida State churns out great linebackers like Wisconsin churns out cheese, but Tampa Bay's Brooks is a cut above the rest.

LEE ROY JORDAN: From 1963-76, the speed of this middle linebacker helped Dallas bring about Doomsday for opponents.

WILLIE McGINEST: Put him on the edge, drop him into coverage, it doesn't matter—McGinest produces big plays when they are needed the most.

DIKEMBE MUTOMBO: If you don't like the finger wagging in your face, don't bring the ball into the lane against Mr. Mutombo. Or at least don't let him block your shot.

JUNIOR SEAU: His last name is fitting because ballcarriers usually "say ow" when this linebacker hits them.

Mutombo

Thomas

F *Derrick Thomas*, unable to get his Alabama No. 55 when he joined the Chiefs in 1989, opted for 58 in honor of then Washington Redskins linebacker Wilber Marshall.

GODZILLA IS A BIG HIT IN JAPAN, NEW YORK

In his first spring training with the Yomiuri Giants in 1993, *Hideki Matsui* chose No. 55 as a tribute to the single-season Japanese home run record set by former Giants great Sadaharu Oh. Ten years and 332 homers later, Matsui chose 55 again, this time as a member of the New York Yankees.

It wasn't the money—a $21 million contract—that prompted Japan's "Godzilla" to come to the U.S. It was the opportunity to test his talents against such major league stars as Barry Bonds and Alex Rodriguez. By adapting to a new culture and facing pitchers he had never seen, Matsui clearly was risking his baseball reputation.

Matsui's signing and New York arrival was greeted by fanfare. Before his first big-league game, he had exchanged quips with David Letterman, answered questions at multiple new conferences and voiced no illusions of becoming the next Babe Ruth and Joe DiMaggio, who, by the way, wore only one 5. His autograph was immediately a collectible, and replica 55 jerseys were flying off the shelf, both in New York and Japan. Could he sustain the marketing frenzy?

Yes and no. In his first three Yankee seasons, left fielder Matsui averaged 23 home runs and 110 RBIs for teams that won three straight East Division titles and played in one World Series. Godzilla did not power his way to the top of the Empire State Building, but he did cement his status as one of the game's top players—anywhere.

Matsui

56
LAWRENCE TAYLOR

It's a stone-cold, no-debate number. LT wore it and you can stop right there. Since 1981, 56 has been the alter ego of the biggest, baddest, angriest linebacker ever to play professional football.

New York Giants fans might remember pre-1981, when the number belonged to center Jim Clack for three seasons. Taylor, 98 during his college days at North Carolina, needed a number in the 50s and latched onto 56 when Clack retired just before his rookie campaign. But the popular Clack came out of retirement in '81 to help an injury-decimated offensive line, and several prominent Giants veterans told Taylor he should return 56 to Clack. But as *Newsday*'s George Willis reported in 1994, Giants general manager George Young thought differently. Young told the veterans Taylor not only would remain 56, he would "take that number to the Hall of Fame." Problem solved. Clack wore 58 for the rest of the season and retired for good.

FAST FACTS

F A much-heralded rookie outfielder in 2003, Tampa Bay's *Rocco Baldelli* wore No. 56 in spring training. After securing a spot on the opening-day roster, Baldelli switched to 5 for the regular season. Put together the pieces: Italian heritage, 56, 5 and a team owner, Vince Naimoli, who idolized Joe DiMaggio. Could this be a giant coincidence? Baldelli says yes, but logic says higher sources might have been choreographing this kid's future.

Baldelli

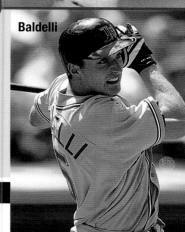

NOTABLE 56s MARK BUEHRLE 56 DANTE LAVELLI 56 JOHN OFFERDAHL 56 HARDY NICKERSON

Elite 56s

CHRIS DOLEMAN: Considering how he plundered offensive lines for sacks and Pro Bowl votes, he was born to be a Viking.

BILL HEWITT: Bears fans always will remember this Hall of Famer as the helmetless end who flipped the game-deciding lateral in the 1933 NFL championship game.

JOE SCHMIDT: He wasn't the NFL's first middle linebacker, but he might have been its first great middle linebacker. Schmidt was a big factor in two of the three NFL titles won by the Lions in the 1950s.

PAT SWILLING: How do you turn around a losing franchise? For the Saints, it meant building a linebacker corps around a guy like Swilling, the NFL's 1991 Defensive Player of the Year.

DARRYL TALLEY: He played his entire career in the shadow of such teammates as Bruce Smith, Thurman Thomas and Jim Kelly, but who ranks as the Bills' career leader in tackles? Yes, Talley.

Zubov

SERGEI ZUBOV: When trying to smooth the transition from Soviet stud to Dallas Star, a Stanley Cup title or two is a pretty good start.

SON'S PLEA OPENS DOOR FOR BOUTON'S RETURN

In 1998, almost three decades after writing his controversial book *Ball Four*, **Jim Bouton** still was persona non grata at Yankee Stadium. Then, unbelievably, he received a phone call inviting him to Old-Timers Day festivities at the stadium.

Bouton, a 21-game winner for the Yankees in 1963, had his son to thank for the Yankees' about-face. Michael Bouton, 34, wrote a heartfelt letter to *The New York Times*, pleading for Yankees boss George Steinbrenner to reconsider the long-standing ban.

"Today is Father's Day," the letter began, "but the date I have circled on my calendar is July 25. That is Old-Timers Day at Yankee Stadium. Traditionally, it is the day when past Yankee stars take their annual curtain call. It is the day when my father, Jim Bouton, No. 56, the Bulldog, is snubbed, and not invited back. Although I know an invitation to attend Old-Timers Day is an honor he can live without, it is what I wish for him this year."

Michael went on to tell about an automobile crash that took the life of his sister, Laurie, the previous August. "I see this as an opportunity to get my father some extra hugs at a time of his life when he could use all the hugs he can get," Michael wrote. "I am not asking for any favors, just reconsideration. ..."

Steinbrenner, indeed, reconsidered, and Bouton's uniform No. 56 was awaiting him when he returned to Yankee Stadium. The 59-year-old prodigal son received a burst of cheers when introduced to the appreciative New York crowd.

Bouton

Bragg

F Well-traveled outfielder *Darren Bragg* has worn No. 56 at several of his stops "because Lawrence Taylor was my favorite professional athlete." Bragg made it a special point to wear 56 in his short 2001 stay with the New York Mets.

F Lawrence Taylor comparisons are not lost on Washington linebacker *LaVar Arrington*, who wears 56 because it puts "a lot of pressure on me, forces me to play with a lot more urgency."

F Detroit middle linebacker *Joe Schmidt*'s 56 jersey was retired for almost three decades before he gave his permission to reactivate it in 1993 for veteran linebacker *Pat Swilling*.

---

56 ANDRE TIPPETT **56** JERRY ROBINSON **56** JEFF LAGEMAN **56** RAY MANSFIELD **56** DINO HACKETT **56** AL WILSON

57
DWIGHT STEPHENSON

It's fair to say that "57" does not offer much variety in the sports numbers jigsaw puzzle. So thank goodness for Dwight Stephenson, an honest-to-god Hall of Famer and mover of mountains—the human variety. Big Dwight, No. 57 in the middle of Miami's offensive line for eight years in the 1980s, was called by his former college coach, Alabama's Bear Bryant, "the greatest center I've ever coached." Dolphins coach Don Shula felt likewise, and numerous opponents willingly testify to his greatness. Film probably still exists showing Miami's 57, both forearms extended, leveling two blitzing New England Patriots at the same time. It's also a testament to Stephenson's greatness that he was elected to the Pro Football Hall of Fame, even after his career was cut short by a serious knee injury.

Elite 57s

TOM JACKSON: Size didn't matter for this undersized, mean and hard-hitting linebacker, who helped the Broncos crush their way to two Super Bowl appearances.

CLAY MATTHEWS: For 16 of his 19 NFL seasons, this talented linebacker delivered big hits and big plays for Cleveland while enduring the agony of The Drive, The Fumble and other frustrating setbacks.

STEVE NELSON: He never got to celebrate a Boston championship, but this linebacker anchored the New England defense like a true Patriot from 1974-87.

JOHAN SANTANA: The changeup can be mightier than the breaking ball. For proof positive, just watch this talented Twins lefthander.

FAST FACTS

Cincinnati lefthander *Johnny Vander Meer* was wearing 57 in 1938 when he fired back-to-back no-hitters—the only one of 13 major league seasons he wore that number.

It took nine NHL seasons, but right wing *Steve Heinze* finally got what he wanted. In 2000-01, when chosen by the Columbus Blue Jackets in the NHL Expansion Draft, he switched to uniform No. 57—thus becoming "Heinze 57."

After pitcher *Darryl Kile* died in a Chicago hotel room in June 2002, his initials and No. 57 became the emotional impetus and inspiration for a Cardinals team that went on to post 97 wins and advance to the NLCS before losing to the Giants.

NOTABLE 57s RICKEY JACKSON 57 MIKE MERRIWEATHER 57 LAMAR LATHON 57 FRANCISCO RODRIGUEZ 57

58

JACK LAMBERT

Maybe you remember that toothless snarl … or the maniacal frenzy … or the leering eyes … or the viciousness with which Lambert attacked offenses as the centerpiece middle linebacker for Pittsburgh's Steel Curtain defense in the 1970s and '80s. If you do, more than a quarter century after the Steelers' four Super Bowl titles in a six-year stretch, then you've made the case for his pick as the best all-time No. 58 over Kansas City Chiefs pass-rushing genius Derrick Thomas. Jack the Ripper, to put it simply, was memorable. His facial contortions, missing teeth and intimidating glare made him one of the most recognizable defensive players in NFL history. His chilling intensity made him one of the most feared. And Steelers fans loved him for it. More than 10 years after his retirement in 1984, Lambert's 58 remained Pittsburgh's best-selling replica jersey.

Elite 58s

PETER BOULWARE: He might not dominate games sideline-to-sideline like Ravens teammate Ray Lewis, but he can get to the quarterback when he's healthy.

WILBER MARSHALL: Mike Ditka, his former coach, called him the best outside linebacker in football. Marshall's quick feet paid off both on the field and in Da Bears' "Super Bowl Shuffle."

DERRICK THOMAS: A quarterback's worst nightmare on third and long, he played linebacker for the Chiefs from 1989-99.

JESSIE TUGGLE: This Hammer dropped more often on ballcarriers than any other in Falcons history.

FAST FACTS

F When utility infielder **Dave Berg** joined the Marlins in 1998, he blanched when issued uniform No. 58. "The only thing it's missing is the word 'Batboy' above it," he said.

F Before he was No. 45, St. Louis righthander **Bob Gibson** was 58. That's the number he wore as a 1959 rookie, when he compiled a 3-5 record in 13 games.

F Linebacker **Shane Conlan,** who wore 58 from 1987-92 with Buffalo, had to switch to 56 from 1993-95 with the Rams because 58 already was taken by linebacker **Roman Phifer.**

NOTABLE 58s MIKE STRATTON 58 WALLY HILGENBERG 58 KIM BOKAMPER 58 DEWEY SELMON 58 CARL BANKS

59

JACK HAM

As the "other Jack" in Pittsburgh's famed Steel Curtain defense of the 1970s, Ham must have questioned his sanity. Not the lack of it; the overabundance in relation to his nine-year partner and havoc-wreaker at linebacker.

While Jack Lambert was snarling, sneering and intimidating in the middle, Ham was plotting, strategizing and making plays on the outside. Nos. 58 and 59 in your program; possibly the best linebacker tandem in football history. Pittsburgh's Jack-o-meter suggests fans celebrated and were motivated by Lambert's venom-spitting intensity, but they appreciated and valued Ham's discipline and steadying influence. They also appreciated and valued the four Super Bowl championships this Jekyll-and-Hyde duo helped the Steelers capture from the 1974 season through the 1979 campaign.

FAST FACTS

Horace Gillom, the NFL's first black punter and a two-time league leader in punting average for the Cleveland Browns, wore No. 59 from 1947-51 before the league's new numbering system prompted a switch to 84.

Linebacker **London Fletcher**, who completed his fourth season with Buffalo in 2005, already ranks as the best Bills player to wear 59. His competition: **Bob Lettner**, **Paul Guidry**, **Doug Allen**,

Fletcher

NOTABLE 59s TODD JONES 59 BOB BRUDZINSKI 59 BRIAN WILLIAMS 59 JOHN GRIMSLEY 59 DERRICK

Elite 59s

GREAT POTATO CAPER HAS HAPPY ENDING

He was an anonymous backup catcher with strictly minor league talent. But fans in Williamsport, Pa., will never forget *Dave Bresnahan*. The "great potato caper" he pulled off in a 1987 Class AA Eastern League game, his final as a professional, will live in baseball lore.

On August 31, a Reading runner advanced to third in the fifth inning and Bresnahan went into action. Feigning a problem with his mitt, he went to the dugout, retrieved a peeled potato and returned with it hidden in his glove. As the next pitch came homeward, Bresnahan switched the ball-shaped potato to his right hand, caught the pitch and fired the potato high over the third baseman's head.

The runner headed home, only to find Bresnahan waiting with the ball. The umpire was not amused and called the runner safe. Bresnahan's manager, Orlando Gomez, immediately fined him $50. And the parent Cleveland Indians, when informed of the prank, branded Bresnahan's act "unprofessional" and released him.

The story quickly drew national attention, and Bresnahan's prominence grew locally. Williamsport team officials, always looking for a good public relations opportunity, invited Bresnahan back for a promotion. Fans carrying a potato got in for $1, and Bresnahan paid his fine with a sack of potatoes.

In 1988, the Bills retired Bresnahan's No. 59 jersey. "He's probably the only .149 hitter in baseball ever to have his jersey retired," said Ken Weingartner, a team spokesman.

Twice. On the 10-year anniversary of the potato ruse, the Williamsport club retired Bresnahan's No. 59 again.

Shane Nelson, *Joey Lumpkin*, *Stan David*, *Steve Maidlow*, *Mitch Frerotte*, *Don Graham* and *Sam Rogers*.

F *Cato June*, who tumbled a long way numerically from the 2 he wore as a free safety at Michigan, is giving new meaning to the 59 he now wears as a linebacker for the Indianapolis Colts.

Edwards

June

MATT BLAIR: This Vikings' special-teams kamikaze (1974-85) was so proficient at blocking kicks that the NFL outlawed his running-start technique. But Blair wasn't just a kick-blocking specialist—he also was a great all-around linebacker who intimidated anyone who lined up across from him.

DONNIE EDWARDS: Some players and coaches are just meant to be together. Edwards has always been at his best playing for Marty Schottenheimer, whether for the Chiefs or the Chargers.

SETH JOYNER: Overshadowed in the early 1990s by such players as Reggie White, Jerome Brown and Clyde Simmons on Philadelphia's "Gang Green Defense," linebacker Joyner never received the recognition he deserved. But he did get plenty of playoff disappointment.

CHARLIE WEAVER: This linebacker and second-round draft pick anchored Detroit's front seven from 1971-81.

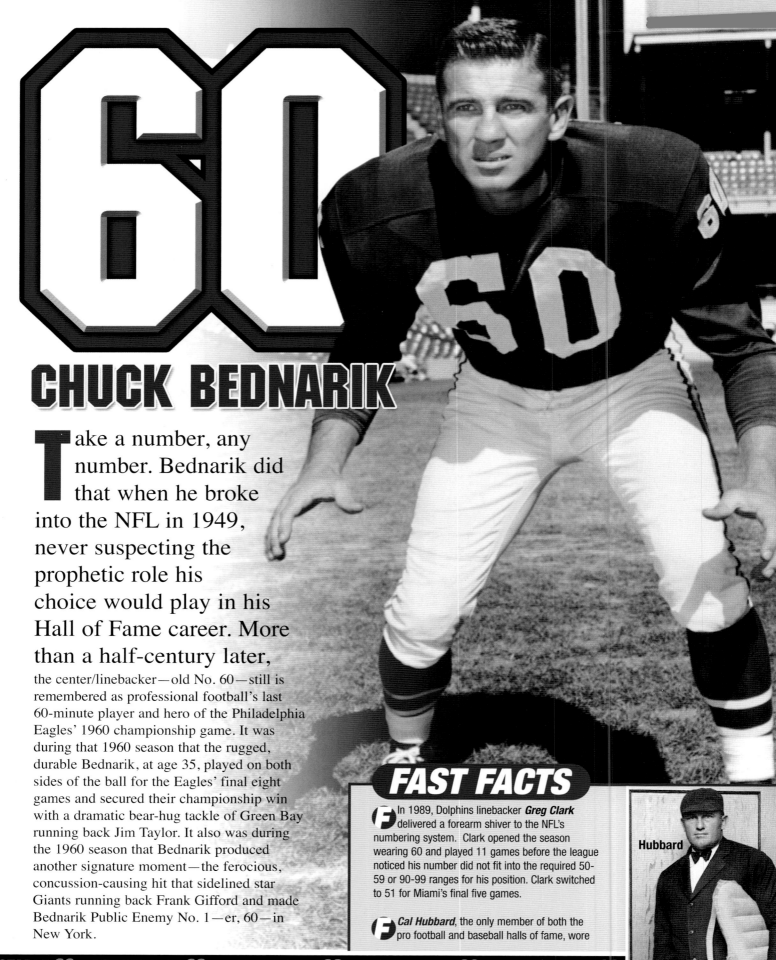

60

CHUCK BEDNARIK

Take a number, any number. Bednarik did that when he broke into the NFL in 1949, never suspecting the prophetic role his choice would play in his Hall of Fame career. More than a half-century later, the center/linebacker—old No. 60—still is remembered as professional football's last 60-minute player and hero of the Philadelphia Eagles' 1960 championship game. It was during that 1960 season that the rugged, durable Bednarik, at age 35, played on both sides of the ball for the Eagles' final eight games and secured their championship win with a dramatic bear-hug tackle of Green Bay running back Jim Taylor. It also was during the 1960 season that Bednarik produced another signature moment—the ferocious, concussion-causing hit that sidelined star Giants running back Frank Gifford and made Bednarik Public Enemy No. 1—er, 60—in New York.

FAST FACTS

F In 1989, Dolphins linebacker *Greg Clark* delivered a forearm shiver to the NFL's numbering system. Clark opened the season wearing 60 and played 11 games before the league noticed his number did not fit into the required 50-59 or 90-99 ranges for his position. Clark switched to 51 for Miami's final five games.

F *Cal Hubbard*, the only member of both the pro football and baseball halls of fame, wore

Hubbard

Elite 60s

TOMMY NOBIS: First he brought prominence to the number as a middle linebacker for Texas' 1963 national championship team. Then he locked it into Atlanta football lore during 11 outstanding seasons with the NFL's lowly Falcons. How can the Hall of Fame keep passing him by?

OTIS SISTRUNK: He bypassed college and attended the University of Mars. In other words, big Otis did it the hard way and then made life equally hard on NFL offensive linemen from 1972-79. Only the Raiders could have unearthed this dominant tackle.

JOSE THEODORE: This Patrick Roy clone floated like a butterfly in net for Montreal before moving on to Colorado.

EMOTION OF 1991 STILL LINGERS IN DETROIT

In Detroit's long football history, no season triggers a more emotional response than 1991.

Through a November 10 loss at Tampa Bay, it was just another season. The Lions were 6-4, having lost two consecutive games, and playoff hopes were fading. Then, in a November 17 game against the Los Angeles Rams at the Pontiac Silverdome, disappointment turned to shock.

Guard *Mike Utley*, falling while trying to block a defender, snapped his neck on the artificial turf and was paralyzed. Utley, who would be confined to a wheelchair the rest of his life, gave a thumbs-up signal to his teammates as he was carried off the field—a show of courage that inspired the Lions for the remainder of the season.

Wearing No. 60 on their helmets in tribute to their fallen comrade, the Lions won that game and their last five, finishing 12-4. Their emotional run ended with a 41-10 loss to Washington in the NFC championship game—but the grief continued in a stunning offseason.

First, assistant coach Len Fontes died of a heart attack. Then guard Eric Andolsek was killed when a runaway truck ran over him as he worked in the yard at his Louisiana home.

Out of respect for the players, the numbers 60 and 65 were not issued for the next seven seasons. Defensive end Paul Spicer became the first player to wear Utley's 60 in 1999, and guard Kerlin Blaise took Andolsek's 65 the same season.

Theodore

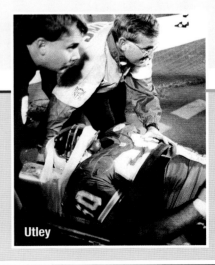

Utley

No. 60 in 1936 when he played offensive and defensive tackle for the New York Giants. It was one of eight numbers Hubbard wore in his three-team NFL career. Later, he was a standout umpire in baseball's American League.

F The number 60, thanks to such linebacking greats as *John Treadwell, Tommy Nobis, Britt Hager and Brian Jones*, is revered at Texas. Top linebackers occasionally will wear it for a special occasion, like in 2004 when *Derrick Johnson* discarded his normal 11 to wear 60 in his final home game.

SCOTT SCHOENEWEIS *60* LARRY GRANTHAM *60* CHRIS SAMUELS *60* DAN ALEXANDER *60* MATT HERKENHOFF *60*

61

BILL GEORGE

All right, he was only the warmup act in Chicago for Dick Butkus. But you have to give George the benefit of historical perspective. He was pro football's first true middle linebacker, the innovative middle guard who dared to stand up, take a step back and draw up a position blueprint for future generations. The Bears' No. 61 did not snarl and snort with Butkus-like intensity. But he prepared meticulously for every game, called defensive signals and used his explosive quickness to diagnose and shut down plays. He was the anti-Butkus who preferred brains over brawn, the defensive captain of George Halas' 1963 championship team. Ironically, George's 14th and final season with the Bears was 1965, the same year a rookie named Butkus began turning heads—both figuratively and literally—in Chicago's training camp.

Elite 61s

CURLEY CULP: The Chiefs of the late 1960s and early '70s had three terrific linebackers in Bobby Bell, Willie Lanier and Jim Lynch. But without Culp in the middle of the defensive line, that trio wouldn't have had room to roam.

LIVAN HERNANDEZ: It's hard to find a more savvy pitcher than Hernandez, who can hit, too.

NATE NEWTON: Large enough to have eaten a horse, it seems only fitting that Newton opened holes big enough for Emmitt Smith to gallop through.

JESSE SAPOLU: A rock in San Francisco's offensive line for 15 seasons, Sapolu kept Joe Montana and Steve Young healthy—and won four Super Bowl rings because of it.

FAST FACTS

F When young Florida righthander **Josh Beckett** wore uniform No. 61 in 2001, '02 and part of '03, everyone thought it was in honor of former Marlins star **Livan Hernandez**. Not so. Beckett wanted 19 when he got to Miami, but it was taken by third baseman **Mike Lowell**. So he flipped 19 and got 61, which he later changed to 21.

F When 21-year-old lefthander **Jesse Orosco** made the Mets' roster out of spring training in 1979, it was so unexpected the club didn't have a uniform ready for the season-opening game at Wrigley Field. So Orosco wore No. 61—with no name on the back. Shortly thereafter, he was wearing "Orosco 47."

F Korean righthander **Chan Ho Park**, who wore 16 throughout his amateur career, took 61 when he signed with the Dodgers in 1994 because it was the reverse of organization pitching guru **Ron Perranoski**'s 16. "Every time I see my reflection in the mirror," Park said, "it's still 16."

NOTABLE 61s *TIM GRUNHARD 61 CORY STILLMAN 61 BRONSON ARROYO 61 BOB DeMARCO 61 BLAINE NYE 61*

62

CHARLEY TRIPPI

Pass. Run. Kick. Catch. Return. Defend. Versatility was high on No. 62's resume, which explains why Trippi was a college and professional football icon in a war-weary America. Forget those triple-threat stars of the old single-wing sets. Trippi was a sextuple-threat halfback and defensive back who sent shivers down the spines of admiring Georgia fans. No wonder! The Bulldogs were 31-3 in Trippi's three varsity seasons, and he was the star of their 1943 Rose Bowl win over UCLA. Then, after toying with professional baseball briefly—he hit .334 for Class AA Atlanta—Trippi signed pro football's first $100,000 contract in 1947 and immediately led the Chicago Cardinals to an NFL championship.No. 62 is one of four numbers retired by Georgia, which obviously is picky about its football heroes. Trippi also is a member of four halls of fame—pro football, college football, Rose Bowl and the state of Georgia.

FAST FACTS

F When the Sacramento Kings traded backup center **Scot Pollard** to Indiana before the 2003-04 season, he had to give up his No. 31—it already was taken by a guy named **Reggie Miller**. So the colorful Pollard took the unusual number 62—"31 times 2."

F If guard **Glenn Parker** doubted that his 12-year career was coming to an end in the summer of 2002 after being warned by the New York Giants they were going to cut him, the truth hit home when two young players wore his No. 62 in a minicamp. Parker was cut a week later.

F **Jim Parker**, Ohio State's first Outland Trophy winner in 1956 and a future Pro Football Hall of Famer, wore No. 62 in college, 77 as a professional.

Elite 62s

MARK BORTZ: From 1983-94, this guard opened holes for Walter Payton, protected Jim McMahon and performed valuable trench work for one of the greatest teams in NFL history.

JIM LANGER: The perfect center for the perfect team. Langer, a member of the Pro Football Hall of Fame, was the glue that held Miami's outstanding line together for 10 seasons.

DAN NEIL: From 1997-2004, Neil was part of a Denver Broncos offensive line that churned out a steady stream of 1,000-yard rushers.

NOTABLE 62s **ELLIS JOHNSON** 62 **JERRY FONTENOT** 62 **GUY McINTYRE** 62 **JEFF CHRISTY** 62 **ADAM TIMMERMAN**

63

WILLIE LANIER

Fans from Kansas City and Tampa can give you 63 good reasons why their man—Lanier or Lee Roy Selmon—should get the nod here, but they don't get to vote. So we're going for the 245-pound stud in the fire-engine red jersey with the big, white 63 front and back—a sleek look that gave Chiefs opponents the willies from 1967-77.

Lanier was the premier middle linebacker of the American Football League when he broke in, a quick, smart and fierce defensive quarterback who reached Butkus and Nitschke-like status after the AFL-NFL merger. The key for K.C.'s No. 63 is those two Super Bowls, the second of which produced one of the classic's biggest upsets. Selmon? Like Lanier, he's merely one of the best players ever to step on a football field.

FAST FACTS

Thurston

F Yes, William Shakespeare went to Notre Dame and wore No. 63 as a do-everything halfback and punter. In a battle of unbeaten juggernauts in 1935, "The Bard" wrote a dramatic script when he threw a game-deciding TD pass to *Wayne Millner* in an 18-13 comeback victory at Ohio State.

F Guard *Fuzzy Thurston*, who anchored the left guard position for Green Bay's powerful

NOTABLE *63s* **BILL MAAS** 63 **DICK STANFEL** 63 **FRANKIE ALBERT** 63 **DOUG WILKERSON** 63 **BRUNO BANDUCCI** 63

Elite 63s

SELMON A MAN OF MANY FIRSTS—AND TALENTS

His 63 is the most memorable number in franchise history, and *Lee Roy Selmon* holds Tampa Bay distinction for several other reasons: He was the first player drafted by the Buccaneers, the first to have his uniform number retired and the first to be enshrined at the Pro Football Hall of Fame.

For the first nine years of the Buccaneers' existence, Selmon was the face of the franchise. He was the No. 1 overall pick out of Oklahoma in 1976, a defensive end who lived up to his hype and delivered big-play performances even though he was the target of double- and triple-team blocks. Selmon was equally celebrated off the field, where he won over fans with his soft-spoken, gentlemanly demeanor and willingness to give back to the community.

In the same '76 draft that netted Lee Roy, the Bucs also grabbed older brother Dewey in the second round. The brothers played together on defense for five years and were part of the 1979 Tampa Bay team that shockingly won the NFC Central Division title and advanced to the NFC championship game before losing to the Los Angeles Rams.

Lee Roy, a 1975 consensus All-American who played for two national championship teams while wearing No. 93 at Oklahoma, played through 1984 before retiring because of a back injury. The only 63 in franchise history was elected to the Hall of Fame despite playing for a team that was 44-88-1 during his tenure.

Dawson

DERMONTTI DAWSON: Not only did he carry on the Steelers' legacy at center, his pulling ability redefined the way the position was played.

JAY HILGENBERG: How about a long snapper who turns into a seven-time Pro Bowler? Ditka and Da Bears discovered a gem.

ERNIE HOLMES: If Greene, Lambert and Ham were the Steel Curtain, this hard-working

defensive tackle was a curtain rod. A very strong curtain rod.

MIKE MUNCHAK: Defenders who shot for the Moon had to get past this Oilers bulldog, who played in nine Pro Bowls from 1982-93.

GENE UPSHAW: From 1968-81, the road to success ran through the left side of Oakland's line, where guard Upshaw and tackle Art Shell blew away defenders.

offensive line from 1959-67, wore uniform No. 63.

Ⓕ Hall of Fame lineman *Mike Michalske* wore nine numbers in his eight seasons with the Packers, from a low of 19 in 1932 to a high of 63 in 1934.

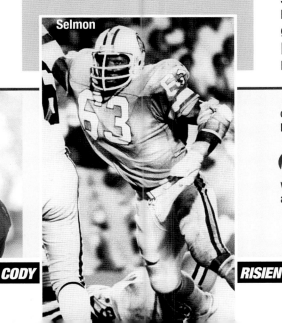

Selmon

Upshaw

CODY   RISIEN 63 ART SPINNEY 63 TOOTIE ROBBINS 63 MIKE BARNES 63 BARRET ROBBINS

64

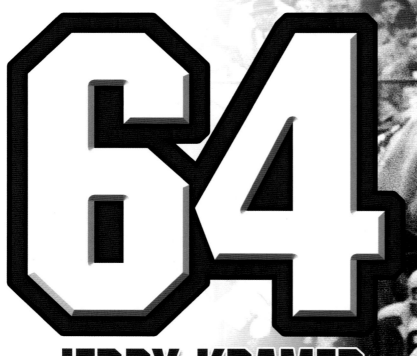

JERRY KRAMER

For years now, we've been watching big No. 64 throw one of the most memorable blocks in football history. Over and over and over, courtesy of NFL Films, we see Kramer clear a path for Green Bay quarterback Bart Starr's game-ending touchdown dive in the Packers' 1967 Ice Bowl championship victory over Dallas.

That signature moment aside, it's hard to think of Kramer without recalling him leading the vaunted Packers' sweep, a runaway truck pounding aside would-be tacklers with trauma-inflicting ease. For 11 seasons, he powered a running game that helped the Pack win five championships, prompting praise-challenged coach Vince Lombardi to declare him the greatest guard in the NFL. Given that endorsement and the Green Bay championship aura, it's no coincidence that the prestige number for offensive linemen in the 1960s and '70s was— you guessed it, 64.

FAST FACTS

Dwight Gooden was assigned No. 64 in 1984 spring training, but unexpectedly won a roster spot with the Mets. The 19-year-old righthander was reissued uniform 16 before opening day and went on to win 17 games in his rookie season.

Dismissed by Detroit's equipment manager with the words, "You're not going to be here very long anyway," linebacker **Joe Schmidt**, a seventh-round draft pick in 1953, was assigned No. 64 in his rookie

NOTABLE 64s   JIM RAY SMITH 64   DAVE WOHLABAUGH 64   ANDY HECK 64   ED NEWMAN 64   JIM BURT 64

Elite 64s

JEFF HARTINGS: He prepped in Detroit before replacing Dermontti Dawson in Pittsburgh. The Steelers' center legacy continues.

RANDALL McDANIEL: Put his name up there with the best offensive linemen of all-time. His 12 Pro Bowl invitations certainly convinced Vikings and Bucs fans.

DAVE WILCOX: They say this Pro Football Hall of Famer's hits could have been recorded on the Richter scale. Before San Francisco's Super Bowl run in the 1980s, this superb outside linebacker provided a blueprint for success.

Hartings

DEMANDING HACKSAW CUTS OFF TRADE TALKS

Athletes paying big money for uniform numbers is a recent phenomenon, but the sense of identity and empowerment players associate with their digits isn't new. New York Giants general manager Ernie Accorsi can cite one instance where a number got in the way of a proposed trade.

Accorsi was a member of the Baltimore Colts' front office in the late 1970s when the team worked out a deal to obtain *Hacksaw Reynolds*, the Los Angeles Rams' colorful and unpredictable middle linebacker.

"We were in training camp," Accorsi recalled, "and Reynolds told us he wanted No. 64. We already had a 64, a starting offensive lineman named David Taylor who was a very good, solid player. We had won divisional titles (1975, '76 and '77) and were not just going to take a number off a regular player. We told Reynolds no.

"So then he said, 'Well, if I can't have 64, I want no number.' Well, you can't play without a number. And then he said, 'I also want exclusive rights to my own trademark, and the NFL and NFL Properties have no rights over me at all.' In other words, you wouldn't be able to print a picture in a program without his permission. So finally we said this isn't worth the trouble. Ted Marchibroda, our coach at the time, said, 'Enough is enough.' "

The trade fell through, and Reynolds remained with the Rams through the 1980 season.

training camp. Schmidt would go on to Hall of Fame glory as No. 56.

F From October 22, 1989, through the 1999 season, the Vikings never took the field without left guard *Randall McDaniel*—No. 64—in their starting lineup.

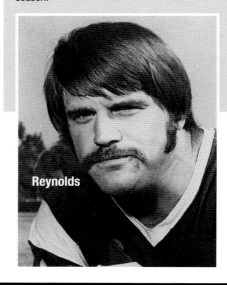

Reynolds

McDaniel

ELVIN BETHEA

In numbers-speak, 65 translates to "warrior." Bethea certainly qualified. So did Tom Mack, Gary Zimmerman and Abe Gibron, fellow NFL trenchmen. Houston fans who watched Bethea do battle from his defensive end position for 16 years still speak the "65 language" fluently. Only one Houston Oilers player, defensive end Gary Greaves, wore the number before Bethea— and he had it for seven games. Bethea had it from 1968-83, his entire Hall of Fame career, and it was retired well before the Oilers relocated to Tennessee in 1997. It wasn't until 2002, 20 years after Bethea, that Houstonians saw a different 65—center Ryan Schau, who wore that jersey for the expansion Houston Texans. With no disrespect to Schau, the quickness, relentless determination and grizzly-bear toughness of Bethea, the ultimate 65, was lost in translation.

Elite 65s

DAVE BUTZ: The 6-7, 295-pound defensive tackle, one of the biggest players of his time, appeared in three Super Bowls and won two rings.

TOM MACK: He never missed a game in 13 seasons with the Rams and earned 11 Pro Bowl invitations. The road to success in the 1960s and '70s passed through left guard.

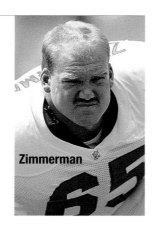

Zimmerman

GARY ZIMMERMAN: This solid offensive tackle stayed around long enough to help Denver win its first Super Bowl after the 1997 season. No such luck in his earlier life with the Vikings.

FAST FACTS

Chuck Noll, the future Pittsburgh Steelers coach, wore No. 65 when he played guard for Cleveland coach **Paul Brown** from 1953-59.

Washington has retired only one uniform number—**Sammy Baugh**'s 33—but several others are unofficially out of circulation, including defensive tackle **Dave Butz**'s 65.

NOTABLE 65s MAX MONTOYA 65 LES BINGAMAN 65 VINCE PROMUTO 65 HOUSTON ANTWINE 65 BART OATES

66

MARIO LEMIEUX

It didn't come to him in a vision while standing on his head. It was more of a tribute to professional hockey's greatest player, Wayne Gretzky, after the Great One took a 15-year-old aspiring superstar to dinner and a night out. Appropriately awestruck, Lemieux asked the Pittsburgh Penguins for a No. 99 sweater four years later and was informed, sarcastically, there is only one No. 99 in hockey. But a clever agent suggested an upside-down 99 might be appropriate and, six scoring titles later, Super Mario ranked among the game's all-time greats. At least to most fans. When Lemieux decided to end his more than three-year retirement during the 2000-01 season, he reportedly had trouble convincing 4-year-old son Austin to switch over from his favorite hockey jersey—Penguins teammate Jaromir Jagr's No. 68.

Elite 66s

KEVIN GOGAN: Call him dirty—his contemporaries did—but this guard was a stalwart on any of the five offensive lines on which he played. Three Pro Bowl selections and two Super Bowl rings confirm that.

LARRY LITTLE: There was nothing little about the contribution this outstanding guard made to the Dolphins' offense in the 1970s.

RAY NITSCHKE: He was a ball-seeking missile who brought Butkus-like intensity to the middle of Green Bay's defense in the championship-filled 1960s.

CLYDE TURNER: The aptly named "Bulldog" put serious bite in the middle of George Halas' game plans. Turner became an icon as a center/linebacker for four Bears championship teams.

FAST FACTS

F Canadian-born **Derek Aucoin**, a 6-7, 235-pound pitcher, didn't have any problem getting his number of choice as a 1996 rookie for the Expos. Aucoin asked for 66, a tribute to his hockey hero, **Mario Lemieux**. But he didn't have Super Mario's staying power. Aucoin was 0-1 in his only two major league games.

F Big 66 **Gene Hickerson**, one of the NFL's original pulling guards, opened holes for Hall of Fame backs **Jim Brown** and **Leroy Kelly** as well as a 1973 Cleveland rookie named **Greg Pruitt**.

F In 1999, offensive guard **Billy Shaw**, Buffalo's original No. 66, became the first player elected to the Pro Football Hall of Fame who played exclusively in the AFL.

NOTABLE 66s BILL BERGEY 66 JOE JACOBY 66 TOM NALEN 66 CONRAD DOBLER 66 GEORGE ANDRIE 66

67

BOB KUECHENBERG

Call him the invisible man. But don't underestimate Kuechenberg's impact on Miami's success from 1970-83, a period in which the Dolphins posted an amazing .706 winning percentage and recorded their perfect 1972 season.

Invisible is in the mind of the beholder. Many elite defensive linemen of the period had nightmares in which No. 67 systematically destroyed them in one-on-one confrontations. Fellow guards John Hannah and Joe DeLamielleure made it a point to study 67—his blocking and pass-protecting techniques—early in their Hall of Fame careers. And Dolphins coach Don Shula claims the man wearing that number "contributed more to our winning than anyone else."

Yeah, Kooch was part of that "no-name" mentality that defined those Miami teams of the 1970s. But he never was invisible after the ball was snapped.

FAST FACTS

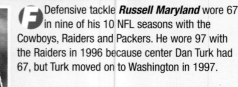

Hull

F Defensive tackle **Russell Maryland** wore 67 in nine of his 10 NFL seasons with the Cowboys, Raiders and Packers. He wore 97 with the Raiders in 1996 because center Dan Turk had 67, but Turk moved on to Washington in 1997.

F Quarterback Jim Kelly grew accustomed to **Kent Hull**'s No. 67. Hull was Kelly's exclusive center in Buffalo during parallel careers that lasted from 1986-96.

NOTABLE 67s STAN BROCK 67 LES RICHTER 67 LUIS **SHARPE 67 DUVAL LOVE 67 KENT HULL**

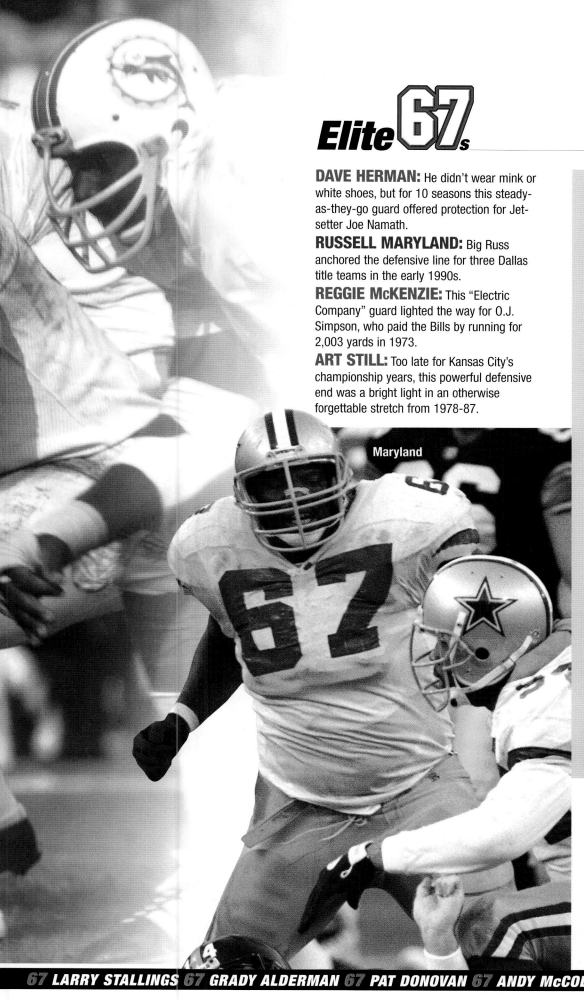

Elite 67s

DAVE HERMAN: He didn't wear mink or white shoes, but for 10 seasons this steady-as-they-go guard offered protection for Jet-setter Joe Namath.

RUSSELL MARYLAND: Big Russ anchored the defensive line for three Dallas title teams in the early 1990s.

REGGIE McKENZIE: This "Electric Company" guard lighted the way for O.J. Simpson, who paid the Bills by running for 2,003 yards in 1973.

ART STILL: Too late for Kansas City's championship years, this powerful defensive end was a bright light in an otherwise forgettable stretch from 1978-87.

Maryland

STRAHAN EXCHANGES 'UGLY' 67 FOR 92

When you check out the 92s of the sports world, New York Giants defensive end *Michael Strahan* ranks high, but well behind all-world defensive end Reggie White. It could have been different if Strahan had stuck with his original NFL number—67.

Strahan, however, says there's no way that was going to happen. In a 2005 story by Gary Myers in the *New York Daily News*, the pass-rushing Giant explained why he switched to No. 92 in the summer of '93:

"Because I had No. 67 when I first got here and saw my picture in the paper after my first day and said, 'That's one ugly number on me,' " Strahan said. "So I went in there and asked for another number and 92 was available. I took it."

So how ugly was 67?

"Go back and look at my rookie card, man," Strahan said. "That was the ugliest thing. Oh my goodness, when I put it on it looked like they were ready to cut me. I wanted to cut myself with that number."

Strahan

68

JAROMIR JAGR

A uniform number seldom has intrinsic value beyond the mystique a player might bring it. No. 68 is different. It has been a source of inspiration for Czech star Jagr, who came to the United States in 1990 to play for the Pittsburgh Penguins and asked for the number to honor a grandfather he never met. The number represents 1968, the year Russian tanks stormed Jagr's country, the former Czechoslovakia, to quell an uprising against Communist rule. His grandfather, also named Jaromir, was imprisoned amid the rebellion and died shortly after his release, almost four years before his grandson was born. Jagr's affection for No. 68 is not about goals and assists, which he has piled up at an amazing rate (537 and 772 entering the 2005-06 season) as an NHL star. It's about the much loftier concept of freedom.

Elite 68s

GALE GILLINGHAM: His first two seasons as a Packers guard were Super, and the next eight weren't too shabby, either.

L.C. GREENWOOD: L.C. and Mean Joe formed a formidable wall on the left side of Pittsburgh's Steel Curtain defensive line.

RUSS GRIMM: Go ahead and call him a Hog. The former Redskins guard won't mind a bit.

KEVIN MAWAE: They're restless in New York and still sleepless in Seattle now that the Pro Bowl center is a Titan.

Greenwood

FAST FACTS

F From 1973-85, guard **Joe DeLamielleure** wore 68 with Buffalo and 64 with the Browns. But if not for the NFL's numbering system, he might well have worn 13. DeLamielleure's last name has 13 letters, he played 13 NFL seasons and he was elected to the Hall of Fame in 2003, his 13th year of eligibility.

F Chiefs guard **Will Shields** has started every game since replacing injured **Dave Szott** in 1993. Big No. 68 had made a Kansas City-record 207 consecutive starts through the 2005 regular season.

F Middle guard **Jim Stillwagon**, who in 1970 became the first player to win the Outland Trophy and Lombardi Award in the same season, wore No. 68 en route to two consensus All-American citations at Ohio State.

NOTABLE 68s RUBIN CARTER **68** DENNIS HARRISON **68** HOWARD MUDD **68** ALEX SANDUSKY **68** KYLE TURLEY

69

LARRY COSTELLO

He played with Wilt Chamberlain on the Philadelphia 76ers team that won the 1967 NBA championship and coached the Lew Alcindor-led Milwaukee Bucks to the league crown in 1971, but Costello's association with 69 has much deeper roots. All the way back to February 21, 1953, in fact, when Costello, a two-handed set shot artist and playmaker, became a fixture in Niagara University's basketball lore. Costello, a junior wearing his familiar No. 24 in a game against Siena, played 69 minutes, 40 seconds and scored three late baskets in the six-overtime thriller won by the Purple Eagles, 88-81. Coach Taps Gallagher, thrilled with the win, changed Costello's number to 69, which he wore the final year of his college career but never again. Costello's yeoman effort has not been forgotten: The 69 jersey is officially retired and now hangs from the ceiling of Niagara's Gallagher Center.

Elite 69s

WOODY PEOPLES: Being a good blocker for the 49ers didn't mean as much from 1968-77, but at least he got to the Super Bowl with the Eagles before he retired.

JON RUNYAN: He's big, strong and nasty—everything you want in an offensive tackle.

KEITH SIMS: Dan Marino never had much of a running game to help him out, but at least he had Sims protecting his blind side.

FAST FACTS

F In his 12 NFL seasons with Washington and Denver, guard *Mark Schlereth* reportedly endured 30 surgeries, almost half the No. 69 he wore on his uniform.

F Defensive tackle *Tim Krumrie*'s No. 69 is not officially retired by the Bengals, but nobody has worn it since his retirement in 1994. Krumrie is best remembered for the broken leg he suffered in the first quarter of Super Bowl 23.

NOTABLE 69s SHERRILL HEADRICK *69* REVIE SOREY *69* JARED ALLEN *69* ROD MILSTEAD *69* BILL FORESTER

70

JIM MARSHALL

I t's an NFL Films classic: Minnesota's big No. 70, cradling a ball, lumbers 66 yards downfield and crosses the goal line. Marshall attained football—as well as numerological—infamy on that October day in 1964 when San Francisco fans at Kezar Stadium watched in disbelief as the Vikings' defensive tackle recovered a 49ers fumble and rumbled for what he thought was a Minnesota touchdown, only to discover he had run the wrong way. New Yorkers might argue for linebacker Sam Huff, and Colts fans might favor defensive tackle Art Donovan as more worthy No. 70s, but Marshall is much more than a football faux pas. He also set an NFL record and secured his status atop the 70 charts by playing 282 consecutive games from 1960-79. Exposure, exposure, exposure. If you want to be seen, you have to answer the bell—and Marshall, the only No. 70 in Vikings history, certainly did that.

FAST FACTS

F When *Joe Maddon* was hired to manage Tampa Bay after the 2005 season, he decided to keep the No. 70 he had worn for 28 years with the Angels organization. Maddon said he wore 20 in 1985 but had to give it up when Hall of Fame pitcher Don Sutton was acquired. He took 70, figuring no one would want that number.

F What a difference a year makes! Young shortstop *Gookie Dawkins*, considered the heir apparent to

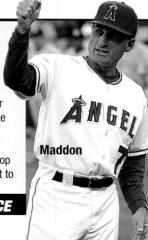

Maddon

Elite 70s

ART DONOVAN: His ability to dominate on the field was matched only by his ability to keep teammates loose off it. Donovan was at his best in the 1950s with the Colts.

Donovan

CHARLIE KRUEGER: This defensive tackle left his heart along with two good knees and a lot of blood, sweat and tears in San Francisco. Krueger could only watch with envy when Bay Area football life improved in the 1980s.

MICHAEL SINCLAIR: He played from 1992-2001 for the Seattle Seahawks, which explains why a lot of people don't remember him. Ask a quarterback who was on the receiving end of one of his sacks; he'll remember.

ERNIE STAUTNER: Mean Joe Greene wasn't the first great Steelers defensive tackle. Despite being Lilliputian by today's standards, Stautner made nine Pro Bowls from 1950-63.

AL WISTERT: This outstanding tackle plowed a path for Steve Van Buren and two Eagles championship teams in the late 1940s.

RAYFIELD WRIGHT: This tight end-turned-tackle anchored the Cowboys' lines in the 1970s.

Barry Larkin in 2002, was issued No. 3 by the Reds in spring training. In 2003 spring training, the same Dawkins wore 70. He was placed on waivers before the regular season.

(F) Dennis Rodman, who wore 10 and 91 through most of his NBA career with the Pistons, Spurs and Bulls, finished his 14-year career in 1999-2000 by playing 12 games as No. 70 for the Mavericks.

RETIRED NUMBER NOT PART OF HUFF'S WORLD

His uniform No. 70 was at the center of the pro football universe from 1956-69. *Sam Huff* glamorized the linebacker position with his engaging personality and the intense hand-to-hand combat he waged against two of the game's most celebrated runners—Cleveland's Jim Brown and Green Bay's Jim Taylor. Huff was a New York icon whose star also rose over a nation that saw him featured, at age 24, on the cover of Time magazine and in a CBS television documentary, *The Violent World of Sam Huff.*

So why haven't the New York Giants—the team that won an NFL championship and played in five other title games during his eight-year tenure—retired his number? They have retired 11 others, including those of quarterbacks Charley Conerly and Y.A. Tittle and running back Frank Gifford from Huff's era. One answer might be the hurt and bitterness Huff displayed toward the Giants long after they traded him to Washington in 1964.

Huff

The Redskins at least kept No. 70 out of circulation for a period after Huff's retirement. The Giants have issued it indiscriminantly since his departure.

Leonard Marshall wore 70 from 1983-92 for the Giants and again in 1994 for the Redskins. He didn't realize the significance of the number until Giants fans let him know.

"People said, 'Sam Huff wore that number. Maybe you'll be as great a player as Sam Huff was,'" Marshall said. "I had thought of it as being Gary Jeter's (his New York predecessor's) number."

71

ALEX KARRAS

For his forearm-shivering, horse-punching flair, Karras gets the call at No. 71. Granted, his memorable "Mongo love Sheriff Bart" proclamation in the Mel Brooks movie hit *Blazing Saddles* had absolutely nothing to do with football, but it had everything to do with the defensive tackle mentality he acquired over 12 seasons (1958-62, 1964-70) with the Detroit Lions. It wasn't the football that brought Karras instant recognition, though he was an outstanding player; it was the football movie that he made in 1968. Karras, playing himself and wearing No. 71, helped re-create author George Plimpton's memorable NFL insider experience in *Paper Lion* before going on to later movie and television fame. Karras is best remembered in football circles for his 1963 suspension, along with Green Bay star Paul Hornung, for betting on games. But post-football, he'll always be Mongo … or Webster's burly former football-playing surrogate father.

FAST FACTS

F When **Deion Sanders** reported to the Yankees for his first spring training in 1989, he was issued No. 71. Sanders asked for a lower number and was switched to 30 and eventually 44. When Sanders played 14 regular-season games later that year, he wore 24.

F When Taiwanese righthander **Chin-hui Tsao** was called up by the Rockies in

Tsao

Elite 71s

WILLIE ANDERSON: This is one tough Bengal. How many offensive tackles can play a season with torn knee cartilage, not miss a game and still make the Pro Bowl? Anderson did in 2004.

TONY BOSELLI: He was the first player picked by two new teams—Jacksonville in the 1995 NFL draft and Houston in the 2002 expansion draft. Boselli opened eyes—and plenty of holes.

Boselli

MARCIS' RESOLVE KEEPS FANS REVVED UP

He won only five Winston Cup races in 35 years, the last in 1982. But when *Dave Marcis* and his No. 71 Realtree Chevrolet finished 42nd in the 43-car Daytona 500 field on February 17, 2002, he was given a rousing retirement sendoff by appreciative NASCAR fans, officials and fellow drivers.

Few competitors on the Cup circuit could have earned such popularity without a long winning resume. Marcis did it with determination and durability. When Marcis started his 33rd Daytona 500 in 2002, he broke a tie with Richard Petty for career starts in the showcase event. When the race ended with engine trouble on lap 79, Marcis owned records for miles run in the Daytona 500 (12,345) and the Pepsi 400 (10,800), and he ranked second all-time behind Petty in career starts.

"It's fantastic," said the 60-year-old Wisconsin native. "To start here in '68 and be able to make the race in 2002 and go out on my own terms—how many guys get to do that?"

Marcis had been tied with Petty since 1999, when he started in his record 32nd consecutive Daytona 500. But he failed to qualify in 2000 and 2001. Marcis and his 71 Chevy started from the 14th position in 2002 after finishing seventh in the 125-mile Gatorade 125-mile qualifier.

GEORGE CONNOR: He earned All-Pro honors with the Bears at three positions (offensive tackle, defensive tackle and linebacker) in the 1950s—an amazing accomplishment.

SANTANA DOTSON: Where's the beef? You didn't have to look far for that answer when the Packers won Super Bowl 31. Tall, strong Dotson and heavyweight Gilbert Brown provided a beefy combination at defensive tackle.

Dotson

2003, he wore No. 71 because first baseman *Todd Helton* had his preferred 17. Tsao's choice prompted this Helton quip to Denver Post writer Irv Moss: "If I go to Taiwan to play, I'll wear No. 71."

F Offensive tackle *Mark Tuinei* wore No. 71 for the Cowboys for 15 years—long enough to block for running backs *Tony Dorsett*, *Herschel Walker* and *Emmitt Smith*.

Marcis

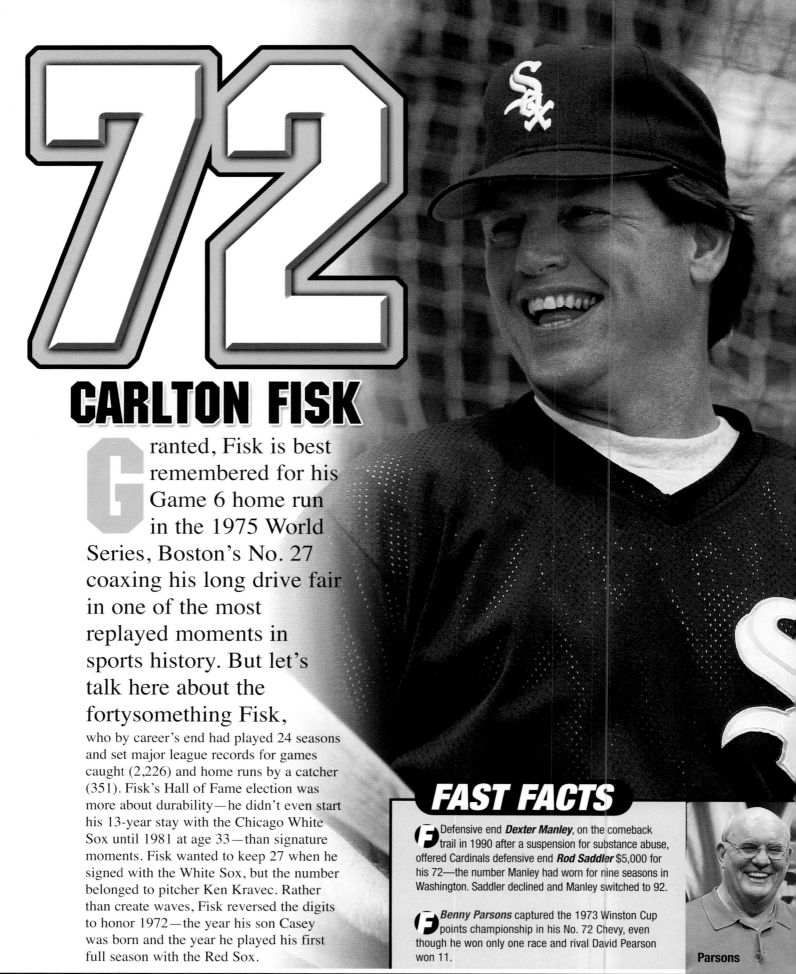

72

CARLTON FISK

Granted, Fisk is best remembered for his Game 6 home run in the 1975 World Series, Boston's No. 27 coaxing his long drive fair in one of the most replayed moments in sports history. But let's talk here about the fortysomething Fisk, who by career's end had played 24 seasons and set major league records for games caught (2,226) and home runs by a catcher (351). Fisk's Hall of Fame election was more about durability—he didn't even start his 13-year stay with the Chicago White Sox until 1981 at age 33—than signature moments. Fisk wanted to keep 27 when he signed with the White Sox, but the number belonged to pitcher Ken Kravec. Rather than create waves, Fisk reversed the digits to honor 1972—the year his son Casey was born and the year he played his first full season with the Red Sox.

FAST FACTS

F Defensive end **Dexter Manley**, on the comeback trail in 1990 after a suspension for substance abuse, offered Cardinals defensive end **Rod Saddler** $5,000 for his 72—the number Manley had worn for nine seasons in Washington. Saddler declined and Manley switched to 92.

F **Benny Parsons** captured the 1973 Winston Cup points championship in his No. 72 Chevy, even though he won only one race and rival David Pearson won 11.

Parsons

NOTABLE 72s DIRON TALBERT 72 LEON SEARCY 72 DON MOSEBAR 72 LINCOLN KENNEDY 72 BRAD

Elite 72s

Jones

'FRIDGE' HAS MELTDOWN AFTER A HOT START

From 308 pounds to rumored highs of 390, *William Perry*'s weight always provided food for thought for Chicago Bears coach Mike Ditka. Defensive coordinator Buddy Ryan, on the other hand, took one look at the rookie "Refrigerator" in 1985 and declared him overweight and a wasted first-round pick.

Perry trimmed down a bit, put on his No. 72 jersey and proved Ryan wrong. He earned a starting job at defensive tackle for a team that finished the regular season 15-1 and won the Super Bowl. And he also took on extra duty as the heftiest blocking/running back in NFL history when Ditka became enamored with his surprising quickness and acceleration.

By the time that 1985 season ended, the gap-toothed Perry was a national folk hero. He was engaging and lovable as a run-stopping and space-eating defender. But he was fascinating when lined up with Walter Payton in a goal-line offense. Fans chanted for the Fridge; companies lined up for commercial endorsements.

Perry didn't disappoint. In 1985, he carried and caught the ball for touchdowns and cleared paths to the end zone for Payton. His big moment came in Super Bowl 20 when he romped for a TD.

But unable to keep his weight in check, the bigger and slower Perry soon was relegated to defensive duty. He fumbled in his only carries of 1986 and '87 and his popularity eventually diminished. Big No. 72, who remained with the Bears until 1993 and played the rest of that season and one more in Philadelphia, never rekindled the magic of 1985.

Perry

DAN DIERDORF: It was a Cardinal sin to underestimate the bruising Dierdorf, who might have been the best offensive tackle of the 1970s.

ED JONES: Fans called him Too Tall, but it easily could have been Too Strong, Too Fast or Too Good.

JOHN MATUSZAK: The Tooz created havoc—both on and off the field—for two Oakland Super Bowl champions from 1976-81.

BENNY PARSONS: From taxi driver to NASCAR champ to broadcaster—what a ride!

HOPKINS 72 EARL DOTSON 72 BOB HEINZ 72 JERRY SHERK 72 BOB VOGEL 72 JOE NASH 72 GIL MAINS 72

73

JOHN HANNAH

Oh brother! You're the best guard in the National Football League, some say the greatest offensive lineman in NFL history, and the ring you're admiring says, "Hannah, 73." Right name, right number ... but wrong Hannah. "I was green with envy," New England star John Hannah admitted to *Chicago Tribune* writer Sam Smith after checking out younger brother Charley's Super Bowl ring, which he won after the 1983 season while playing left guard—John's position—for the Oakland Raiders. John never won a ring, although he did play for the Patriots in a Super Bowl loss to the Chicago Bears after the 1985 campaign. But he can take consolation in that Hall of Fame plaque, which probably makes Charley turn different colors, and the fact that few other 73s could even approach his talent level. Only Ron Yary and Leo Nomellini came close.

Elite 73s

LARRY ALLEN: Sonoma State? What an unlikely starting point for one of the NFL's best offensive linemen of the last decade.

JOE KLECKO: The firm of Gastineau and Klecko presided over the New York Sack Exchange. Their specialty: hostile takedowns.

RON YARY: This warrior tackle blocked out pain and cleared a path to four Super Bowls in the 1970s. The Vikings never won, but they reveled in the intense work ethic of their premier blue-collar blocker.

Rodman

FAST FACTS

F In 23 games with the Lakers in 1998-99, *Dennis Rodman* wore No. 73—the 7 a tribute to his seven rebounding titles, the 3 signifying the championship rings he won in consecutive seasons with the Bulls.

F Two-way tackle *Leo Nomellini,* the first draft pick by NFL newcomer San Francisco in 1950, wore 73 for his final 12 seasons after wearing 42 in 1950 and '51. Leo the Lion, a 10-time Pro Bowl pick, switched when the NFL introduced its new numbering system in 1952.

F *Joe Klecko*, part of a starting defensive line that combined to record 53½ sacks in 1981, is one of three Jets to have his uniform number retired. Klecko, No. 73, was joined on that line by *Marty Lyons*, *Abdul Salaam* and *Mark Gastineau*.

NOTABLE 73s DOUG DIEKEN 73 BOB BAUMHOWER 73 NORM EVANS 73 MARK MAY 73 ARNIE WEINMEISTER 73

74

BOB LILLY

Forget the NFL's numbering system! Mr. Cowboy should have been allowed to wear No. 1. He was the first draft pick in Dallas franchise history, the team's first Ring of Honor member and its first Hall of Famer. And any all-time list of NFL defensive tackles is likely to have Lilly ranked No. 1. But the big Texan with the furious pass rush and incredible strength will have to be content as the all-time No. 1 No. 74. Another noted 74, Hall of Fame defensive tackle Merlin Olsen, might dispute that honor, but those flower commercials and that Father Murphy gig kind of tarnish his Fearsome Foursome image. And yet another 74, Hall of Famer Ron Mix, loses points because he was—c'mon, pay attention now—an offensive lineman. Lilly is, and always will be, the only player to wear No. 74 for the Cowboys.

Elite 74s

HENRY JORDAN: Five championship rings and Hall of Fame recognition: Not bad for a balding, undersized Green Bay defensive tackle.

BRUCE MATTHEWS: Matthews will tell you his longevity and outstanding play are all in the genes. And with a father (Clay Sr.) and a brother (Clay Jr.) who also made a living in the NFL trenches, who can argue?

RON MIX: It's not uncommon today for an offensive lineman to get called for two holding penalties in a game. San Diego's "Intellectual Assassin" was flagged for two in his career.

MERLIN OLSEN: Like clockwork, Olsen showed up and Olsen dominated. You wouldn't expect any less from the leader of the the Rams' Fearsome Foursome defensive line.

FAST FACTS

F Offensive lineman **Bruce Matthews**, who played in 14 straight Pro Bowls, wore No. 74 for the Oilers/Titans franchise for an amazing 19 seasons. He retired after the 2001 season at age 40.

F On second thought. ... When future Hall of Fame tackle **Ron Mix** retired in 1969 after 10 seasons with the Chargers, team owner **Gene Klein** retired his No. 74. But gratitude quickly turned to disgust. Mix came out of retirement in 1971 to play for the hated Raiders, prompting Klein to "unretire" his number.

NOTABLE 74s PAUL GRUBER 74 TOM KEATING 74 MIKE McCORMACK 74 MIKE REID 74 DERLAND MOORE 74

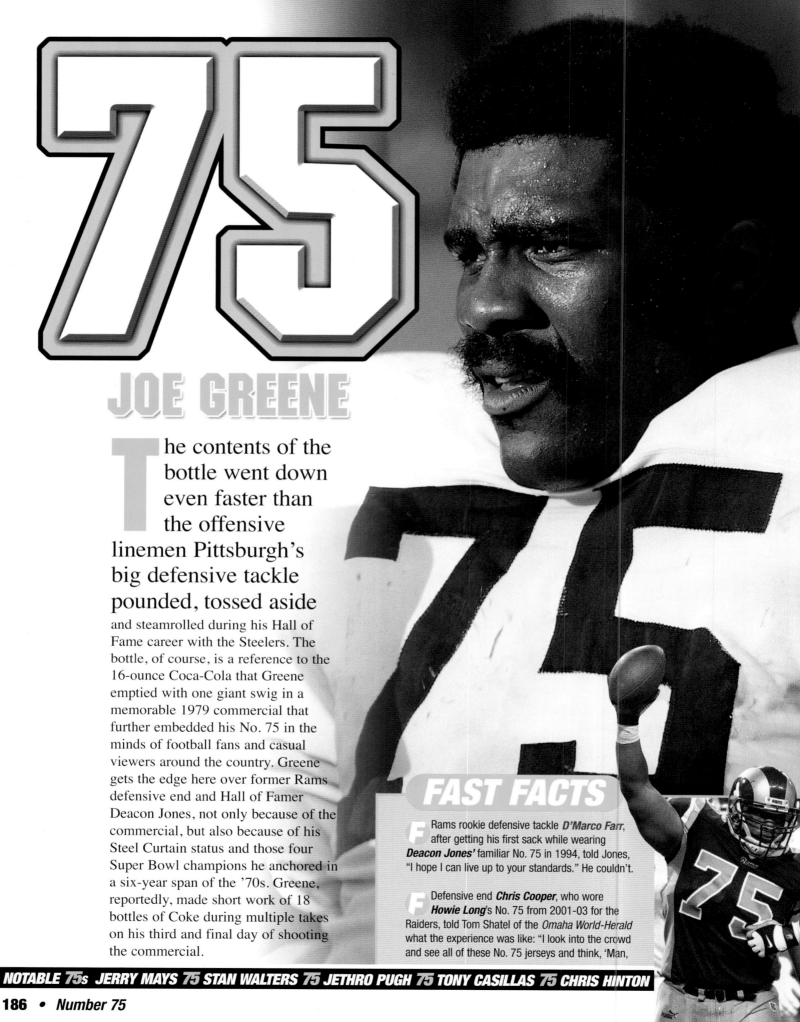

75

JOE GREENE

The contents of the bottle went down even faster than the offensive linemen Pittsburgh's big defensive tackle pounded, tossed aside and steamrolled during his Hall of Fame career with the Steelers. The bottle, of course, is a reference to the 16-ounce Coca-Cola that Greene emptied with one giant swig in a memorable 1979 commercial that further embedded his No. 75 in the minds of football fans and casual viewers around the country. Greene gets the edge here over former Rams defensive end and Hall of Famer Deacon Jones, not only because of the commercial, but also because of his Steel Curtain status and those four Super Bowl champions he anchored in a six-year span of the '70s. Greene, reportedly, made short work of 18 bottles of Coke during multiple takes on his third and final day of shooting the commercial.

FAST FACTS

F Rams rookie defensive tackle **D'Marco Farr**, after getting his first sack while wearing **Deacon Jones'** familiar No. 75 in 1994, told Jones, "I hope I can live up to your standards." He couldn't.

F Defensive end **Chris Cooper**, who wore **Howie Long**'s No. 75 from 2001-03 for the Raiders, told Tom Shatel of the *Omaha World-Herald* what the experience was like: "I look into the crowd and see all of these No. 75 jerseys and think, 'Man,

NOTABLE 75s JERRY MAYS 75 STAN WALTERS 75 JETHRO PUGH 75 TONY CASILLAS 75 CHRIS HINTON

Elite 75s

Jones

LOMAS BROWN: In front of every great running back is a great offensive lineman; just ask Barry Sanders about his good buddy Lomas.

MANNY FERNANDEZ: The ever-intense run-stopper in Miami's "No-Name Defense" became a big name.

FORREST GREGG: Technique. Technique. Technique. Quickness, finesse and hard work translated into stardom for this offensive tackle, who anchored the line for five Green Bay championship teams.

that's cool. They're wearing my jersey.' Then they turn around and it says 'Long.' "

F Offensive tackle **Ken Ruettgers** was no **Forrest Gregg**, but he wore Gregg's No. 75 well over a 12-year Packers career that ended when a knee injury forced him to retire after the 12th game of 1996—a Super Bowl championship season for Green Bay.

FOR LEFTY, 75 CONVEYS STRUGGLE TO SUCCEED

Jim Crowell has no illusions about 20-win seasons and a long, prosperous major league career. The 6-4 lefthander got a taste of the majors with Cincinnati in 1997, but most of his 11-year career through 2005 had been spent in the minors battling frustration, major elbow surgery and anonymity.

So it wasn't a lark in May 2004 when Crowell, who had just been called up by Philadelphia to replace injured Roberto Hernandez in the Phillies' bullpen, chose to wear 75—generally disdained as a football number. Crowell took it as a reminder of how difficult it is to get back to the majors after attending numerous spring camps as a nonroster player wearing afterthought numbers.

"I'll wear it forever," promised Crowell, who pitched in only four games that season and appeared in four more with the Marlins in 2005.

The road to 75 was much easier for Oakland's **Barry Zito**, who spent only one full season and part of a second in the minor leagues. Zito, who arrived in Oakland in 2000, had posted 86 wins through 2005, and he earned the 2002 American League Cy Young Award with a 23-5 record. So why such a high number?

The sometimes-mysterious lefty wore 34 at USC and wanted to keep that number in Oakland, but it was retired for Rollie Fingers. "So I just went for a number I could keep my entire career," Zito said. "In case I go to another team, I'm pretty sure No. 75 will be available."

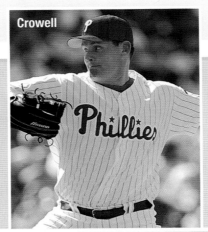

Crowell

WINSTON HILL: It's no coincidence that this tackle's Jets career coincided with the NFL life expectancy of Joe Namath. Hill earned eight Pro Bowl invitations.

DEACON JONES: During his 14-year harassment of NFL quarterbacks, this Fearsome Foursome defensive end coined the term "sack"—"you know, like you sack a city, you devastate it."

HOWIE LONG: For 13 years, he showed quarterbacks his silver-and-black mean streak. Then he showed TV viewers his softer side as a Radio Shack pitchman.

JONATHAN OGDEN: No wonder Ravens back Jamal Lewis has run for thousands of yards, including 2,066 in 2003.

Long

75 JIM KATCAVAGE **75** GEORGE KUNZ **75** KEITH MILLARD **75** GEORGE MARTIN **75** DOUG BETTERS **75** RULON JONES

76

LOU GROZA

For brute force and head-slapping proficiency, it's hard to ignore such NFL heavyweights as Steve McMichael, Big Daddy Lipscomb and Orlando Pace. But our search for the ultimate 76 takes us beyond the grunting and grabbing brigade.

It focuses on the most unusual two-way performer in football history, an offensive tackle/kicker known affectionately as "The Toe." Groza, who wore No. 46 as an original member of the Cleveland Browns in the late 1940s, was a Hall of Fame tackle who could step back and drill a 45-yard game-winning field goal. He revolutioned the kicking game over a durable 21-year career in which he played for eight championship teams and produced a still-standing Browns record of 1,608 points. To many, this gentle giant remains the quintessential Brown, which explains the address of the team's training facility in Berea, Ohio: 76 Lou Groza Boulevard.

FAST FACTS

F In 1950, two years before the NFL introduced a numbering system, Green Bay's **Tom O'Malley** became the first and last quarterback to wear No. 76.

F Though No. 76 was eventually retired by Cleveland for kicker/tackle **Lou Groza**, running back **Marion Motley** wore it from 1946-51 for the Browns. When the NFL's new numbering system was introduced in 1952, Motley switched to 36 and Groza changed from 46 to 76.

NOTABLE *76s* **JOHN ALT** *76* **ROCKY FREITAS** *76* **FLOZELL ADAMS** *76* **JERRY SISEMORE** *76* **LEN ROHDE** *76* **ROGER**

Elite 76s

Pace

JUMBO ELLIOTT: The nickname fits this oversized tackle, who did his best work on the New York stage for the Giants and Jets.

ROOSEVELT GRIER: First, Rosey was a Giant. Then he was a member of the Rams' Fearsome Foursome defense. "Giant" and "fearsome" capture the essence of the big defensive tackle.

GENE LIPSCOMB: Big Daddy was the prototype for the modern defensive lineman—big, quick, fast, nasty and larger than life. But his appetite for winning was surpassed by his appetite for partying, and he paid the price.

STEVE McMICHAEL: He anchored the middle of the Bears' defensive line for 13 seasons, and his intensity personified one of the NFL's all-time best defenses in 1985.

MARION MOTLEY: With his size and speed, this Hall of Fame back would be almost as unstoppable today as he was for the Browns in the 1940s and '50s.

ORLANDO PACE: The Greatest Show on Turf needed a strongman, and Pace ranks among the best left tackles in the game.

STEVE WISNIEWSKI: Being labeled one of the dirtiest players in the NFL didn't stop offensive guard Wisniewski from earning eight Pro Bowl invitations.

F "Offsides, No. 76, defense." That probably sounds familiar to Buffalo fans and former Bills nose tackle *Fred Smerlas*, who became famous for his encroachment penalties from 1979-89.

Smerlas

BRADLEY GETS INTO THE SPIRIT OF 76

It seemed only fitting. When Philadelphia grabbed BYU center *Shawn Bradley* with the second overall pick of the 1993 NBA draft, the 245-pounder requested uniform No. 76. "I looked at the team logo (76ers), and saw my height (7-6) listed next to my name, and thought it might be a pretty neat idea," he explained.

Neat, as in a nice marketing ploy for the 76ers' $44 million (over eight seasons) man. Not so neat as a target for burly centers and taunting fans. Shaquille O'Neal twisted Bradley like a pipe-cleaner, and Rony Seikaly, Patrick Ewing and other physical centers manhandled him.

Bradley was skinny, and just couldn't seem to add bulk; he was helpless when the massive Shaq decided to clear the lane. Inexperience was a factor, too. He had played one season at BYU, taken two years off for a Mormon mission and jumped to the NBA.

Bradley averaged 10.3 points and 6.2 rebounds as a rookie, 9.5 and 8.0 in his second season. His strength was on the defensive end, where he blocked 421 shots in those two seasons. But the 76ers, who had mortgaged the farm to get and sign him, did a quick about-face in November 1995 and traded him to New Jersey.

Bradley switched to No. 45 with the Nets and spent the last eight-plus seasons of his 12-year career wearing 44 for Dallas. Never dominant, he was a solid role player for the Mavericks.

Bradley

77

RED GRANGE

The Galloping Ghost was an honest-to-God hero in the 1920s, maybe the first superstar to be associated with a uniform number and one of the first to endorse products.

There were Red Grange teddy bears, candy bars, sweaters, caps and ginger ale; the most passionate fans could even eat Red Grange meatloaf. In a decade otherwise dominated by the likes of Babe Ruth, Jack Dempsey, Bobby Jones and Big Bill Tilden, Grange performed elusive, legacy-building running feats, first for the University of Illinois, then for the NFL's Chicago Bears. He energized his sport and gave it national appeal, prompting Bears owner and coach George Halas to say that no player had a greater impact on football, college or professional, than Grange. So why 77? Because, Grange once explained, the guy in front of him got No. 76 and the guy behind him got 78.

FAST FACTS

F **Dontrelle Willis,** the high-kicking lefthander who won 22 games for the 2005 Marlins, was No. 77 in his first spring training in 2003. He wore No. 35, his current number, when he made his major league debut later that season.

F No. 77 is retired by the Portland Trail Blazers in honor of former coach **Jack Ramsay,** who presided over the team's 1977

Stringer

NOTABLE _77_s DICK SCHAFRATH _77_ **JIM TYRER** _77_ **ADAM OATES** _77_ **ERNIE LADD** _77_ **A.J.**

Elite 77s

LYLE ALZADO: This macho strongman of the 1970s and early '80s introduced the term "steroids" to the sports vernacular.

PAUL COFFEY: Sevens were wild for this high-scoring defenseman, who wore one of them for seven years with the powerful Oilers (1980-87) and two of them for most of the rest of his career (1987-2001) with eight other teams. Coffey wore 74 in his final season with Boston.

JIM JEFFCOAT: This Cowboy rode out the storm of the late 1980s and helped Dallas win two Super Bowls in the early '90s. Twelve years with one team for a defensive end is impressive.

KARL MECKLENBURG: A post-draft trade brought John Elway to the Broncos in 1983. A 12th-round pick brought Mecklenburg the same year. Mecklenburg became the versatile

Mecklenburg

cornerstone of Denver's defense.

JIM PARKER: Some say he was the greatest offensive guard ever to play in the NFL. Others say he was the greatest tackle. All Colts coach Weeb Ewbank asked of Parker was to keep defensive linemen away from Johnny Unitas. He did that and much more in his Hall of Fame career.

WILLIE ROAF: A Saint and a Chief. NFL life has been good for big Willie, who forces defensive linemen to spend big parts of every game looking up at the sky.

7 OR 77, BOURQUE LEAVES AN IMPRESSION

Ray Bourque's No. 77 hangs from the rafters of Boston's TD Banknorth Garden and Colorado's Pepsi Center, a reminder that the two NHL franchises once provided home ice for one of the best two-way defensemen of all-time. But from 1979-87, Bourque was only half the player he was for the remainder of his 22-year career. He was No. 7 for the Boston Bruins.

It seemed natural in 1979 that the prized rookie should inherit the number worn with distinction for eight-plus seasons by Phil Esposito with the Bruins. Esposito was a five-time league scoring champion for the Bruins and a key figure for two Stanley Cup champions. Bourque figured to be the defensive anchor for years to come.

But in 1987, the Bruins decided to honor Esposito by raising his No. 7 to the Boston Garden rafters. Bourque, the current No. 7, was asked to present the old No. 7 jersey at mid-ice to Esposito.

Esposito and 14,451 fans were shocked when Bourque threw in a little twist. He handed Esposito the old jersey as planned, but then he peeled off his No. 7 and handed that to him, too. Underneath his 7 was a 77 sweater—the number he would wear permanently.

"Nobody knew about it, so we decided to really surprise him and surprise a lot of people with it," Bourque said.

Esposito was floored. "What this young man did tonight is something that I'll never ever, ever forget, no matter what happens in my life," he said.

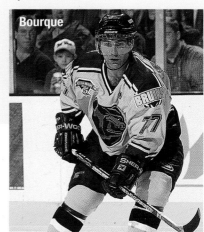

Bourque

NBA championship season.

The Minnesota Vikings have retired 77 in honor of offensive tackle *Korey Stringer*, who collapsed in the team's 2001 training camp and died the next day of heat stroke complications.

Pierre Turgeon, No. 7 throughout his junior hockey days in Quebec, was gratified when Buffalo officials handed him a 77 jersey after taking him with the first overall pick of the 1987 NHL entry draft. "I liked it because I liked 7," he said.

DUHE 77 CHRIS GRATTON 77 DICK MODZELEWSKI 77 GHEORGHE MURESAN 77 BRUCE BOSLEY 77 STEW BARBER

78
ANTHONY MUNOZ

"His head alone weighs 200 pounds," proclaimed one scout in a 1980 draft-day exaggeration. But there was no exaggerating the huge, powerful legs that anchored the 6-6 Munoz and provided leverage for his ferocious blocks.

Cincinnati's big No. 78 didn't just attack defenders, he destroyed them. And his physical onslaughts usually continued until somebody was on the ground. Because there has been no better offensive tackle in NFL history, it stands to reason Munoz also is the world's greatest No. 78—an easy pick over such NFL heavyweights as Art Shell, Bruce Smith, Stan Jones and Bobby Bell. Those who had to eat the pancakes and waffles he handed out for 13 Hall of Fame seasons certainly agree. As do quarterbacks Ken Anderson and Boomer Esiason, who benefited most from his big brother-like protection. It's no coincidence that Munoz and the Bengals played in two Super Bowls in the 1980s.

FAST FACTS

F Rams offensive tackle *Jackie Slater* is one of two NFL players to wear the same number for the same team 20 straight seasons. Slater wore 78 for the Rams, and *Darrell Green* wore 28 for the Redskins.

F Offensive tackle *Greg Skrepenak*, explaining why he left the Raiders in 1996 to sign a free-agent contract with Carolina: "I was No. 78 with the Raiders, and automatically Art Shell was always the comparison. That's kind of unfair to a player like me

Slater

NOTABLE *78s* **MARION CAMPBELL** *78* **BUBBA SMITH** *78* **JOHN DUTTON** *78* **JIM DUNAWAY** *78* **MIKE KENN**

Elite 78s

Shell

BOBBY BELL: He was a 1960s athlete in a 1990s body. Bell did his damage as a defensive end and outside linebacker, but coach Hank Stram claimed he could have played any of the 22 positions—and played it well.

STAN JONES: The Bears' two-way lineman, one of the first NFL players to lift weights, was the strongest player of his era. He powered his way to Canton.

ART SHELL: From 1968-81, Raiders tackle Shell and guard Gene Upshaw formed

… because he's a Hall of Fame tackle. And I was only a couple of years in the league, and they're saying, 'Well, he's no Art Shell.' "

Ⓕ Rams quarterback *Jim Everett* after a 1992 game against Buffalo and defensive end *Bruce Smith*. "I didn't get much time to see much else besides No. 78. The onions he had before the game were killing me. I was smelling them all day."

EMOTIONAL BILLS FANS WELCOME BACK NO. 78

There he was, wearing his familiar No. 78 and pushing aside blockers in his never-ending pursuit of quarterbacks and ballcarriers. But this time *Bruce Smith* was wearing a burgundy and gold uniform and feeding off the frenzy of 73,000-plus opposing fans, many of whom were decked out in the blue No. 78 Buffalo jersey that used to be his trademark.

This strangely inspirational October 19, 2003, homecoming was both bizarre and understandable. Smith had played 217 games in 15 seasons for the Bills, earning 11 Pro Bowl invitations and leading the team to four consecutive Super Bowl appearances. Chants of "Bruuuce, Bruuuce, Bruuuce" cascaded through Ralph Wilson Stadium as the big defensive end, now wearing the colors of the Washington Redskins, returned to his old stomping grounds for the first time in four years.

"It was certainly an emotional experience for me coming back and seeing so many fans yelling and chanting," said Smith, who at age 40 needed two sacks to slip past all-time NFL leader Reggie White. Smith got close, pressuring quarterback Drew Bledsoe several times, but didn't get a sack as his Redskins lost, 24-7.

The record-setting sacks came later. On this day, Smith settled for his reaffirmation as one of the most beloved sports figures in a football-crazed city. His long Buffalo stay had ended in 1999 when he was released by the Bills as a cost-cutting move.

the most formidable blocking combination in NFL history.

JACKIE SLATER: The Rams might not always have known who was running or throwing during Slater's two decades, but at least they knew who would open the holes and stop pass rushers.

RICHMOND WEBB: Anybody looking to blindside Dan Marino had to get through Webb, which explains why Marino had the time to complete all those passes for all those yards and touchdowns.

DWIGHT WHITE: He was a playmaker for Pittsburgh's Steel Curtain defense, even if he was overshadowed by linemate Mean Joe Greene.

Smith

79
ROOSEVELT BROWN

It doesn't take long to call roll on No. 79. Brown looms large, just as he must have on the football field in the 1950s and '60s as a 6-3, 255-pound offensive tackle for the New York Giants. It really wasn't his size that intimidated opponents—it was the speed, quickness and relentless determination with which he knocked the bejabbers out of them in his never-ending quest to make life easier for his teammates. He was a new breed, the most mobile lineman of his era. The sight of big No. 79 pulling around end made some defenders rethink their life calling; his agility and quickness while handling bigger and stronger defensive tackles in pass protection set the standard for future generations of linemen. Nobody appreciated the future Hall of Famer more than running back Frank Gifford and quarterback Charley Conerly, key members of the Giants' 1956 title team.

FAST FACTS

F Defensive guard *Rich Glover*'s 79 is one of 16 jerseys retired by the University of Nebraska. Glover won both the Lombardi Award and Outland Trophy in 1972.

F Only one player other than *Jim Lee Hunt* has worn No. 79 for the Patriots—defensive end *Al Richardson* briefly in 1960. Defensive tackle Hunt wore 79 for all 11 seasons that the team was known as the "Boston" Patriots.

NOTABLE 79s HARRIS BARTON 79 ROSS BROWNER 79 DAVE SZOTT 79 TEX COULTER 79 RAY CHILDRESS 79 COY BACON

Elite 79s

RUBEN BROWN: This talented offensive guard Buffaloed opponents for eight straight Pro Bowl seasons before moving on to Chicago.

JIM LACHEY: For a portion of his seven-year stay with the Redskins, Lachey was the best left tackle in the NFL.

HARVEY MARTIN: A member of the

AS A PACKER, HE'S 'THE INCREDIBLE BUST'

He wore No. 79 as a consensus All-American at Michigan State and as a solid tackle for the Indianapolis Colts eight years later. In between, *Tony Mandarich* was a shockingly disappointing No. 77 for the Green Bay Packers.

Mandarich had a can't-miss tag when he left college with expectations that rivaled his 6-6, 315-pound frame. He was featured on the cover of *Sports Illustrated* with the headline, "The Incredible Bulk," and the magazine billed him as "the best offensive line prospect ever." After Dallas took quarterback Troy Aikman with the first pick of the 1989 draft, the Packers grabbed Mandarich, ignoring Barry Sanders, Derrick Thomas and Deion Sanders.

Trouble surfaced quickly. Mandarich was a training camp holdout, made bold predictions and insulted Packers fans by calling Green Bay a "village." The arrogant, underachieving Mandarich spent parts of three seasons floundering and another on the sideline with a parasitic infection before he was released.

It took four years for Mandarich to regain his football enthusiasm. Given a tryout by the Colts in 1996, he displayed maturity and a work ethic he never showed at Green Bay. He played three strong seasons with Indianapolis and would have continued as young Peyton Manning's primary protector if not for a shoulder injury.

In the end, attitude and immaturity—not uniform numbers—defined Mandarich, one of the biggest draft busts in National Football League history. But for superstitious types, the 79 factor is certainly hard to ignore.

elite 20-sack fraternity, defensive end Martin also was the anchor of the Cowboys' Doomsday II Defense and co-MVP of Super Bowl 12.

BOB ST. CLAIR: The 6-9, 265-pound 49ers offensive tackle ate raw meat and any defenders who got in his way en route to the Hall of Fame.

Martin

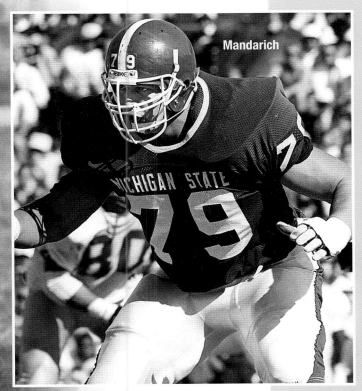

Mandarich

Glover

79 **BARNEY CHAVOUS** 79 **RON McDOLE** 79 **JACOB GREEN** 79 **RUBEN BROWN**

80

JERRY RICE

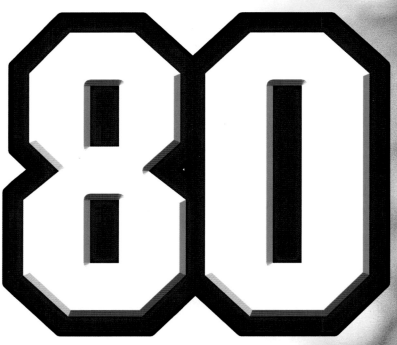

He always will be No. 80, even when he's 19. If you think that's confusing, consider the late-career travels of superstar receiver Jerry Rice and his legendary numeral.

After 16 record-setting seasons in San Francisco, Rice signed a free-agent contract with Oakland in 2001 and was handed No. 80, even though the team still was negotiating with the 2000 owner of that jersey, Andre Rison. When Rice was traded to Seattle in 2004, he boldly asked for 80, the number Seahawks receiver Steve Largent had worn to Hall of Fame distinction. Largent graciously agreed to "unretire" the number. But Rice said he never considered asking for 80 when he signed in 2005 with Denver. Good thing: The number belongs to Broncos all-time receptions leader Rod Smith, who said in a Sirius satellite radio interview, "That's like somebody saying this guy over here is a better husband and father than you, why don't you give him your wife." Rice opted for 19 in training camp—then abruptly retired.

FAST FACTS

F Detroit's **Brett Hull** wore No. 80 for two 2003-04 preseason games as a tribute to **Herb Brooks**, the 1980 U.S. Olympic hockey coach who had died in August 2003. Hull later donated the signed jerseys to the Herb Brooks charity foundation.

F Since 1983, Rams uniform No. 80 has belonged to **Henry Ellard** and **Isaac Bruce**, two of the best wide receivers in franchise history.

F **Wayne Chrebet** chose No. 80 as a Jets receiver because his favorite player as a youngster was Seattle's Steve Largent.

NOTABLE 80s CRIS COLLINSWORTH 80 LEN FORD 80 ROD SMITH 80 JEREMY SHOCKEY 80 TROY BROWN 80 TONY

Elite **80**s

ISAAC BRUCE: Great hands and acrobatic catches provide marquee value in the Greatest Show on Turf.

CRIS CARTER: This pass-catching demon wasn't that fast—but he was extremely precise. Just watch tape of him running routes during his prime with the Vikings.

HENRY ELLARD: The student always becomes the teacher. That's what happened in St. Louis, where Ellard coaches Rams wide receivers.

Carter

IRVING FRYAR: The Patriots' former No. 1 overall pick (1984) ranks among the NFL's top 10 all-time in receptions and yards.

TOM FEARS: The prototypical possession receiver of the 1950s once caught 18 passes for the Rams in a single game—a record that stood for many years.

STEVE LARGENT: Short and slow, Largent used savvy and hard work to become the NFL's most prolific wide receiver until that Jerry Rice fellow came along.

Chrebet

JAMES LOFTON: A big-play speed receiver who could make a quarterback look good. His five-team pass-catching numbers rank high on the NFL's all-time lists.

KELLEN WINSLOW: A wide receiver in a tight end's body. Hall of Famer Winslow helped make Air Coryell a prime-time show in San Diego.

2004 DRAFT YIELDS A DIGITAL BONANZA

Aaron Shea has Mark Campbell's number. Now all he needs is his former teammate's negotiating skills. From 2000 through 2002, the two tight ends wore Nos. 80 and 83 for the Cleveland Browns. When Campbell was traded to Buffalo before the 2003 season, he managed to retain his 83, never dreaming the uniform number would one day reap a bonanza. Neither did Shea expect his 80 to become lucrative, a double irony made possible by the 2004 NFL draft.

It didn't take long for Shea to hear from Cleveland's first-round pick, *Kellen Winslow Jr.*, after the April draft. Winslow Jr., also a tight end, wanted to wear the No. 80 his father, Hall of Fame tight end Kellen Winslow Sr., had made famous with San Diego. Winslow was willing to pay. And he had a six-year, $40 million contract to draw from.

Shea listened … and listened … and listened as Winslow pestered him about the number. He finally relented, handing over 80 to Winslow just before the regular-season opener. Shea switched to 83 in honor of Campbell but refused to provide details of his transaction.

"I didn't get a deal like Campbell got," he said with a sly grin. "Campbell robbed the guy. I guess I have to work on my negotiating skills."

Shea's reference sent reporters scurrying to check out his Campbell reference. Sure enough, Campbell had switched to 84 after selling his 83 to first-round Buffalo pick Lee Evans, a wide receiver out of Wisconsin. According to reports, Campbell got $20,000.

Winslow Jr.

HILL 80 ANDRE RISON 80 JACK BUTLER 80 CURTIS CONWAY 80 ERIC MOULDS

81
TIM BROWN

When wide receiver Brown played for Notre Dame in the 1988 Cotton Bowl, he chased down and tackled a bigger Texas A&M opponent who had lifted a towel from his belt during a pileup.

"It has my initials and my No. 81," he explained. And it was a gift from a friend. So it stands to reason that Brown would go to any lengths to make his jersey number memorable in the NFL. Over the next 17 seasons, all but one with the Raiders, he performed with Jerry Rice-like flair and made 1,094 receptions for 14,934 yards and 100 touchdowns. When the flashy future Hall of Famer signed with Tampa Bay for a final season in 2004, he let Buccaneers coach Jon Gruden do the chasing. Gruden politely asked veteran tight end Dave Moore to give up his No. 81. Not surprisingly, Moore agreed.

FAST FACTS

F Actor **Lee Majors**, TV's "Six Million Dollar Man," wore uniform No. 81 as an offensive and defensive tackle in the early 1960s at Eastern Kentucky University. Majors, known as Harvey Lee Yeary during his undergraduate days, had his football career shortened by a back injury.

F When **Torry Holt** played for N.C. State in the late 1990s, he couldn't get his old high school No. 9, so he wore 81—as in 8 +1 = 9. Apparently

Holt

NOTABLE 81s RUSS FRANCIS 81 CARL PICKENS 81 ANDY ROBUSTELLI 81 TERANCE MATHIS 81

DOUG ATKINS: Big, bad and mean, defensive end Atkins attacked blockers and quarterbacks with the power of a runaway locomotive.

CARL ELLER: The 6-6 defensive end fought the cold war in Minnesota for 15 years, swallowing so many quarterbacks he could have been tried for cannibalism.

ROY GREEN: It was a Cardinal sin to underestimate this big-play receiver, who recorded three 1,000-yard seasons and a career average of 16.0 yards per reception.

TORRY HOLT: For a talented receiver like Holt, getting drafted by the Rams must have seemed like winning the lottery.

NIGHT TRAIN LANE: The Godfather of Cornerbacks. Nobody inflicted punishment like the Night Train, who ran over ballcarriers, stripped receivers and played with Hall of Fame passion for the Rams, Cardinals and Lions.

ART MONK: Every Posse needs a leader. The Redskins had a good one.

MIROSLAV SATAN: What's scarier, his name or his ability around the net? Only the Sabres know for sure.

JACKIE SMITH: His dropped pass in Super Bowl 13 proved costly for the Cowboys and his reputation, but Smith was the best tight end in the NFL for most of his 16 seasons.

Satan

the addition still worked in 2002, when Holt traded in his 88 Rams jersey for 81—thanks to the departure of **Az-Zahir Hakim**, St. Louis' former 81.

In the late 1960s and early '70s, 81 (**Carl Eller**) + 88 (**Alan Page**) + 77 (**Gary Larsen**) + 70 (**Jim Marshall**) equaled the Purple People Eaters, the Minnesota Vikings' famed defensive line.

IN PHILADELPHIA, FANS SHOW NO BROTHERLY LOVE FOR T.O.

When Philadelphia officially cut ties with wide receiver **Terrell Owens** midway through the 2005 season, Eagles fans washed their hands of everything T.O., and sporting goods and apparel stores took a bath on merchandise they had invested thousands of dollars to acquire.

Owens was suspended four games without pay for "conduct detrimental to the team" after his steady stream of public criticism toward quarterback Donovan McNabb and Eagles management. Coach Andy Reid also told reporters Owens would not return to the team after the end of his suspension.

Fans showed full support of the team's action. Prior to the November 14 Monday night game against Dallas, a Philadelphia radio station staged a mock funeral near Lincoln Financial Field and invited fans to toss replica No. 81 jerseys and other Owens-related memorabilia into a coffin for burial. The response was overwhelming.

T.O. jerseys virtually disappeared in Philadelphia. Fans who had clogged roads around the Eagles' training camp in 2004 to get a look at Owens quickly severed any remaining emotional ties. By November 20, the No. 81 Owens jersey that was NFLShop.com's top seller in July was no longer in its top 10.

Nothing associated with Owens was selling, forcing store owners to slash $75 replica jerseys to $20 and down. Merchandisers said they had never witnessed such an abrupt drop in popularity.

RAGHIB ISMAIL 81 **HOWARD TWILLEY** 81 **O.J. McDUFFIE** 81 **AMANI TOOMER** 81 **WARREN WELLS** 81 **ERNEST GIVINS**

82
RAYMOND BERRY

How could he lose? Wide receiver Berry's No. 82 always will be linked to quarterback Johnny Unitas' 19 in that never-ending search for professional football's top passing combination.

Yeah, John Stallworth had Terry Bradshaw, Andre Reed had Jim Kelly, Shannon Sharpe had John Elway and Marvin Harrison has Peyton Manning. But Unitas to Berry— No. 19 to 82—still has, four decades later, that aura of near-perfection that might be approached, but never topped. Amazingly, the sanctity of 82 was tested in 1984 by the very franchise that had retired the number years earlier. Short of jerseys in the 80s—the range designated for wide receivers and tight ends by the NFL—the Colts "unretired" 82 and 89 (Hall of Famer Gino Marchetti's number) and assigned them to journeymen tight ends Mark Bell and Dave Young. But an outcry of indignation by fans and media prompted the team to do a quick about-face.

FAST FACTS

F When tight end *Shannon Sharpe* left Denver for Baltimore after the 1999 season, he tried to talk new teammate *Jermaine Lewis* out of his No. 84. When that failed, Sharpe offered Lewis two Rolex watches. Again Lewis refused, saying he could buy the watches himself. Sharpe settled for 82.

F *Raymond Berry's* No. 82 was retired by the Colts, but fellow Hall of Famers *John*

Sharpe

NOTABLE 82s DON BEEBE 82 JAMES JETT 82 VINCENT BRISBY 82 MARTIN STRAKA 82 YANCEY

Elite 82s

Johnson

DANTE HALL: Don't let the Human Joystick touch the ball. Kansas City's receiver/return specialist is a threat to score at any time.

VANCE JOHNSON: Denver's John Elway wasn't blessed with a great running attack in the 1980s, but at least he had Johnson and the other two Amigos.

OZZIE NEWSOME: Cleveland's Wizard was a Hall of Fame wide receiver trapped in a tight end's body.

MIKE QUICK: The name captures the essence of this standout Eagles receiver, who earned five straight Pro Bowl invitations in the 1980s.

JOHN STALLWORTH: Everybody talks about Lynn Swann, but the other half of Pittsburgh's Hall of Fame duo holds many of the team's receiving records.

JOHN TAYLOR: He'll always be remembered for his winning touchdown catch against Cincinnati in Super Bowl 23—and his role with the 49ers as second fiddle to the best receiver in football history.

Stallworth and *Ozzie Newsome* have not been accorded that honor. Wide receiver *Derek Hill* became the first player since Stallworth to wear 82 at Pittsburgh in 1989; tight end *Irv Smith* became the first player since Newsome to wear 82 at Cleveland in 1999.

After wearing 85 for two years in Cleveland, wide receiver *Derrick Alexander* wore 82 in stops at Baltimore, Kansas City and Minnesota. The number switch was to honor his brother Steven, who died in a 1988 car accident at age 23. Steven had worn No. 82 in high school.

Hall

SURE ENOUGH, SMITH SEES FANS WEARING 82

From the beginning, *Jimmy Smith* has been there. The speedy, big-play wide receiver is the only No. 82 in Jacksonville's NFL history, and there probably never will be another. Smith knows he has become synonymous with the digits, but wants to make one thing perfectly clear: This is not a numerological infatuation.

"It's just a number," he told Alex Abrams of the *Florida Times-Union.* "A number is what you make it. When I came to Jacksonville (in 1995, the team's expansion season), I liked 82. It fit me, and I said, 'Hey, you know what? I'm going to make this number so I could look up in the stands and see a bunch of 82s.' "

Smith has accomplished that goal. He leads the Jaguars in virtually every career receiving category and finished the 2005 regular season with 862 career catches for 12,287 yards and 67 touchdowns. After 11 seasons as Jacksonville's go-to receiver, Smith can look into the Alltel Stadium stands and spot numerous No. 82 replica jerseys. He admits now that he might be willing to pay for the number if he ever switches teams—but he would never sell it.

"No amount of money now," he said, "but if (a player) would have caught me the first couple of years (in Jacksonville), yeah."

Smith

THIGPEN 82 ANTWAAN RANDLE EL 82 PAUL COFFMAN 82 LIONEL ALDRIDGE 82 JIM HOUSTON 82 RODNEY HOLMAN

83

TED HENDRICKS

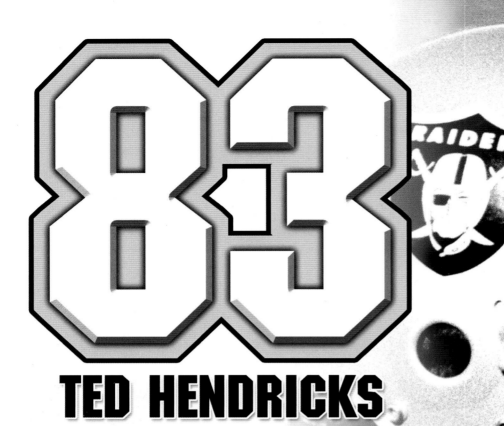

Defensive lineman Ben Davidson was to the early Raiders what linebacker Hendricks was to a later version—big, rowdy, mean, flamboyant and No. 83. The Mad Stork, all 6-7 and 220 pounds of him, sought out Davidson when he arrived in Oakland in 1975 and asked permission to use the number, which he had worn in a previous four-year stop at Baltimore. Big Ben, the story goes, twitched his handlebar mustache in delight over the prospect of such a world-class player and carouser doing him this honor. Stories abound about Hendricks' off-field antics. On the field, he was creative and unpredictable, which contributed to his effectiveness. The Stork was one of the great pass and kick blockers of all time, thanks to his long arms, and he collected four Super Bowl rings during a Hall of Fame career that ended in 1983—one while playing with the Colts and three with the Raiders.

FAST FACTS

F World class hurdler **Renaldo Nehemiah** wore No. 83 from 1982-84 with the 49ers, catching 43 passes and scoring four touchdowns. Apparently, not even **Joe Montana** was capable of turning a track star into a great receiver.

F **Mark Clayton**, **Dan Marino**'s go-to receiver for 10 seasons in Miami, wore No. 37 instead of his familiar 83 in training camp before his final season with Green Bay. Near the end of camp, Clayton got his 83 when rookie wideout Orlando McKay generously switched to 81.

NOTABLE 83s MORRIS STROUD 83 BOBBY WALSTON 83 GOLDEN RICHARDS 83 STEPHONE PAIGE 83 J.J. STOKES 83

Elite 83s

REED CHOOSES NOT TO BE A BEGGAR

For *Andre Reed*, it was simply a matter of respect. In 15 seasons as the go-to receiver in Buffalo, he had caught 941 passes for 13,095 yards and 86 touchdowns. He was the Bills' honored No. 83, a veteran of four Super Bowls and quarterback Jim Kelly's longtime favorite target. Reed even had an 83 tattooed on his shoulder.

So why, after signing with Denver before the 2000 season, was the veteran begging for his career-long uniform number? Reed was reduced to No. 81 in training camp because second-year Broncos receiver Travis McGriff, who had caught three passes as a 1999 rookie, wouldn't give up 83.

"Give" is the key word. McGriff was perfectly willing to sell it—for "a whole lot of money." Reed said no to that idea, suspecting that his outstanding career was nearing its end anyway. He said his No. 83 tattoo would remain with him long after his playing stint with the Broncos.

McGriff, who claimed an affection for the number 3 dating to his college career at Florida, smiled when he heard about the tattoo. "That's why you don't get the tattoo of a girl's name or a football number," he said, " 'cause stuff like this happens."

Reed was smart to keep his money. Released by the Broncos before the season, he quickly signed with Washington, where he found his 83 aspirations blocked again, this time by starting wide receiver Albert Connell. Reed spent his final NFL campaign wearing No. 84.

Gault

Clayton

BEN DAVIDSON: The prototypical Raider, from handlebar mustache and free-spirited lifestyle to nasty temper and brute-force mentality in the AFL trenches.

WILLIE GAULT: Speed kills. Just ask the countless defensive backs burned by this world-class sprinter, or anyone who saw him terrorize the Patriots in Super Bowl 20.

JOHN JEFFERSON: Dan Fouts had a special affinity for Jefferson, who averaged 12 TD catches in his three seasons as an Air Coryell Charger.

Davidson

HARRIS

LOUIS LIPPS: It's never easy replacing a legend, but Lipps stepped in for Lynn Swann as John Stallworth's Pittsburgh running mate in 1984.

GEORGE SAUER: Few teams in the 1960s had the luxury of two 1,000-yard receivers. Joe Namath could pick his poison, Sauer or Hall of Famer Don Maynard.

PAT TILLEY: Great numbers for not-so-great teams. Tilley was a person of interest from 1976-86 with the Cardinals.

STEVE JORDAN *83* FLIPPER ANDERSON *83* RICKY FEACHER *83* ANTHONY MILLER

84

SHARPE BROTHERS
STERLING & SHANNON

We admit it's blatantly unfair to let the brothers Sharpe gang up on such other deserving NFL receivers as Randy Moss, Herman Moore, Gary Clark, Webster Slaughter, Brent Jones and Joey Galloway.

But you have to admit there's a lot to be said for the chemistry and charisma they brought to the game. Shannon is the most prolific pass-catching tight end in history and a member of the trash-talking Hall of Fame; Sterling, who once held the record for receptions in one season, appeared headed for the football Hall of Fame before a neck injury derailed his career after seven seasons with Green Bay. Both are smooth in front of a microphone, and they've always been very competitive. Older brother Sterling got first dibs on No. 84 when he broke in with the Packers in 1988. Shannon couldn't get his 84 until 1992 after spending his first two Denver seasons as 81.

FAST FACTS

F *Billy "White Shoes" Johnson*, the diminutive touch-down-scoring machine who took end zone dancing to a new level with his wobbly-kneed "Funky Chicken" celebrations, wore No. 84 from 1974-80 with the Houston Oilers—his peak years as the most electrifying return man in the NFL.

F Wide receiver *Joey Galloway* has worn No. 84 for three teams covering 11 NFL seasons, most recently Tampa Bay in 2004 and '05.

NOTABLE 84s JACK SNOW 84 CARROLL DALE 84 BOB TRUMPY 84 PAUL WIGGIN 84 FRED ARBANAS 84 WEBSTER

Novacek

MOSS, AS NO. 18, IS QUIET AND EFFICIENT

The old *Randy Moss* wore uniform No. 84 for the Minnesota Vikings and made his job of NFL wide receiver look easy. For six straight seasons, he toyed with defensive backs while catching passes for 1,233 or more yards. For six of his seven years with the Vikings, he recorded double-digit touchdown totals.

Moss, the lanky receiver, was exciting and remarkable. But Moss, the surly and unpredictable personality, was difficult to swallow. There was the $10,000 fine he paid for pretending to moon the Green Bay crowd in a 2005 playoff game. There were sideline altercations with teammates, brushes with the law, incidents on the team bus and other behavior issues. When asked about his one-play-on, one-play-off style, Moss told reporters, "I play when I want to play."

Moss' act eventually wore thin, prompting the Vikings to trade him to Oakland after the '04 season. Moss showed up at an introductory news conference wearing a No. 18 jersey— the number he had worn as a Vikings training camp rookie in 1998. Fellow receiver Jerry Porter, who wears 84 for the Raiders, offered to give his number to Moss, who declined. So when the 2005 season opened, there was No. 18 Moss lining up opposite No. 84. The double dose of Moss didn't transform the Raiders, who struggled to a 4-12 record. For No. 18, it was a quietly efficient season, both off the field and on: He caught 60 passes for 1,005 yards and eight touchdowns.

Moss

GARY CLARK: Every Posse needs a tracker who can home in on passes and make the big play. Clark was that guy for the Redskins from 1985-92.

BRENT JONES: Quarterbacks like Joe Montana and Steve Young dream about tight ends like Jones, who excelled at finding openings underneath.

HERMAN MOORE: He dropped off fast, but Moore's mad rush to the 600-reception plateau with the Lions was remarkable.

JAY NOVACEK: It wasn't the drop-off of Troy Aikman, Emmitt Smith or Michael Irvin that signaled the end of the Cowboys' Super Bowl run in the 1990s—it was the retirement of this underappreciated tight end.

Galloway

F *J.T. Snow*, familiar to San Francisco fans as No. 6 in his nine seasons with the Giants, asked to wear 84 in 2006 as a new member of the Red Sox. The first baseman wore the unusual baseball number as a tribute to his father, Jack Snow, who died early in the year. Jack had worn 84 as a standout receiver for the Los Angeles Rams.

SLAUGHTER 84 ALFRED JENKINS 84 JIM MUTSCHELLER 84 J.T. SMITH 84

NICK BUONICONTI

He ran all over the field, a squat, roundish middle linebacker who inflicted his will on Miami opponents in the 1970s. "Oh yeah, what's his name, No. 85! I remember him." Such was life for the former captain of the Dolphins' vaunted "No-Name Defense"—an undersized overachiever who spent his 14-year professional career under a cloak of anonymity. He was No. 85 for seven years with the AFL's Boston Patriots after NFL teams passed him over in the draft. He was 85 for seven seasons with the Dolphins. What's his name, you know the fiery, proud and passionate leader of the defense that anchored consecutive Super Bowl winners and that perfect 17-0 season in 1972. "His first name was Nick, wasn't it? Last name started with a B, I think." Don't worry. Just look for No. 85 in your Hall of Fame program.

Elite 85s

ISAAC CURTIS: Check out that 17.1-yards-per-reception average this steady Cincinnati wideout posted over a 12-year run that included the team's first Super Bowl appearance.

MEL GRAY: He could run and catch. That lethal combination made him a big-play option in the 1970s and '80s for St. Louis quarterback Jim Hart.

DEL SHOFNER: Y.A. Tittle-to-Shofner set the offensive tone for the Giants from 1961-63, when the team made three straight appearances in the NFL title game. The speedy wideout topped 1,100 yards receiving in each of those seasons.

JACK YOUNGBLOOD: The "John Wayne of Pro Football" played much of the 1979 postseason (three games) with a broken leg. It's hard to measure heart, but the Rams' Hall of Fame defensive end definitely had it.

FAST FACTS

F A Green Bay wide receiver wearing No. 85 caught the first touchdown pass in Super Bowl history. Eleven-year veteran **Max McGee** pulled in a 37-yard first-quarter strike from **Bart Starr** in the Packers' 35-10 victory over Kansas City in Super Bowl 1.

F The number 85 has been retired by the St. Louis Cardinals in honor of longtime owner and president **August A. Busch Jr.** "Gussie" was honored in 1984 in conjunction with his 85th birthday.

F **Petr Klima**, who scored 313 goals for six NHL teams from 1985-99, wore uniform No. 85 to commemorate the year he defected from Czechoslovakia.

86

BUCK BUCHANAN

His real first name was Junious, which might explain why everyone called him Buck. But Mr. Buchanan, by any name, might have been the most feared player in the American Football League. The first player chosen in the 1963 AFL draft, the big defensive tackle from Grambling was measured by a delighted Kansas City coach Hank Stram at 6-7, 286 pounds, and he soon was sending shivers (both the quivering and forearm kind) through the rest of the league. "He revolutionized the game," said former Oakland coach John Madden, who talked Raiders owner Al Davis into drafting offensive guard Gene Upshaw (6-5, 255) just to block him. "Guys that size usually played on the outside. Buck was the first tall guy to play inside." Upshaw had some success blocking Junious, but even he was taken aback. "When you played Buck," he once said, "you couldn't sleep the night before a game."

Elite86s

GARY COLLINS: He caught three touchdown passes from Frank Ryan in the 1964 NFL championship game, endearing himself to Cleveland fans forever. But Collins also made 70 TD catches over an impressive 10-year career.

BOYD DOWLER: It's no coincidence Dowler's career runs parallel to Bart Starr's—they were a near-perfect match.

ANTONIO FREEMAN: Every great quarterback needs a go-to receiver. Brett Favre got plenty of mileage out of Freeman for seven years.

STANLEY MORGAN: Check out the numbers: 534 catches, 10,352 yards and 67 touchdowns. Sir Stanley was a bona fide, died-in-the-wool Patriot.

HINES WARD: It's fitting he's a Steeler because he plays the game the way it's supposed to be played. And he's pretty darn good at it, as a Super Bowl MVP honor attests.

FAST FACTS

F Longtime Eagles fans might remember a two-way end who wore uniform No. 86 in 1951 and '52. That was **Bud Grant**, who went on to greater fame as the coach who led Minnesota to four Super Bowl appearances.

F **Dante Lavelli**, Otto Graham's go-to receiver in the 1940s and '50s, wore No. 86 for the last five years of his Hall of Fame career. Lavelli wore 56 from 1946-51 before the NFL's new numbering system was introduced.

F The **McKeever twins**, Marlin and Mike, retained a spiritual connection by flip-flopping their uniform number digits when they played for USC from 1958-60. Marlin, an end and fullback, wore 86 and Mike, an offensive guard, opted for 68.

NOTABLE 86s **JAKE REED** 86 **DUB JONES** 86 **BOYD DOWLER** 86 **MIKE TICE** 86 **CEDRICK HARDMAN** 86 **BILLY HOWTON**

87

WILLIE DAVIS

The soaring, fingertip grab that turned No. 87 into a household highlight also makes Dwight Clark the sexy pick here. But it would be remiss to ignore the career-long consistency and durability that helped the Green Bay Packers and Davis earn five championship rings. In the 1960s football Camelot ruled by Vince Lombardi, the Packers' No. 87 was an undersized but relentless and crafty end on an impenetrable defensive wall. He, too, had a flair for the big play, though his "moments" came with sacks and tackles and not spectacular catches and touchdowns. Give Clark his due: The Catch, dramatic and memorable, secured San Francisco's 28-27 title game win over Dallas and a berth for the 49ers in Super Bowl 16. But Davis, after all, is a Hall of Famer. If you disagree with the pick, just say cheeeeese!

Elite 87s

BUCK BAKER: The NASCAR pioneer who won 46 races and the second of consecutive Winston Cup titles while driving an 87 Chevrolet in 1957 might be better known for the Buck Baker Driving School, where many drivers learned their craft.

BILL CARPENTER: The "Lonely End" in Army coach Red Blaik's innovative split end formation of 1958 and '59 opted for a military career over pro football, eventually rising to the rank of general.

DAVE CASPER: The free-spirited tight end was a ghost story for Raiders opponents from 1974-80 and later as an Oiler.

BEN COATES: A pass-catching machine for the Patriots from 1991-99, this tight end was a Cinderella story out of Division II Livingstone College.

ED McCAFFREY: He wore 87 only in Denver, where he helped John Elway deliver two Super Bowl titles.

FAST FACTS

When **Donald Brashear** was traded to Philadelphia in 2001, he couldn't get the No. 8 he had worn for five-plus years with the Canucks. So he asked for 7, which the Flyers had retired for **Bill Barber**. Brashear finally opted for 87—a combination of the two.

Center **Sidney Crosby**, the Pittsburgh Penguins' newest high-scoring phenom, wears No. 87 to signify the year he was born.

Titans receiver **Kevin Dyson** was wearing No. 87 when he came up inches short of a game-tying touchdown on the final play of Super Bowl 34. He was halted by Rams linebacker **Mike Jones**.

NOTABLE 87s KEENAN McCARDELL 87 LIONEL TAYLOR 87 CLAUDE HUMPHREY 87 TOM WADDLE 87 TAMARICK VANOVER

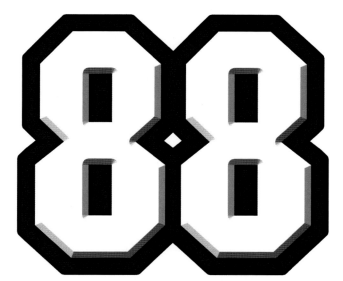

ALAN PAGE

Mardye McDole, Don Hasselbeck, Billy Waddy and Buster Rhymes were bad enough. But Marc May? What in the name of Bud Grant were the Minnesota Vikings thinking in that forgotten decade of the 1980s? McDole, Hasselbeck, Waddy and Rhymes were short-term Vikings who were handed the No. 88 jersey worn by Hall of Fame defensive tackle Page from 1967-78. May was a 1987—quick, cover your eyes—replacement player, the last Viking to wear 88 before it finally was retired for Mr. Purple People Eater a year later. Page, who traded in his football uniform after the 1981 season and later donned the long, black robe of a Minnesota Supreme Court judge, edges out Lynn Swann, Michael Irvin, Tony Gonzalez and Eric Lindros in a close battle of 88s. Note that May is not on that list. But at least he'll always be the answer to a No. 88 trivia question.

Elite 88s

TONY GONZALEZ: Safeties are too small and linebackers too slow for this prototypical tight end, who catches passes and blocks like a demon.

MARVIN HARRISON: Peyton Manning and go-to receiver Harrison are so in sync observers think they must be able to read each others' thoughts. Or maybe they just practice a lot.

MICHAEL IRVIN: Loud, flamboyant and talented, Irvin helped put the "Super" in the 1990s vocabulary of Dallas fans.

JOHN MACKEY: Johnny Unitas used this trend-setting tight end as a deadly weapon in his deep passing game.

DREW PEARSON: Maybe a few Hail Marys would get this Cowboys receiver into the Hall—where many think he belongs.

LYNN SWANN: Numbers don't paint a full picture of this clutch Steelers receiver, whose elegance was captured by his appropriate last name.

FAST FACTS

F When *Jerry Rice* arrived in San Francisco in 1985, he was unable to get the No. 88 he wore at Mississippi Valley State because *Freddie Solomon* had it. So he took 80 and turned it into a 49ers institution.

F When *John Mackey* attended Syracuse, the 44 he wanted (Jim Brown's old number) was being worn by future Heisman Trophy winner *Ernie Davis*. So Mackey doubled his pleasure to 88, never missing an opportunity to inform Davis that he was "twice as good as he was."

F In 1999, *Dale Jarrett*'s 88 Ford became the highest-numbered car to win a Cup Series championship in more than four decades. *Carl Kiekhaefer*'s 300B Chrysler (the number reflected the model) was driven to victory in 1956 by *Buck Baker*.

MIKE DITKA

For almost four decades now, Chicago Bears coaches have been looking for the next Ditka. Even former coach Ditka searched for the next Ditka. No. 89 clearly set the bar high in 1961 when he showed up at Papa Bear's training camp and redefined the tight end position, demonstrating that good blockers also can be great receivers. Through 1966 with the Bears and 1972 with Philadelphia and Dallas, the chubby-faced, crew-cut Ditka opened the doors to the Hall of Fame for tight ends while setting new standards for intensity. A few have matched and even surpassed Ditka's skill level, but none in the city Iron Mike once owned. Quick quiz: What do Terry Stoepel, Bob Wallace, Mitch Krenk, James Coley, Ryan Wetnight and Dustin Lyman have in common? Answer: They are Bears tight ends, all 89s, who weren't the next Ditka.

Elite 89s

WES CHANDLER: The Chargers' Dan Fouts had a lot of weapons at his disposal, none more dangerous than the speedy Chandler from 1981-87.

BOB DEE: Thanks to an end zone fumble recovery in the AFL's first preseason game in 1960, the former Patriots defensive end holds distinction as the first player to score a touchdown for the new league. Dee also was good enough to get his No. 89 retired.

GINO MARCHETTI: Terminator. Dominator. Intimidator. All the names fit Marchetti, the fire-breathing defensive end who introduced fans to the power rush. Marchetti was a demon for Colts teams that won consecutive NFL championships in 1958 and '59.

OTIS TAYLOR: He was an early version of the modern receiver—big, strong and fast. The Chiefs' Taylor showcased those talents on a 46-yard TD catch in Super Bowl 4 against the Vikings.

FAST FACTS

Alexander Mogilny has worn 89 throughout an NHL career that began in 1989, the year he earned freedom by defecting to the United States from the Soviet Union.

Fred Dryer, who played detective Rick Hunter in the 1980s hit television series *Hunter*, wore No. 89 for 13 NFL seasons as a defensive end with the Giants (1969-71) and Rams (1972-81).

Steve Tasker, a 185-pound ninth-round pick by the Houston Oilers in 1985, wore No. 89 in his 12 seasons with the Buffalo Bills and earned seven Pro Bowl invitations as a special-teams player.

NOTABLE 89s MARK BAVARO 89 NAT MOORE 89 BILLY JOE DUPREE 89 MARK CHMURA 89 FRANK WYCHECK

BOB KURLAND

Long before the big bodies of Neil Smith, Jevon Kearse and George Webster flashed the big 9-0 on their uniforms, the number belonged to college basketball star and pioneer Kurland. The suspicion here is that Kurland, one of the game's first 7-footers, probably could have been successful trading blows with the likes of his No. 90 football successors. Kurland was just plain big. And his scoring and superlative rebounding were major reasons why Oklahoma A&M (later Oklahoma State) became the first team to win consecutive NCAA Tournament championships in 1945 and '46. Other credits on Kurland's lengthy resume: Former coach Hank Iba claimed he was the first player to dunk a ball in game competition, and the goaltending rule was passed to negate the shot-blocking tactics of Kurland and DePaul contemporary George Mikan.

Elite 90s

JOE JUNEAU: The speedy center was No. 49 as a high-scoring rookie for the Boston Bruins, No. 90 during his less-spectacular, steady-as-she-goes days with Washington and Buffalo.

NEIL SMITH: The big defensive end, who rushed hard and swung for the fences, played a lot longer in Kansas City but earned two Super Bowl rings with the Broncos.

DICK TRICKLE: This lovable NASCAR loser laughed all the way to the bank during his four-decade career. Trickle piloted Junie Donlavey's No. 90 car for 2½ seasons in the late 1990s.

Smith

FAST FACTS

F No player has worn uniform No. 90 for the New York Jets since 1992, when defensive end **Dennis Byrd** was paralyzed in a game against the Chiefs.

F Hard-charging defensive end **Jevon Kearse**, a three-time Pro Bowler who wore No. 90 in five seasons with the Titans, switched to 93 in 2004 when he signed as a free agent with the Eagles. Kearse couldn't persuade defensive tackle **Corey Simon** to give up 90.

F When **Alonzo Spellman** signed with Dallas in 1999, his familiar No. 90 was being worn by third-round draft pick **Dat Nguyen**, who gladly switched to 45, explaining that the two digits of either number added up to 9—the number he had worn at Texas A&M. Nguyen, a linebacker, later got good news and bad news: He made the Cowboys' season-opening roster, but he had to switch to a number in the 50s to conform to the NFL's numbering system. With 54 unavailable, he settled for 59.

NOTABLE 90s JULIUS PEPPERS 90 ALONZO SPELLMAN 90 EZRA JOHNSON 90 GEORGE WEBSTER 90 TONY BRACKENS

91

SERGEI FEDOROV

It doesn't represent the speed of his slap shot or how fast Fedorov can skate, although he sometimes seems capable of reaching 91 mph. The numeral is much more meaningful to the former Soviet national team center. It represents freedom, as in 1991, when he played his first season with the Detroit Red Wings after defecting to the United States. It's hard to imagine a more naturally skilled hockey player than Fedorov, whose size, free-flowing speed, puck-handling ability and quickness produced 400 goals in 13 seasons and helped Detroit win three Stanley Cup titles and him the hand of Anna Kournikova—temporarily, at least. Never mind that Fedorov defected again, from the MIGHTY Red Wings to the Mighty Ducks, who then traded him after one-plus season to Columbus. That, Fedorov has discovered, is freedom NHL-style.

Elite 91s

LESLIE O'NEAL: Everyone reveres offensive triplets (a star quarterback-running back-wide receiver combination), but end O'Neal was part of a triple-threat Chargers defense that also featured linebacker Junior Seau and safety Rodney Harrison.

ROBERT PORCHER: Quietly and relentlessly, this defensive end fattened up on quarterbacks for 13 seasons and finished as Detroit's career sack leader.

DENNIS RODMAN: The NBA's best pound-for-pound, inch-for-inch rebounder wore this unusual number during three championship seasons with the Bulls because the sum of the digits equaled his original number (10) in Detroit. As for the wedding dress, tattoos and piercings … let's not go there.

FAST FACTS

F Forward **Ron Artest** should have known better. He was wearing No. 91 for Indiana—a tribute to bad boy **Dennis Rodman**—on that fateful fall day in 2004 when he participated in a brawl with Detroit fans that resulted in his suspension for most of the 2004-05 NBA season.

F When defensive end **Leslie O'Neal** and defensive tackle **Chester McGlockton** were signed by the Chiefs in 1998, both requested 91—the number they had worn throughout their NFL careers. O'Neal won out by virtue of seniority (11 years to six), forcing McGlockton to switch to 75.

F Former linebacker **Kevin Greene** wore No. 91 throughout his 15-year NFL career, but only because he proved adept at bribery when he reached San Francisco in 1997. "I was able to bribe the guy who had it," Greene said. "I bought him some furniture. I bought his wife a 10-speed bike. And I got my 91."

NOTABLE 91s **LEONARD LITTLE** 91 **BRIAN NOBLE** 91 **ALFRED WILLIAMS** 91 **JOHNNY STRZYKALSKI** 91 **JEFF WRIGHT**

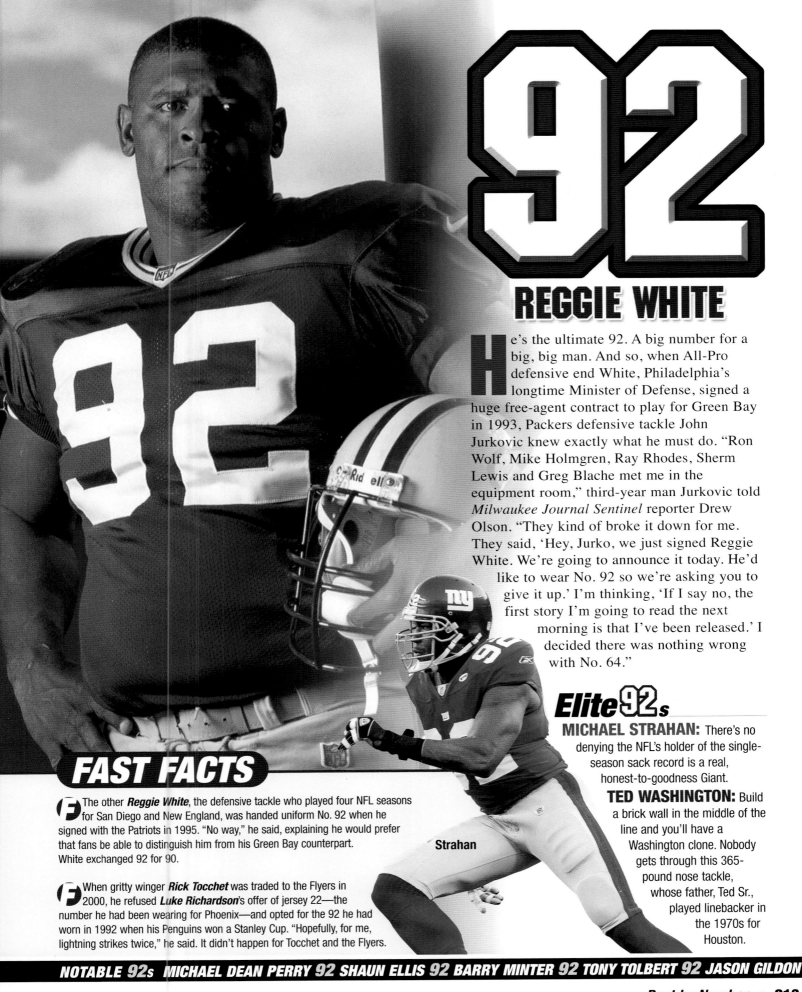

92
REGGIE WHITE

He's the ultimate 92. A big number for a big, big man. And so, when All-Pro defensive end White, Philadelphia's longtime Minister of Defense, signed a huge free-agent contract to play for Green Bay in 1993, Packers defensive tackle John Jurkovic knew exactly what he must do. "Ron Wolf, Mike Holmgren, Ray Rhodes, Sherm Lewis and Greg Blache met me in the equipment room," third-year man Jurkovic told *Milwaukee Journal Sentinel* reporter Drew Olson. "They kind of broke it down for me. They said, 'Hey, Jurko, we just signed Reggie White. We're going to announce it today. He'd like to wear No. 92 so we're asking you to give it up.' I'm thinking, 'If I say no, the first story I'm going to read the next morning is that I've been released.' I decided there was nothing wrong with No. 64."

FAST FACTS

F The other *Reggie White*, the defensive tackle who played four NFL seasons for San Diego and New England, was handed uniform No. 92 when he signed with the Patriots in 1995. "No way," he said, explaining he would prefer that fans be able to distinguish him from his Green Bay counterpart. White exchanged 92 for 90.

F When gritty winger *Rick Tocchet* was traded to the Flyers in 2000, he refused *Luke Richardson*'s offer of jersey 22—the number he had been wearing for Phoenix—and opted for the 92 he had worn in 1992 when his Penguins won a Stanley Cup. "Hopefully, for me, lightning strikes twice," he said. It didn't happen for Tocchet and the Flyers.

Strahan

Elite 92s

MICHAEL STRAHAN: There's no denying the NFL's holder of the single-season sack record is a real, honest-to-goodness Giant.

TED WASHINGTON: Build a brick wall in the middle of the line and you'll have a Washington clone. Nobody gets through this 365-pound nose tackle, whose father, Ted Sr., played linebacker in the 1970s for Houston.

NOTABLE 92s MICHAEL DEAN PERRY **92** SHAUN ELLIS **92** BARRY MINTER **92** TONY TOLBERT **92** JASON GILDON

93

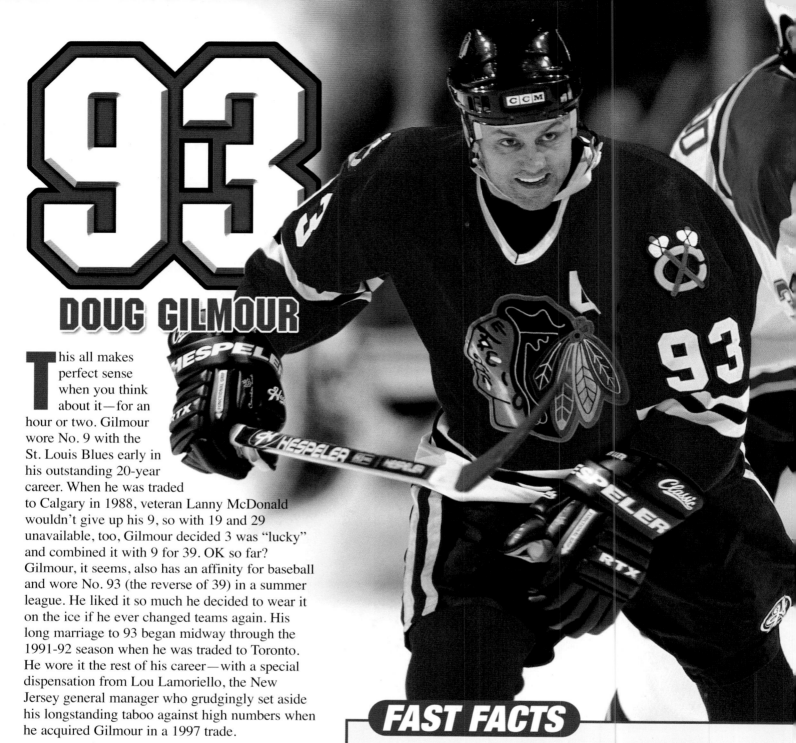

DOUG GILMOUR

This all makes perfect sense when you think about it—for an hour or two. Gilmour wore No. 9 with the St. Louis Blues early in his outstanding 20-year career. When he was traded to Calgary in 1988, veteran Lanny McDonald wouldn't give up his 9, so with 19 and 29 unavailable, too, Gilmour decided 3 was "lucky" and combined it with 9 for 39. OK so far? Gilmour, it seems, also has an affinity for baseball and wore No. 93 (the reverse of 39) in a summer league. He liked it so much he decided to wear it on the ice if he ever changed teams again. His long marriage to 93 began midway through the 1991-92 season when he was traded to Toronto. He wore it the rest of his career—with a special dispensation from Lou Lamoriello, the New Jersey general manager who grudgingly set aside his longstanding taboo against high numbers when he acquired Gilmour in a 1997 trade.

Elite 93s

GILBERT BROWN: It was a long way around this 340-pound defensive boulder, and runners who took this route seldom made it to the Green Bay secondary.

JOHN RANDLE: Fire and brimstone. The motor never stopped for this premier defensive tackle, who sacked, pillaged and taunted with the passion of a real-life Viking.

RICHARD SEYMOUR: No one on Bill Belichick's New England roster is irreplaceable, but defensive tackle Seymour's size, strength, quickness and drive make him as close as a player can get.

FAST FACTS

From 1997-99, the Vikings had two of the NFL's most prominent No. 93s playing side by side on their defensive line. *John Randle*, a career 93, was at tackle; *Jerry Ball*, who wore 96 in deference to Randle, was at nose tackle. Ball had worn 93 for the Lions, Browns and Raiders before coming to Minnesota.

In 1993, Vancouver Canucks center *Petr Nedved* switched from No. 19 to 93 because that was the year the former Czech star became a Canadian citizen.

When the Tampa Bay Lightning grabbed veteran goaltender *Daren Puppa* in the 1993 expansion draft, he celebrated his fresh start by switching to No. 93 and wore it for the last seven seasons of his 15-year career.

NOTABLE 93s KEVIN CARTER 93 GREG TOWNSEND 93 MIKE FOX 93 TRACE ARMSTRONG 93 MARTY LYONS 93

94

CHARLES HALEY

He's the best No. 94 ever to put on a uniform. Remember Haley's outlandish, blatantly sexist reply to a question about his violent ways on the football field? "If they wanted a bunch of women," he said, "they would have made all of us quarterbacks." Tongue in cheek? Only the scowling, contrary Haley knew for sure. But his quarterback bashing didn't end there. The undersized defensive end with the pit-bull mentality ravaged more than a few in his heyday as a premier sackman for the San Francisco 49ers and Dallas Cowboys. The bottom line for this unsmiling, unrelenting purveyor of football mayhem is best conveyed by this career-defining fact: No. 94 is the only player in history to play for five Super Bowl winners.

Elite 94s

Stubblefield

CHAD BROWN: Linebackers who can get to the quarterback typically fare well in the NFL. Brown has thrived for 13 seasons (through 2005) in stops at Pittsburgh, Seattle and New England.

DANA STUBBLEFIELD: A disruptive force when at the top of his game, defensive tackle Stubblefield helped the 49ers win Super Bowl 29.

KEITH TRAYLOR: This massive 340-pound load requires double teams on running plays, even in the twilight of his career. Many have tried to move Tractor Traylor, but only a select few have managed to do it consistently.

FAST FACTS

F **Randy White** wore No. 54 as a Hall of Fame defensive tackle for the Cowboys, but he is remembered as 94 at the University of Maryland, where his jersey number is retired.

F In the long history of the Chicago Bears, no player had worn No. 94 until 1987, when defensive tackle **Dick Chapura** wore it in the first of three seasons with the team.

F **Bill Elliott**, who built his NASCAR reputation driving No. 9 cars, was less successful in a 94 Ford from 1995-2000, when he owned his own team. The 94 was partially a tribute to Elliott's nephew Casey, who used that number as a NASCAR All-Pro Series driver before dying of cancer.

NOTABLE 94s **LUTHER ELLISS** 94 **JOHN ABRAHAM** 94 **JOE JOHNSON** 94 **KABEER GBAJA-BIAMILA** 94 **SEAN GILBERT**

95

RICHARD DENT

"**T**he sackman's comin', I'm your man Dent. If the quarterback's slow, he's gonna get bent." If those words sound familiar, it's because the 265-pound singer was one of the yappin' and rappin' Chicago Bears who took their Super Bowl Shuffle routine to record heights before Super Bowl 20. You can't say the Patriots weren't forewarned. The Bears' powerful 46 defense recorded seven sacks, and the sackman "bent" a little quarterback himself while forcing two fumbles and earning MVP honors in the NFL title game victory. Dent, a defensive end, went on to make No. 95 a Chicago institution, setting Bears records for sacks in a career ($124\frac{1}{2}$), single season ($17\frac{1}{2}$) and single game ($4\frac{1}{2}$) before going to San Francisco in 1994. If not for the Super Bowl Shuffle (and those never-ending Police Academy movies), No. 95 honors might well have gone to Bubba Smith, a defensive lineman who wore it while starring for Michigan State in the mid-1960s.

Elite 95s

WILLIAM FULLER: This mobile pass-rushing machine earned four Pro Bowl invitations—one with the Oilers and three in as many seasons with the Eagles.

CHAD HENNINGS: After the 6-6 Air Force All-American served his country, he served the Cowboys as a defensive end. He got a big rush out of three Super Bowl titles in the 1990s.

GREG LLOYD: This man of steel could rush the passer or drop into coverage, skills verified by his career totals of 54.5 sacks and 11 interceptions. Five Pro Bowl invitations suggest Lloyd was an elite outside linebacker.

BRYCE PAUP: Snap, crackle, Paup. The sounds of an NFL sackmaster.

FAST FACTS

F The Canadiens' 10,000th home-ice goal, scored January 27, 2002, came with an unusual twist. It is believed to be the first in NHL history in which all three players involved wore uniform numbers in the 90s. *Sergei Berezin* (95), the goal scorer, was assisted by *Yanic Perreault* (94) and *Doug Gilmore* (93).

F When Steelers outside linebacker *Joey Porter* excelled while wearing No. 95 in his 1999 rookie training camp, many people told him he reminded them of former outside man *Greg Lloyd*. The comparison spooked Porter, who switched to 55 before the season.

NOTABLE 95s MICHAEL CARTER 95 ALEKSEY MOROZOV 95 JOE SALAVE'A 95 JOHN ENGELBERGER 95 RICK LYLE

96

BILL VOISELLE

A 6-4 righthander known fondly during his 1940s pitching days as "Totsie" or "Big Bill," Voiselle is something of a baseball novelty. He didn't put 96 on the map—it was there long before he showed up—but it's fair to say he gave the number, and his hometown, more publicity than either had received before. Voiselle was from Ninety Six, S.C., which explains why he wore such an odd number with the Boston Braves and Chicago Cubs over the final four seasons of his nine-year career. Voiselle was downright boring (Nos. 19, 5, 17 and 30) during his first five-plus major league seasons with the New York Giants, although he did win 21 games in 1944. But as 96 in 1948, he won 13 times and was part of that "Spahn and Sain and pray for rain" rotation that took the Braves to the World Series. Big Bill started and lost Game 6 of that fall classic.

Elite 96s

Kennedy

SEAN JONES: This hard-charging end recorded 113 career sacks over 13 seasons, nine of them while wearing No. 96 for the Oilers and Packers.

CORTEZ KENNEDY: The Seahawks played only one postseason game from 1990-2000, Kennedy's tenure on the defensive line. But make no mistake: He was a big-time player.

CLYDE SIMMONS: A quarterback nightmare: Reggie White coming at you from one end, Simmons attacking full speed from the other. The Eagles soared on defense from 1986-92 with those bookend bashers.

FAST FACTS

F Japanese righthander *Mac Suzuki*, who wore No. 96 for the Mariners during the springs of 1995, '96 and '97, also wore it in his one major league game during that span (1996). Suzuki chose 96 because his fastball was clocked at 96 mph.

F The first person to wear No. 96 for the Green Bay Packers was a replacement player—defensive end *Tony Leiker*—in 1987.

F When the Red Wings acquired Russian *Dmitri Mironov* late in the 1997-98 season, second-year man *Tomas Holmstrom* gave up his 15—the number Mironov had worn for Anaheim—and switched to 96. Mironov was gone the next season, but Holmstrom decided to remain a 96.

NOTABLE 96s DARRELL RUSSELL 96 HARALD HASSELBACH 96 REGGIE CAMP 96 ADALIUS THOMAS 96 ELLIS WYMS

97

CORNELIUS BENNETT

For all you numbers crunchers, 97 is better than 55. Not higher, better—as in wins, losses and Super Bowls better. Just ask Bennett, who made a strong first impression in the mid-1980s as a consensus All-American and Lombardi Award winner while wearing No. 97 at Alabama. As No. 55 for the first three years of his professional career, Bennett was an outside linebacker for a Buffalo team struggling to join the NFL elite. Reunited with 97 over his last 11 NFL seasons, Bennett was a terrific outside linebacker for Buffalo, Atlanta and Indianapolis teams that carved out a 113-63 regular-season record and appeared in five Super Bowls. Run, jump, tackle, fight off blocks, rush the passer—Bennett just seemed to do everything better as 97. But beware: The power of 97 does have its limits. Bennett also is one of two players who are 0-5 in Super Bowl appearances.

Elite 97s

SIMEON RICE: After surviving a stormy early career in the Arizona desert, the hard-charging defensive end started pillaging quarterbacks for Tampa Bay. Like the rest of the Buccaneers' defenders in 2002, Rice was super.

JEREMY ROENICK: The same qualities that make him superior on the ice—passion, drama and flash—also make him controversial off it. But 1,000-point scorers maybe have the right to speak their mind or be a little different.

BRYANT YOUNG: A potential career-ending broken leg in 1998 only seemed to inspire this powerful defensive stopper, who still was going strong with the 49ers through the 2005 season.

Roenick

FAST FACTS

F Other than the 300-series Chrysler models that won point championships for owner *Carl Kiekhaefer* in 1955 and '56, *Kurt Busch*'s 97 is the highest number to adorn a title-winning car. Busch drove Jack Roush's 97 Ford to victory in NASCAR's 2004 inaugural Nextel Cup championship.

F Ever the free spirit, center *Jeremy Roenick* viewed his 1996 trade from Chicago to Phoenix as a new beginning after eight seasons with the Blackhawks. So he dumped his No. 27 jersey for 97, hypothesizing that "maybe '97 will be my first Stanley Cup." It wasn't, but in 2005-06 Roenick still was wearing 97 in his first year as a King.

F *Art Still*, who took No. 67 to four Pro Bowls as a defensive tackle for weak Kansas City teams in the 1980s, wore 97 for a University of Kentucky team that posted a 10-1 record in 1977. The Wildcats retired his collegiate 97.

NOTABLE 97s TYOKA JACKSON 97 HENRY THOMAS 97 RENALDO TURNBULL 97 DAN SALEAUMUA 97 CHRIS ZORICH

98
TOM HARMON

Old 98. The nickname still resonates, more than 60 years after Michigan great Harmon ran roughshod over college football. So, too, does the story of how it came to be: Harmon, late for his first high school practice, was told by the equipment manager to pick a uniform and get out on the field. He grabbed a new jersey from the pile on a nearby table and joined the team, only to be greeted by a barking coach. "Hey scrub," he yelled. "What are you doing with that jersey? Those belong to the regulars. Get outta here until you're dressed properly." Humiliated and defiant, Harmon returned a few minutes later dressed in a shabby, faded jersey bearing the number 98. Late in a scrimmage pitting scrubs against the varsity, he fielded a punt, sidestepped three tacklers, found daylight and raced for a long touchdown. "Hey," the coach asked, "who's that kid?" The student manager gave him his name. "Well, tell him he's on the varsity now," the coach said, "and tell him to get a new uniform." Harmon refused. And eight years later, he still was wearing his beloved 98 when he won the Heisman Trophy.

Elite 98s

SAM ADAMS: After six years as 98 for Seattle, Adams switched to 95 in 2000 and combined with 98 Tony Siragusa to form a 675-pound body wall on Baltimore's defensive line.

JULIAN PETERSON: As No. 98 for the 49ers, linebacker Peterson hit with abandon, rushed the passer and covered big tight ends—roles he'll maintain in Seattle.

TONY SIRAGUSA: Ray Lewis, Peter Boulware and Jamie Sharper were Baltimore playmakers in 2000—but only because strongman Siragusa was occupying blockers. Without big Tony, those Super Ravens might have said an early "nevermore" in the playoffs.

FAST FACTS

F **Mike Ditka**, traded to Philadelphia in 1967, couldn't get his familiar 89 that season and reversed it to 98, thus becoming the first Eagles player to wear a number in the 90s. Linebacker **Mike Morgan** was gone by 1968, freeing Ditka to return to 89.

F Size doesn't always matter. Before settling on No. 98 when drafted by the Cardinals in 1991, 6-5, 320-pound defensive end **Eric Swann** had asked for 99. He was told the number had been retired for **Marshall "Biggie" Goldberg**, a 5-11, 190-pound halfback who played for the Chicago Cardinals from 1939-43 and 1946-48.

F Linebacker **Jessie Armstead**, who was drafted in the eighth round by the Giants in 1993, knew his days might be numbered when he was assigned uniform 98, a number usually given to defensive linemen. So he "just took the number and ran with it"—all the way to five Pro Bowls in nine seasons with the Giants and two more years as 98 for the Redskins.

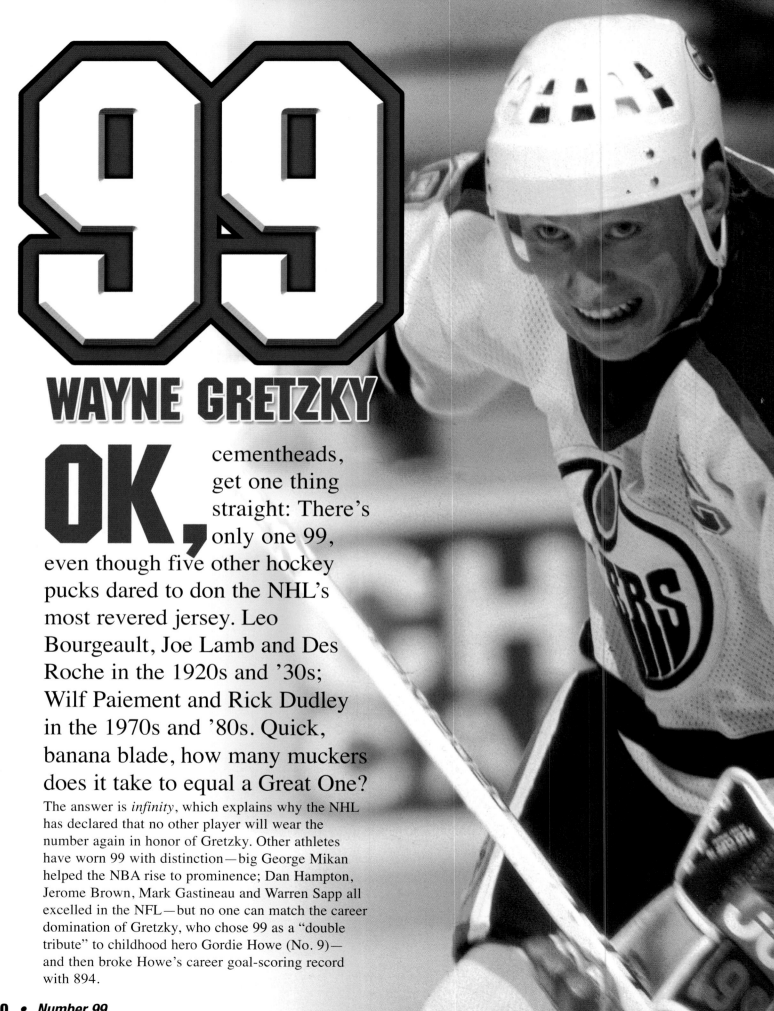

99

WAYNE GRETZKY

OK, cementheads, get one thing straight: There's only one 99, even though five other hockey pucks dared to don the NHL's most revered jersey. Leo Bourgeault, Joe Lamb and Des Roche in the 1920s and '30s; Wilf Paiement and Rick Dudley in the 1970s and '80s. Quick, banana blade, how many muckers does it take to equal a Great One?

The answer is *infinity*, which explains why the NHL has declared that no other player will wear the number again in honor of Gretzky. Other athletes have worn 99 with distinction—big George Mikan helped the NBA rise to prominence; Dan Hampton, Jerome Brown, Mark Gastineau and Warren Sapp all excelled in the NFL—but no one can match the career domination of Gretzky, who chose 99 as a "double tribute" to childhood hero Gordie Howe (No. 9)— and then broke Howe's career goal-scoring record with 894.

PATIENCE LIFTS TAGUCHI TO HIGH PLACES

Nothing about *So Taguchi's* first year in the United States was simple. Signed by the St. Louis Cardinals after playing 10 seasons for Orix in his home country of Japan, Taguchi struggled to adjust to new surroundings while quickly discovering he was overmatched by big-league pitching. Then there was the matter of picking a uniform number.

Taguchi asked for 6, the number he had worn in Japan. The Cardinals explained that 6 had been retired in honor of a guy named Stan Musial. Hoping to remain connected to his old number, Taguchi simply turned it upside down and asked for 9. Sorry, the Cardinals responded, there was this former outfielder named Enos Slaughter.

Taguchi changed direction and asked for the number he wore for Japan in the 2000 Olympic Games—1. That, he was told, was retired for Ozzie Smith. And when Taguchi asked for 66, he learned it already was being worn by pitcher Rick Ankiel. Thinking big, Taguchi countered with 66 upside down. Much to everyone's relief, the Cardinals signed off on 99, which the outfielder has worn since.

On-field struggles forced Taguchi to spend most of 2002 and '03 in the Cardinals' farm system. But hard work and patience eventually paid off, just as it had while playing numbers roulette.

Taguchi played 109 games for the Cardinals in 2004, batting .291. He appeared in 143 games in 2005 as a valuable fill-in for injured starters Larry Walker and Reggie Sanders, hitting .288 with 53 RBIs.

Taguchi

Elite 99s

Mikan

Sapp

JEROME BROWN: Forget his mediocre sack totals. Big Jerome's primary responsibility from 1987-91 was to plug up the middle of the Eagles defensive line and keep blockers from focusing on quarterback-crushing ends Reggie White and Clyde Simmons.

MARK GASTINEAU: The former CEO of the New York Sack Exchange also topped the NFL's single-season sack-leader corporation until Michael Strahan initiated a hostile takeover.

MARSHALL GOLDBERG: "Biggie" was

FAST FACTS

F When veteran linebacker *Levon Kirkland* signed with Seattle in 2001, his No. 99 already was being worn by defensive end *Matt LaBounty.* So Kirkland did a little homework on LaBounty, discovered he was an avid outdoorsman and made an offer he couldn't refuse: some cash and an expenses-paid fishing trip. He got his number.

F *Mitch Williams,* the eccentric lefthanded closer dubbed "Wild Thing," was wearing 99 for the 1993 Phillies when he surrendered the World Series-ending home run to Toronto's Joe Carter.

Williams

JOEL SMEENGE 99 RAYLEE JOHNSON 99 LEE

Upon joining the Mets in 1997, reliever *Turk Wendell* would have preferred the number 13 he had worn the previous four seasons with the Cubs. But his new team already had a 13 (infielder Edgardo Alfonzo) and 99 seemed a logical option. Wendell did have a passion for the number 9, and 99 was the number worn by Charlie Sheen's quirky character, Rick "Wild Thing" Vaughn, in the movie *Major League*.

As it turned out, 99 was a fortunate choice. Wendell pitched well enough from 1997-2000 to earn a big contract that he spiced with a distinct 99 flavor. He signed a three-year deal with yearly salaries of $3 million, $2.85 million and $3.25 million plus a signing bonus of $299,999.99. An additional $600,000 in bonuses brought the contract's potential value to $9,999,999.99.

But 99 magic eventually ran dry. Late in 2001, Wendell was traded to the Phillies, who were making a pennant run. Wendell struggled badly in his new 99 uniform and finally traded it in for a 13 model, which he got from infielder Tomas Perez for a Rolex watch. The season ended badly for the Phillies, and Wendell spent much of the next two years battling injuries before signing on for a final 2004 fling with Colorado—wearing No. 99.

Early in his career, Wendell brushed his teeth between innings and wore a necklace made from the teeth of wild game he had hunted. Stories abounded about his off-the-wall habits, but Wendell claimed they had nothing to do with superstition.

Why, he pointed out, would anybody who's superstitious wear No. 13?

a popular, all-purpose star for the Cardinals' last championship team in 1947.

DAN HAMPTON: Bears fans called him "Danimal" because he was half "Dan" and half "animal." But few defenders and no amount of zookeepers could keep this focused and intense defensive lineman from wreaking havoc—or earning a bust in Canton.

GEORGE MIKAN: If he wasn't the tallest No. 99 ever, he certainly was the most imposing. The 6-10 Hall of Fame center revolutionized the post position while dominating college basketball at DePaul and the professional game from 1946-56. His Minneapolis Lakers won six championships in a seven-year span.

WARREN SAPP: Say what you want about the loose-lipped, ever-controversial Sapp. But you can't deny his impact on the Tampa Bay Bucs and their rise to defensive prominence. Sapp, one of the most dominant tackles of his era, helped the Bucs attain Super status in 2002.

F The original Wild Thing? *Charlie Sheen's* 100-mph-throwing character *Rick Vaughn,* who wore No. 99 in the 1989 movie *Major League*. The fictional off-beat righthander pitched for the Cleveland Indians.

F Defensive end *Hugh Douglas* was not well versed on the legend of *Mark Gastineau* when he signed with the New York Jets in 1995 and took uniform No. 99. Soon he was hearing the inevitable comparisons, pressure he apparently did not want. When Douglas was traded to the Eagles in 1998, he switched to 53, his college number.

F Dolphins 99, defensive end *Jason Taylor,* reportedly was cruising on his 99-foot yacht in the summer of 2005 when he got a shore-to-ship call from coach Nick Saban assuring him he would not be traded.

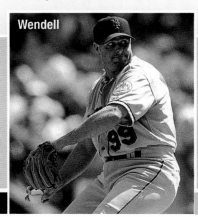

Wendell

WILLIAMS 99 **ALVIN WRIGHT** 99 **CHRISTIAN PETER** 99 **AL NOGA** 99 **MIKE BELL** 99